Intelligent Data Analytics for Terror Threat Prediction

Scrivener Publishing
100 Cummings Center, Suite 541J
Beverly, MA 01915-6106

Publishers at Scrivener
Martin Scrivener (martin@scrivenerpublishing.com)
Phillip Carmical (pcarmical@scrivenerpublishing.com)

Intelligent Data Analytics for Terror Threat Prediction

Architectures, Methodologies, Techniques and Applications

Edited by

**Subhendu Kumar Pani,
Sanjay Kumar Singh, Lalit Garg,
Ram Bilas Pachori and Xiaobo Zhang**

Scrivener
Publishing

WILEY

This edition first published 2021 by John Wiley & Sons, Inc., 111 River Street, Hoboken, NJ 07030, USA and Scrivener Publishing LLC, 100 Cummings Center, Suite 541J, Beverly, MA 01915, USA
© 2021 Scrivener Publishing LLC
For more information about Scrivener publications please visit www.scrivenerpublishing.com.

Wiley Global Headquarters
111 River Street, Hoboken, NJ 07030, USA

For details of our global editorial offices, customer services, and more information about Wiley products visit us at www.wiley.com.

Limit of Liability/Disclaimer of Warranty
While the publisher and authors have used their best efforts in preparing this work, they make no representations or warranties with respect to the accuracy or completeness of the contents of this work and specifically disclaim all warranties, including without limitation any implied warranties of merchantability or fitness for a particular purpose. No warranty may be created or extended by sales representatives, written sales materials, or promotional statements for this work. The fact that an organization, website, or product is referred to in this work as a citation and/or potential source of further information does not mean that the publisher and authors endorse the information or services the organization, website, or product may provide or recommendations it may make. This work is sold with the understanding that the publisher is not engaged in rendering professional services. The advice and strategies contained herein may not be suitable for your situation. You should consult with a specialist where appropriate. Neither the publisher nor authors shall be liable for any loss of profit or any other commercial damages, including but not limited to special, incidental, consequential, or other damages. Further, readers should be aware that websites listed in this work may have changed or disappeared between when this work was written and when it is read.

Library of Congress Cataloging-in-Publication Data

ISBN 978-1-119-71109-4

Cover image: Pixabay.Com
Cover design by Russell Richardson

Set in size of 11pt and Minion Pro by Manila Typesetting Company, Makati, Philippines

Contents

Preface

Intelligent data analytics for terror threat prediction is an emerging field of research at the intersection of information science and computer science. Intelligent data analytics for terror threat prediction is a new era that brings tremendous opportunities and challenges due to easily available criminal data for further analysis. The aim of this data analytics is to prevent threats before they happen using classical statistical issues, machine learning and artificial intelligence, rule induction methods, neural networks, fuzzy logic, and stochastic search methods on various data sources including social media, GPS devices, video feeds from street cameras and license-plate readers, travel and credit-card records and the news media, as well as government and propriety systems. Intelligent data analytics is to ensure the efficient data mining techniques to get solutions for crime investigation. Prediction of future terrorist attacks according to city, attack type, target type, claim mode, weapon type and motive of attack through classification techniques, facilitates the decision making process by security organizations, as well as to learn from the previous stored attack information and then rate the targeted sectors/areas accordingly for security measures. Intelligent data analytics models with multiple level of representation in which at each level the system learns raw to higher abstract level representation. Intelligent data analytics-based algorithms have demonstrated great performance to a variety of areas including data visualization, data pre-processing (fusion, editing, transformation, filtering, and sampling), data engineering, database mining techniques, tools and applications, etc.

This edited book, titled "Intelligent Data Analytics for Terror Threat Prediction" emerges as a consequence of the vital need for public safety in various domains and parts of the world. It is particularly targeted at resource constrained environments such as in developing nations, where crime is growing at a frightening rate across various domains of life and impeding economic growth. By source constrained situation, we mean environments where crime intelligence skilled personnel are limited and inadequate technological solutions are in place to gather operational safety information for citizens' security. In particular, of interest is the quest to realize the nature, scope and level of impact of present crime mining solutions across various domains and to develop novel paradigms for a more comprehensive solution. This will present innovative insights that will help to obtain interventions to undertake emerging dynamic scenarios of criminal activities. Further, this book presents emerging issues, challenges and management strategies in public safety and crime control development across various domains. The book will play a vital role in improving human life to a great extent. All researchers and practitioners will highly benefit from reading this book, especially those who are working in the fields of data mining, machine learning, and artificial intelligence. This book is a good collection on the state-of-the-art approaches for intelligent data analytics. It will be very beneficial for the new researchers and practitioners working in the field to quickly know the best performing methods.

Organization of the Book

This book consists of 14 chapters. It includes quality chapters that present scientific concepts, framework and ideas on intelligent data analytics for terror threat prediction across different crime domains. The editors and expert reviewers have confirmed the high caliber of chapters through careful refereeing of the papers. For the purpose of coherence, we have organized the chapters with respect to similarity of topic addressed. The topics addressed range from crime mining issues pertaining to cyber-crime, cyber-crimes on social media, intrusion detection system, cryptography Internet of Things (IoT) and machine to machine comm. and analysis of crime scenarios.

Chapter 1, "Rumor Detection and Tracing its Source to Prevent Cyber-Crimes on Social Media" by Ravi Kishore Devarapalli, Anupam Biswas, presents the different automated rumor detection systems in social networks and techniques to trace the source of rumor.

Chapter 2, "Internet of Things (IoT) and Machine to Machine (M2M) Communication Techniques for Cyber Crime Prediction" by Jaiprakash Narain Dwivedi presents a response to crime issues by offering a novel security structure that is based on the examination of the "limits and capacities" of M2M devices and improves the structures headway life cycle for the general IoT natural framework.

In Chapter 3, "Crime Predictive Model Using Big Data Analytics" by Hemanta Kumar Bhuyan and Subhendu Kumar Pani presents detailed information on the methods of machine learning to develop different techniques to catch criminals based on their track of activities.

Sushobhan Majumdar presents an important discussion and analysis in Chapter 4 on "The Role of Remote Sensing and GIS in Military Strategy to Prevent Terror Attacks". He focuses on the role of RS and GIS in constructing defense strategies to prevent terror attacks.

In Chapter 5, Supriya Raheja and Geetika Munjal present "Text Mining for Secure Cyber Space". The chapter presents an expert system for extracting similarity score of cyber-attack related keywords among various resources. The proposed work uses text mining approach for making a secure cyber space.

R. Arshath Raja, N. Yuvaraj, and N.V. Kousik provide an insightful discussion and analysis in Chapter 6 on "Analyses on Artificial Intelligence Framework to Detect the Crime Pattern". The chapter describes the performance of the proposed clustering model for crime pattern investigation and is compared with time series analysis, support vector machine, artificial neural network. The analysis is carried out against various performance metrics that includes: accuracy, specificity, sensitivity and f-measure.

In Chapter 7, Ebrahim A.M. Alrahawe, Vikas T. Humbe, and G.N. Shinde present the issue of "Biometric Technology-Based Framework for Tackling and Preventing Crimes". The chapter provides an insight into the possibility of integrating surveillance systems with biometric systems at a single system in order to predict crime by identifying criminals and crime tools.

In Chapter 8, Supriya Raheja, Geetika Munjal, Jyoti Jangra, and Rakesh Garg provide a useful discussion "Rule-Based Approach for Botnet Behavior Analysis". The chapter also proposes that botnet traffic in any network is a matter of serious concern. They are used for many activities of malicious type like distributed denial of service (DDOS) attacks, mass spam, phishing attacks, click frauds, stealing the user's confidential information like passwords and other types of cyber-crimes.

Abhishek Goel, Siddharth Gautam, Nitin Tyagi, Nikhil Sharma, and Martin Sagayam present an important discussion and analysis in Chapter 9 on the role of "Securing Biometric Framework with Cryptanalysis". The chapter investigates the different contentions for and against biometrics and argues that while biometrics may present real protection concerns, these issues can be satisfactorily ameliorated.

In Chapter 10, Galal A. Al-Rummana, Abdulrazzaq H.A. Al-Ahdal and G. N. Shinde present "The Role of Big Data Analysis in Increasing the

Crime Prediction and Prevention Rates". The chapter discusses different big data analysis techniques.

Dipalika Das and Maya Nayak present an important discussion and analysis in Chapter 11 on the "Crime Pattern Detection Using Data Mining". The chapter discusses how statistical data related to crime are monitored and analysed by various investigating bodies so that various strategies can be planned to prevent crimes from happening.

In Chapter 12, Nikhil Sharma, Ila Kaushik, Vikash Kumar Agarwal, Bharat Bhushan, and Aditya Khamparia present the role of "Attacks & Security Measures in Wireless Sensor Network". The chapter presents different layer attacks along with security mechanisms to avoid the effect of attack in the network. Security is considered as one of the main constraints in any type of network so it becomes very important to take into consideration the key elements of security which are availability, integrity and confidentiality.

Hemanta Kumar Bhuyan presents an important discussion and analysis in Chapter 13 on the role of "Large Sensing Data Flows Using Cryptic Techniques". The chapter discusses the replicated crimes using cyberspace by criminals.

In Chapter 14, Chandra Sekhar Biswal and Subhendu Kumar Pani present the role of "Cyber-Crime Methodology and its Prevention Techniques". The chapter places the emphasis on various frauds and cyber-crime happening in India, as well as the different types of cyber-crimes along with the probable solutions for that.

Dr. Subhendu Kumar Pani
Department of Computer Science & Engineering, Orissa Engineering College, BPUT, Odisha, India

Dr. Sanjay Kumar Singh
Department of Computer Science and Engineering, Indian Institute of Technology Campus, BHU, Varanasi, Indore, India

Dr. Lalit Garg
Department of Computer Information Systems at University of Malta, Msida

Dr. Ram Bilas Pachori
Department of Electrical Engineering, Indian Institute of Technology Campus, Indore, India

Dr. Xiaobo Zhang
School of Automation, Guangdong University of Technology,
China
November 2020

Rumor Detection and Tracing its Source to Prevent Cyber-Crimes on Social Media

Ravi Kishore Devarapalli* and Anupam Biswas†

Department of Computer Science Engineering,
National Institute of Technology Silchar, Assam, India

Abstract

Social media like Facebook, Twitter, WhatsApp, Sina Wiebo, Hike, etc. play an important role in the information spreading in today's world. Due to large scale connectivity, some of the cyber criminals are choosing these platforms to implement their criminal activities such as rumor spreading which is popularly known as rumor diffusion. In a pluralistic society like India, rumors that spread over various social networking platforms are much more vulnerable. It is challenging for even public, government and technical experts working on social media to find these cyber-crimes and its origin to punish the culprit. Nowadays, some cyber criminals are choosing different platforms and paths to accomplish their plans to escape brilliantly from those activities. Thus automated detection of rumor and tracing its source has great importance.

This chapter surveys the different automated rumor detection systems in social networks and techniques to trace the source of rumor. Detection of rumors on social networking platforms is possible through analysis of shared posts and comments wrote by followers. After detection of rumors, next job is to 1) prevent the rumors from further spreading and 2) identification of culprit i.e. the originator of rumor. This chapter covers both these aspects. The opinion of an influential person in the group influences others very easily. Cyber criminals may use separate communities in social media to fulfil their activities. Thus, it is important to trace the most influential person in community to prevent further spreading. This chapter aims to discuss the recent techniques that are developed for identifying influential persons in the group. The chapter also aims to study the various techniques developed for identifying the culprit, which are based on factors like

---

**Corresponding author*: ravikishoredevarapalli@gmail.com
†*Corresponding author*: abanumail@gmail.com

Subhendu Kumar Pani, Sanjay Kumar Singh, Lalit Garg, Ram Bilas Pachori and Xiaobo Zhang (eds.)
Intelligent Data Analytics for Terror Threat Prediction: Architectures, Methodologies, Techniques and Applications, (1–30) © 2021 Scrivener Publishing LLC

network structure, diffusion models, centrality measures, etc. The chapter will also discuss the various challenges including real-life implementation, evaluation, and datasets in respect to both rumor detection and rumor source tracing.

Keywords: Rumor, rumor source detection, centrality measures, social networks, diffusion models

1.1   Introduction

Social media like Facebook, Twitter, Sina Wiebo, YouTube and WhatsApp are becoming major online businesses. Social media uses computer-based technology with internet to ease the sharing of ideas, thoughts, and information by building of virtual networks and communities [1]. Nowadays, social media plays an important role for information diffusion [2]. Social networking sites like Facebook, Twitter, and WhatsApp have become popular over a short period of time with their user-friendly features [3]. It has advantages as well as disadvantages too [4]. Advantages of Information diffusion are, enable users to upload and share photos, videos, comment and like them, without hurting any communities, religions, or political parties, etc. The other side where people may share abusive photos, videos, terror activities or sensitive information about country, which are criminal activities come under cyber-crime.

Cyber-crime is a criminal activity which involves a computer and internet as part of it [5]. There are many activities that fall under cyber-crime such as passing rumors, online harassment, hacking emails, websites or databases, etc. [6]. To detect whether given data is rumor or fact, use text classification algorithms like Naïve Bayes theorem and support vector machine [7]. These classical algorithms are mainly used for classification purpose, and classify text data based on features and dimensions [8].

Detection of these cyber-crimes and finding the culprit involved becomes challenging for public, government and police departments as it is very difficult to detect and even hard to prove. As technology progresses, people can remotely access networked computer devices from different locations. Detection of Rumor Source in social media is also difficult as people can use various devices, IP addresses and emails to bully online, such as posting offensive images, videos or any rumors about others. So detection of these cyber-crimes and origin of those as early as possible in social networks will be helpful to combat the further diffusion and also punish the culprit involved [9]. After detection of rumors in social network it is required to combat them by finding people who spread first and punish them. Rumor source identification in social networks become very difficult as discussed earlier many techniques have been introduced, but very few become popular in finding origin of rumor.

Before going to find rumor source, there is a need of considering factors such as diffusion models, network structure, evaluation metrics and centrality measures [10]. Topology associates with Network structure is in tree or graph, and observation of network example complete observation, snapshot observation, and monitor observation, etc. [11]. If network topology is tree or graph use maximum likelihood (ML) estimator to estimate source [9]. Next factor consider diffusion models to get how fast information diffusing over network [10]. There are four diffusion models namely Susceptible-Infected-Susceptible (SIS), Susceptible-Infected (SI), Susceptible-Infected-Recoverable-Susceptible (SIRS) and Susceptible-Infected-Recoverable (SIR). SI model considers each node in any one of two states susceptible or infected [12]. SIS model considers three states susceptible-infected-susceptible, where infected node can again susceptible in future [13, 14]. SIR model also has three states but susceptible-infected-recovered, where infected node can be recovered by having immune power or taking medicines [15]. SIRS has four states of nodes such as susceptible-infected-recovered-susceptible, where recovered node may be susceptible in future [16]. Another factor consider in source detection is centrality measures [17]. There are several centrality measures such as degree centrality, closeness centrality, and betweenness centrality are popularly considered. All these factors considered to detect source in network are explained in following section.

Rumor source detection approaches are broadly divided into two main categories: 1) single source detection approach and 2) multiple sources detection approach [10]. Single source detection approaches are query-based, anti-rumor-based, network observation, etc. Multiple source detection approaches are network partitioning, ranking-based, community-based, approximation-based, etc. Single source detection using network observation again has three types of observations such as snapshot, complete and monitor observations, etc. Query-based observation allows to find source of rumor by asking queries to neighbors about rumors [18], anti-rumor-based is by diffusing anti-rumors into the network can get information about network using monitor-based observation and use this information to find rumor source [19]. Multiple sources of rumor is also a challenging task, and can be done by network partitioning using rumor centrality metric [20], community-based which follows SIR model and reverse diffusion [21]. All these models are useful to find rumor source in online social networks. Rumor source identification and punishing the culprit reduces further diffusion of rumors and cyber-crimes in social networks. This survey explains in the rest of the chapter social networks and their features in Section 1.2. What is cyber-crime, various cyber-crimes and their impacts, cyber-crimes in social networks are discussed in Section 1.3. Rumor detection using classification models in Section 1.4. Factors consider in rumor source identification and its classifications are discussed in Section 1.5. Rumor source detection categories such as single source and multiple sources of rumor in network are discussed in Section 1.6. Summary of this survey is discussed in Section 1.7.

1.2   Social Networks

A social network is a website that allows people to make social interactions and personal relationship through sharing information like photos, videos, messages and comments, etc. [22].

1.2.1   Types of Social Networks

There are many social networking sites, among these some sites like Facebook, WhatsApp, Twitter and Instagram that have become popular platforms over a short period for social interaction across the world [3]. But the options available in these networking sites are limited even though they are popular. There are other social networks, which are having more number of options but not popular. All these social networks are classified based on the options like sharing photos, videos, thoughts of personal or professional which are available for people to interact and collaborate each other. The following categories explain about how each one classified based on available options. Figure 1.1 depicts various social networks available online.

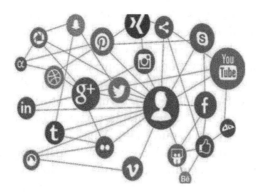

Figure 1.1 Social networks [23].

The major benefit of social networks is keeping in touch with family members and friends. The following list shows the most widely used social networks for building social connections online. Table 1.1 shows users for each network in millions.

Table 1.1 Social network users [24].

Service	Active users (in millions)
Facebook	2,320
YouTube	1,900
WhatsApp	1,600
Facebook Messenger	1,300
WeChat	1,098
Instagram	1,000
QQ	807
Qzone	532
TikTok	500
Sina Wiebo	462
Twitter	330
Reddit	330
Douban	320
LinkedIn	303
Biadu Tieba	300
Skype	300
Snapchat	287
Viber	260
Pinterest	250
Discord	250
LINE	203
Telegram	200

Facebook: Facebook is arguably the most popular social media service, providing users with a way to build relationships and share information with people and organizations that they choose to communicate with online [3].

WhatsApp: It is a real-time social network that arrived later than Facebook but has evolved in a short time by offering user-friendly features such as quick messaging, sharing photos, videos, documents, voice and video calling, group chatting and protection for all these, etc. [3].

Twitter: Share your thoughts and keep ahead of others through this platform of real-time information [3].

YouTube: YouTube is the world's largest social networking site for video sharing which allows users to upload and share videos, view them, comment on them, and like them. This social network is available throughout the world and even enables users to create a YouTube channel where they can share all of their personal videos to show their friends and followers [3].

Google +: The relatively new entrant to the social interaction marketplace is designed to allow users to establish communication circles with which they can communicate and which are integrated with other Google products [3].

MySpace: Though it initially began as a general social media site, MySpace has evolved to focus on social entertainment, providing a venue for social connections related to movies, music games and more [3].

Snapchat: This is social image messaging platform which allows you to chat with friends using pictures [3].

Interface through social network sites between online users is one of the major common computer-based activities. Facebook is most a dominant platform over a short span of time for social interaction across the world. Even though it stays the largest social networking site, sites like YouTube, Twitter, Google+ and Sina Wiebo all have lively and busy user populations that maintain social interactions in their own ways, with new features springing up all the time. With the help of inventive research methods and theoretical case studies, inventors can better realize how these networks work and measures their influence on various kinds of social interactions as well as the associated risks and benefits. Like sharing information which can be useful to public without hurtling other communities, religions, or political parties, etc. and the other is where people may share abusive photos, videos or sensitive information about country. For more advantages and disadvantages see Ref. [4].

1.3   What Is Cyber-Crime?

1.3.1   Definition

Cyber-crime is also called as computer-oriented crime, as this crime involves computer and network. It can be defined as "Offences that are committed against individuals or groups of individuals with a criminal motive to intentionally harm the reputation of the victim or cause physical or mental harm, or loss, to the victim directly or indirectly, using modern telecommunication networks such as Internet (networks including chat rooms, emails, notice boards and groups) and mobile phones (Bluetooth/SMS/MMS)" [25].

1.3.2   Types of Cyber-Crimes

Nowadays, there are many ways that cyber-crimes may occur using computers and network [5]. Some of the cyber-crimes such as hacking, cyber bullying, buying illegal things and posting videos of criminal activity are explained in following subsections.

1.3.2.1   Hacking

Hacking is nothing but attacking/accessing devices like computers and mobiles without the permission of owner. It can be done by people called as hackers, who attack/access our systems without permission. Hackers are basically computer programmers who hack by intruding programmes called as virus into our systems. These viruses may steal our data like username, password, documents, files, etc. stored in computer [6]. Hacking is not limited to individual computers but can even damage computers which are in network, as well as username, password, information of emails, bank accounts, social networking sites, etc. So there is a need to concentrate on these attacks to prevent them and punish the culprit.

1.3.2.2   Cyber Bullying

Cyber bullying is bullying that happens over digital devices like cell phones, computers, and tablets [26]. It can occur by sending emails, messages through social networks like Facebook, Twitter, Instagram, WhatsApp and software services like Gmail, Yahoo, etc. where a group of people are connected and sharing social information. Some people are misusing these facilities and bullies by sharing abused photos, videos, or negative information about others, etc. [27]. It is very harmful to the society and needs attention to combat and find culprit.

1.3.2.3 Buying Illegal Things

Buying illegal things like Bit coins and drugs belong under criminal activities in India and many other countries. So this is also a one of the cyber-crime that needs attention to prevent and find the source of user who bought those [6].

1.3.2.4 Posting Videos of Criminal Activity

Posting/sharing videos of criminal activities such as abused photos, videos, and disinformation on online social networks is also under cyber-crime [5]. There are some other activities like sharing security issues of country and posts against some religions and communities also falls under this cyber-crime.

These are some popular cyber-crimes but are not limited to many others such as Denial-of-Service attack, Email bombing, spamming, Cyber stalking, etc. [6]. So there is a need to focus on these cyber-crimes and how to prevent and punish the culprits.

1.3.3 Cyber-Crimes on Social Networks

Nowadays, social networks like Facebook, Twitter, WhatsApp, Sina Wiebo, etc. are become very popular in sharing and diffusing any kind of digital information. But sharing all kinds of information is not legal in any social networks. If anyone is sharing illegal information in social networks then it is considered as cyber-crime. Some of the cyber-crimes on social networks are listed in the section below.

A. Posting Rumors
   Posting/sharing any misinformation (unknown) or disinformation (wontedly wrong) is called as rumors. The diffusion of rumors is very fast comparing to the actual news in social networks [5]. Finding whether particular post content is rumor or not is a challenging task, and if it is a rumor, detecting the source of rumor is also becomes a big challenge to many people like government, police and experts who are working on social networks. Therefore, it is important to put

more effort on how to control rumors in social networks and also detection of rumor source to punish them.

B. Sharing Abusive Photos/Videos
   Sharing any kind of abusive photo or video of anyone is illegal activity and treated as cyber-crime [6].

C. Posting Comments Against Religions, Communities or Country

D. Movie Release Online Without Permission.
   These are other occurring cyber-crimes in social networks but are not limited to these four important cyber-crimes. Whatever it may be, there is a need to prevent them and if anyone has done these, a need to find and punish them. In the next section, a discussion is given about how to detect whether a given data is rumor or fact-based on some classification algorithms.

1.4 Rumor Detection

Rumor is a currently trending topic which contains an unverified content. This content may be either wrong information (misinformation) or intentionally wrong information (disinformation) [31]. Social media is capable of diffusing the information rapidly in the network as these rumors are also disseminated over the network. Some people may not know the difference between rumor and fact and may share the same rumor to other communities.

It is observed that rumors (about politics, religions, communities, etc.) diffuse very fast when compared to normal news. Thus, it is important to stop diffusion of rumors in social media, which requires detecting whether the information is rumor or not. Nowadays, rumor detection becomes a challenging task and many researchers are working on it. How a information can be classified rumor or non-rumor is shown in Figure 1.2. The figure shows how a rumor is classified as true or false and if it is false how it is classified as misinformation or disinformation.

1.4.1 Models

In order to classify whether given data is rumor or not, follow the procedure as shown in Figure 1.3.

Initially, we consider a rumor dataset (messages) from social network. Next, to process the data, data processing is used. After processing, it is

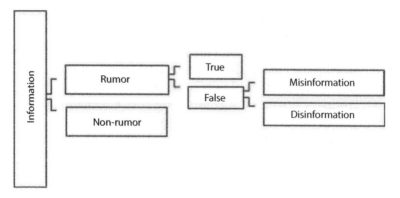

Figure 1.2 Classification of rumor and non-rumor.

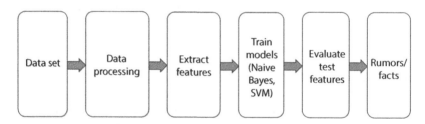

Figure 1.3 Rumor classification process.

required to extract features like user features, Tweet features, and comment features from processed Twitter data as shown in Table 1.2. Later, use any classification algorithm to classify rumors based on these features. Classification models classify and produce results. In order to detect whether a given text is a rumor or not, the most common approach is to simply tokenize the text and apply classification algorithms. There are many classification algorithms that exist, but only few algorithms give better results. They are algorithms like Naïve Bayes, SVM, Neural network with TF, Neural network with Keras, decision tree, random forest, Long Short Term Memory, etc. In this section two major classification algorithms are discussed.

1.4.1.1   Naïve Bayes Classifier

In machine learning, Naïve Bayes classification algorithm is a very simple algorithm which is based on a combination of Bayes theorem and naïve assumption. A Naïve Bayes classifier assumes that presence of one feature is unrelated to the other features presented in same class [30]. Generally the

Table 1.2 Dataset features [31].

User features in social networks	Tweet features in Twitter	Comments features in social networks
No of followers	No of records	No of replies
No of friends	No of words	No of words
User has location in his profile	No of characters	No of characters
User has URL?	Tweet contains URL?	Comments contain URL?
User is a verified user?	Source of tweet	Source of comment
Ratio of friends/followers	Length of tweet	Length of tweet
Age of the user account	No of hash tags	No of question mark
Ratio of statuses/followers	No of mentions	No of pronouns
	No of pronouns	No of URLs
	No of URLs	No of exclamation mark
	No of question mark	Polarity
	No of exclamation mark	Presence of colon symbol
	Polarity	
	Presence of colon symbol	

assumptions made by Naïve Bayes are not correct in real situations, and even independence assumption never correct, but it works well in practice [29].

It can be done using the following Bayes theorem,

$$P(c/x) = \frac{P(x/c) * P(c)}{P(x)} \tag{1.1}$$

Where

- P(c/x) is the posterior probability of class.
- P(c) is the prior probability of class.

- P(x/c) is the likelihood which is the probability of given class.
- P(x) is the prior probability of predictor.

Naive Bayes classifier is a combination of Bayes theorem and Naïve assumptions. This algorithm calculates assumption values even though use multiple parameters as input. Rumor detection is purely based on either classification of text or images. For example, try rumor detection in social networks like Twitter or Facebook, then it is required to consider several features like User features, Tweet features, and Comment features. All these features deal with text data [32]. If Tweet or post or comment includes these features then one can apply Naïve Bayes classifier algorithm to classify them whether it is a rumor or not. These features are classified into three categories. Some of dataset features are listed in Table 1.2.

First, consider user features, number of followers or friends to a particular person are more, then it may be considered as truth, otherwise it is a rumor. Because, in survey it is observed that many people who share rumors may have less number of followers or friends in their social networking accounts. Second, there are many features to be considered as Tweet features from which one can detect whether it is rumor or not. For example, consider number of retweets, number of words or number of characters. If count of any one of these or all of these are more than average range in size, then the tweet may be rumor, otherwise it is truth. Third one is comment features. These are very much important features used in rumor detection. This feature is based on comments given by many people who are already infected by the particular post or tweet. If found comments like Is it real? Impossible? How it is possible? Or I can't believe this, then the particular post/tweet may be a rumor. There have many other features to distinguish whether a post/tweet is rumor or not. Figure 1.4 below gives a brief idea about how Naïve Bayes algorithm classifies different classes of data points.

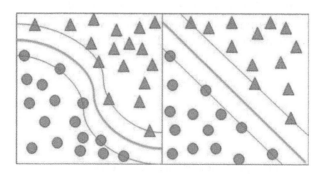

Figure 1.4 Naïve Bayes classifier.

It can be observed that there are two classes of data points and how they are classified with maximum distance.

Two classes are

    i.   Circle
   ii.   Triangle.

Adding more parameters in input dataset reduces the accuracy when compared to using less parameter. To increase the accuracy use another popular model SVM.

1.4.1.2 Support Vector Machine

Support vector machine (SVM) is a one of the best machine learning algorithm used for both classification and regression, widely it is used for classify given data points even though those input vectors are mapped non-linearly [8]. In social networks data available in many forms so to detect rumors it is required to classify given text data using classification algorithms based on dataset features. Classifying dataset which has multiple features and multiple dimensions is a challenging task, so using SVM will give better results.

The main objective of the SVM is to find a hyper plane in an N-dimensional space that distinctly classifies the data points. Rumor detection in social networks is mainly depending on text classification, using SVM algorithm it can be done. It is shown in Figure 1.5, how a SVM classifier classifies the

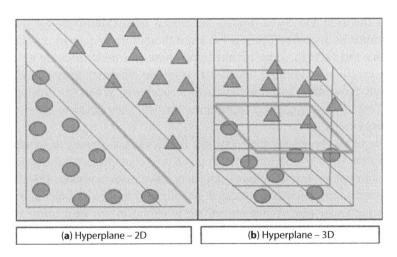

Figure 1.5 Hyperplane in 2-D and 3-D.

given dataset that has multiple features and dimensions. SVM classifies as large margin in between two types of data: first one is in circle shape and the second one is in triangle shape. These two data points have been classified with maximum distance (thick line) between them. The large margin shown in Figure 1.5(a) says that it is classifying those circles and triangles equally from that point, which means distance between those two data types is maximum through that margin. As shown in Figure 1.5(b), SVM also supports multi-dimensional data.

1.4.1.2.1 Cost Function and Gradient Features

SVM algorithm looks to maximize the margin between the data points and the hyper plane. The loss function that helps maximize the margin is hinge loss [8] and is defined as follows:

$$c(x,y,f(x)) = \begin{cases} 0, & \text{if } y*f(x) \geq 1 \\ 1 - y*f(x), & \text{else} \end{cases} \tag{1.2}$$

If predicted value and expected value have the same sign then the cost function is 0.

1.4.2 Combating Misinformation on Instagram

Classification of shared contents by users in social media is prevalent in combating misinformation. Baseline classification algorithms like Naïve Bayes theorem and SVM models have been used extensively for detecting rumor as discussed Section 1.4. Even though these algorithms classify rumors and facts in some manner, still there is a need to come up with some excellent techniques which may improve efficiency in rumor classification. Nowadays, social networks like Facebook, WhatsApp, Instagram and Twitter are using good techniques, but still they failed to classify the rumors exactly.

One of the popular social network, Facebook, has started in Instagram application (in US) to detect whether given post contains fact-information or false-information through some third party called as fact-checkers [33]. These third-party-fact-checkers are located globally and find rate of fact and false about particular post. When something is wrong in any post immediately fact-checkers check ratio of fact or misinformation.

If any post contains more false ratio then immediately it labels as "False information" otherwise no. Now it is the user's responsibility to view or not

Figure 1.6 Combating misinformation in Instagram [33].

that particular post based on false ratio and fact ratio, about share to their friends, communities or not. Using third-party-fact-checkers, Instagram is trying to combat misinformation on social networks. Figure 1.6 will give you brief idea about this method.

1.5   Factors to Detect Rumor Source

Rumor detection is not only a solution to prevent these cyber-crimes in social media, but finding source plays an important role to prevent further diffusion and punish the culprit. Initially, finding source of rumors in network discussed by Ref. [9]. Later, much research has been done and has introduced several factors which are to be considered in RS identification. There are mainly four factors considered namely, diffusion models, network structure, evaluation metrics, and centrality measures. Each factor has been explained in the following section with examples. After rumor detection, consider these factors and find rumor source using source detection methods in social networks are explained in Section 1.5.2.

1.5.1   Network Structure

Network structure can be derived from two parameters: network topology and network observation [9]. Network topology describes the structure of network either in tree or graph. Source identification is more complex in the graph topology than tree topology, as tree has exactly one root node and no loops are allowed, Graph doesn't have any root node and loops are allowed in network. Network observation is the second type of network structure and it is useful to observe the network during rumor propagation to get the knowledge about states of nodes in particular time. Network can be observed possibly in following three ways [11]: Complete, Snapshot and Monitor.

1.5.1.1   Network Topology

In computer networks, network topology is defined as design of physical and logical network. Physical design is the actual design of the computer cables and other network devices. The logical design is the way in which the network appears to the devices that use it.

In complex networks, network topology is the arrangement of network in generic graph or tree. In general, many domains like medical, security, pipeline of water, gas, and power grid are available in graph structure. These graphs are required to restructure two topologies as d-regular trees and random geometric trees [34]. Initially, rumor source identification is discussed and introduces methods for general trees and general graphs based on rumor source estimator. Rumor source estimator plays a key role in finding the exact source of rumor. Source estimator mainly based on Maximum likelihood (ML) estimation is the same as a combinatorial problem [9, 35]. The following section will explain required techniques such as rumor source estimator, ML estimator, rumor centrality, and message passing algorithms to detect rumor source in trees.

1.5.1.2   Network Observation

In rumor source identification, network structure plays an important role. When structure of network is known, it is easy to find how a rumor is spread in network using diffusion models such as SI, SIS, SIR and SIRS. If back track these diffusion models then rumor source can be detected easily. To know the structure of network another model is used called network observation, which provides information about states of each node present in network at particular time. Those states are in a susceptible node—able to being infected, infected node—that can widen the rumor more while recovered node—that is alleviates and no longer infected [10]. If information of each node likely is susceptible, infected or recovered is observed then it is easy to generate structure of network from that knowledge. Network observation can be done in three ways: complete observation, snapshot observation and monitor observation.

1.5.1.2.1   Complete Observation

Complete inspection of network presents broad information like whether a node is susceptible, infected or recovered at each time of interval in network [11]. It is not enough to know about state of node at one time only and requires multiple time intervals. Complete observation will give this knowledge even in different time intervals. Complete observation of small scale network is easy as size of network is small but it is hardly possible in large scale networks. Figure 1.7 depicts knowledge about this problem, as shown in Figure 1.7(a) regular tree with 7 nodes considered as small scale network and complete observation of network can be possible like root node, leaf nodes, degree of nodes, etc. In Figure 1.7(b) a generic graph is shown with many nodes and multiple connections between each node treated as large scale network and observation is not easy as finding the root node, leaf nodes and degree of nodes are difficult in these kind of large scale networks. It is observed that complete observation gives better results to provide knowledge about states of nodes but works only in small scale networks [39] not in large scale network. To overcome this problem another model is used called as snapshot observation.

1.5.1.2.2   Snapshot Observation

It provides limited information about states of nodes in network at given time interval. To avoid this problem, instead of one or two snapshots, taking multiple snapshots will give better knowledge about nodes in different time intervals. Disadvantages of taking multiple snapshots may consume much time, and although it provides correct information about lone

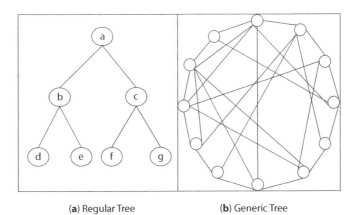

(a) Regular Tree   (b) Generic Tree

Figure 1.7 Network topology.

contaminated nodes, it cannot distinguish between recovered or susceptible [37]. So it is difficult to understand about nodes in these states i.e. either they received rumor and ignored it or not received yet.

1.5.1.2.3   Monitor Observation

Monitor observation means monitoring the network by inserting monitor or sensor nodes in it which works as an observer in network [36]. These sensor nodes gather information about states of nodes and pass this to administrator. The administrator will maintain all gathered data about each node state in a database. But there is chance of missing information in monitor observation as sensor nodes are inserted in a few places of network. Also, there may be a loss of information about some nodes where sensor nodes are not available. Due to unavailability of information of some nodes in network it reduces the accuracy of system, as system is based on number of nodes. If number of nodes increases then accuracy may increase but reduces performance of system due heavy load on network.

These are three types of network observations which help to understand states of nodes and network structure. Network topology and network observation both are used to understand the structure of network. Network structure is one of the best factors that are considered in source identification. Other factors also considered are diffusion model which is mandatory in source identification as discussed in Section 1.5.2.

1.5.2   Diffusion Models

Diffusion models are also one of the factors considered in source identification as they give information about how fast information diffusion occurs in network [2]. There are four diffusion models namely susceptible-infected (SI), susceptible-infected-susceptible (SIS), susceptible-infected-recovered (SIR), and susceptible-infected-recovered-susceptible (SIRS). All these come under epidemic models, which can spread deceases widely from person to other or group of people. These epidemic models are discussed in the following section as well as how they spread and the differences between them.

1.5.2.1   SI Model

SI model is one of the oldest epidemic models where S stands for susceptible and I for infected. Initially, for complex networks SI model was proposed by Ref. [12]. If complex networks use SI model then state of nodes

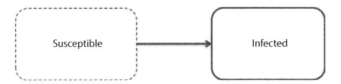

Figure 1.8 SI model.

is either susceptible or infected. Once a node is infected it could remain in same state throughout life as shown in Figure 1.8. But this model is not practical. There is little chance that a susceptible infected node can be recovered and again in future. In social networks once rumor is received by any user, he/she believes it at that particular time and in the future they may know the truth and recover from it, which is not possible in SI model. The models SIS, SIR and SIRS deal with this issue and these models are discussed in the succeeding sections.

1.5.2.2   SIS Model

The SI model is not practically applicable, as it doesn't allow infected users to be recovered. The SIS model addresses this problem [13, 14], and focuses on number of persons infected and number of persons cured as well. Once anyone is infected they may be cured and become susceptible in the future. Figure 1.9 explains the same problem where susceptibility of infection is possible [38]. In social networks once a rumor is received by a user he/she may believe or ignore as they knew fact and can become susceptible in the future.

1.5.2.3   SIR Model

SIR model is one of the simplest diffusion models. It has three states where S stands for number of susceptible, I for number of infectious, and R for number of recovered or removed. Total number of people is considered collectively from these three states susceptible, infected, and recovered [15].

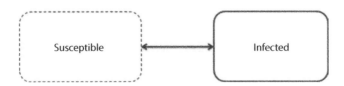

Figure 1.9 SIS model.

Figure 1.10 SIR model.

In social networks, once rumor is diffused and received by any user he/she becomes infectious if doesn't know truth about rumor. If they knew truth, he/she recover by ignoring rumor or not passing to neighbors. This is ignored in SI and SIS models. Recovery from rumors is only between SIR and SIS models. Figure 1.10 shows how users are transforming from one state to other.

1.5.2.4   SIRS Model

In SIR model once a person recovered from disease he/she remains in same state in future. In general once a person is cured from any disease there is chance that they may be reinfected with same decease in future, which is ignored in SIR model. SIRS model addresses this problem where once a person is infected and have recovered by having immunity or medical treatment, they couldn't be in same recovered state in future. After recovery, there is possibility that again infected by same decease [16].

In social networks, once a rumor is diffused and received by any user, if believed, user is infected; otherwise if fact is known about rumor, user recovers by ignoring or not passing to neighbors. There is possibility that this recovered node again will be reinfected in the future on social networks. For further details see Figure 1.11.

All these diffusion models are explained in Ref. [41]. There are independent cascade models to find rumor sources by analyzing network diffusion in reverse direction [42].

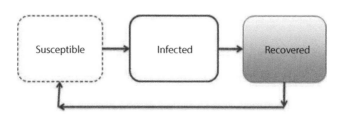

Figure 1.11 SIRS model.

1.5.3   Centrality Measures

In rumor source identification centrality measures are also considered as one of the important factors. Centrality measures are computed to assign a score to each node, which influences the diffusion process [43]. There are several centrality measures discussed in Ref. [17], such as Degree centrality, Closeness centrality, and Betweenness centrality and are explained in following sections.

1.5.3.1   Degree Centrality

It is defined as the total nodes connected to a node in network or graph. Currently, eminent people like politicians, actors, and sports players are having excellent degrees of centrality with others in the network [40]. Social networks like Facebook and Twitter are proving this as many famous people having more number of friends and followers in their accounts. Figure 1.12(a) illustrates this degree of centrality measures.

1.5.3.2   Closeness Centrality

It is defined as smallest distance among a node and other nodes in the graph [46]. See Figure 1.12(b) for more details, where closeness centrality is shown as node with black color and having the same distance with all other nodes in graph.

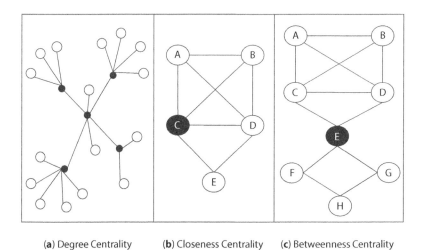

(a) Degree Centrality   (b) Closeness Centrality   (c) Betweenness Centrality

Figure 1.12 Centrality measures.

1.5.3.3 Betweenness Centrality

It is defined as a node i.e. bridge between any other two nodes and has the shortest path between them among it. It is observed that a node with better betweenness centrality may not have better degree which is necessary in information diffusion [47]. Figure 1.12(c) depicts how a betweenness centrality chosen, node in black color acts as a bridge between others. For more details about rumor centrality measures see Refs. [44, 45].

1.6 Source Detection in Network

Rumor source identification in social networks is an emerging topic, introduced by Ref. [9]. In order to find the rumor source in network, first task is to classify given data rumor or not, then apply source detection techniques on network which contain nodes that are infected by rumors. The following Figure 1.13 will give idea about how a rumor is classified from given data using classification algorithms and how rumor sources are classified based on metrics. Initially, it is needed to collect dataset of sender and receiver messages (rumor) from social network, do data processing like removing urls, hashttags, stopwords, etc. and annotation. Next construct propagation graph finds rumor or misinformation, and selects any suitable diffusion model to get information about how a rumor is diffused in network, suitable metrics for source detection and evaluation. It also classifies sources based on metrics available, do validation and analysis of results.

Source detection approaches are classified into two most important categories: single source detection and multiple source detection [10].

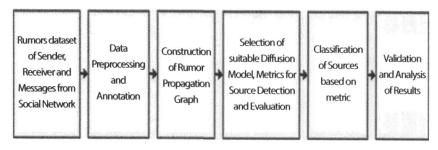

Figure 1.13 Rumor source detection process.

1.6.1   Single Source Detection

This section explains detection of single source of rumor in social networks. Major research work has been performed on single source detection and proposed many techniques. All these techniques have been classified again as anti-rumor based, query based, and network observation, etc.

1.6.1.1   Network Observation

Network observation is discussed in Section 1.5.1.2. The three types of observation techniques are complete, snapshot, and monitor observations which are very useful in source identification. The three methods and how they used in detection of rumor source are explained in following sections.

1.6.1.1.1   Complete Observation

First, Rumor source identification in networks was proposed in Ref. [9], to find source in network, consider a tree-like network as structure of network is one of the factors to detect source. The authors assume a node receives information from its neighbor nodes in trees. SIR model considered to find how this information is diffusion occurs from one node to other. Next factor to be considered is centrality measures, and gives knowledge about rumor centrality of one node, it is defined as a number of links from source node. If any node is having better rumor centrality it is considered as source of rumor diffusion. For more details see Ref. [45]. Rumor source estimator and maximum likelihood estimators are explained in following section.

A. Rumor Source Estimator

To find rumor source estimator first need to know how rumor spreading over network? Rumor spreading model gives solution to this problem. There are many models like SI, SIS, SIR and SIRS uses as diffusion models to spread rumor over the network. These models are applied to diffuse information in online social networks. In this section a simple example is discussed on how a rumor can spread over the network.

Let's consider an undirected graph G (V, E), where V is a countable infinite set of nodes, and E is the set of form (i, j) for some i and j in V, and consider the case where initially only one node v^* is the rumor source. For the rumor spreading model, use popular model subject to infected or SI representation which does not permit for any nodes to get well, i.e. once a node with the rumor, it remains such forever. Once a node i with the rumor, it is able to widen it to another node j if and only if there is an edge among them, i.e. if (i, j) $\in E$. A node i needs the time to widen the rumor to node j is modeled by an exponential random variable τij has the rate λ. Suppose there is no loss of generality that $\lambda = 1$. All τij's are autonomous and identically distributed [9].

B. Rumor Source Estimator: Maximum Likelihood (ML)
   Suppose that the rumor has widen in G (V, E) refer to diffusion model i.e. SI model and all N nodes with the rumor. Infected nodes are symbolized by rumor graph G_N (V, E) which is a sub graph of G (V, E). It has been observed that actual rumor source (v^*) may differ than rumor estimator $(\tilde{v})$. By using all these variables v^*, $\tilde{v}$ and $G_{N,}$ rumor source estimator is given as follows,

$$\tilde{v} = \arg\max P(G_N / v^* = v) \qquad (1.3)$$

$$v \in G_N$$

Where $\tilde{v}$ = rumor estimator
         v^* = rumor source.

In general trees, evaluation of P $(G_N \mid v^* = v)$ is difficult. However in case of regular trees this evaluation is simple because every node has same degree. As the network is tree structure it is possible to spread rumor through unique sequence only. So that finding rumor source is also become simple. Evaluate P $(G_N \mid v)$ for all $v \in G_N$ and then select one with maximal value.

The authors consider general network, random tree, and d-regular tree to find rumor source. For d-regular and random trees it is easy to get information how rumors are diffusing in network as explained earlier but in general network it is difficult. So, they uses Breadth-First-Search (BFS) technique in general networks to convert them into BFS trees. Initially assume every node as a source node which means starting point for BFS. To find origin they used BFS tree with infection probability p. After finding, node which has higher probability considered as source node. For more details see Ref. [9].

1.6.1.1.2   Snapshot Observation

This observation gives limited information as discussed earlier in Section 1.5.1.2.2. It is useful for single rumor source detection on social networks, if multiple snapshots are taken in various time intervals. Single snapshot gives limited information about network and states of nodes whereas multiple snapshots give more information about these. Single source detection by applying rumor centrality metric and multiple observations is discussed [37]. They consider tree-like network and used SI model for rumor diffusion, they proves that multiple observations always improve detectable performance. Even two independent snapshot observations increases probability of source detection compare to single snapshot observation. The authors shown that source detection performance increases for multiple observations and decreases with number of infected nodes. After multiple observations use maximum likelihood estimator to find rumor centrality and from it to find rumor source in tree-like network and graph network. Graph network uses BFS technique to transform graph into BFS tree as discussed in above section. The problem in snapshot observation is if SIR model is used for information diffusion, it cannot distinguish between susceptible and recovered nodes.

1.6.1.1.3   Monitor Observation

Monitor observation is possible by inserting sensor nodes in network, and monitor these nodes behavior. Sensor nodes placed in network gather information about states of nodes as discussed in Section 1.5.1.2.3. Monitor observation is one of the factors and is useful in identifying source in network. There is chance of missing information about some nodes where sensor nodes are not placed and if number of sensor nodes increases then system performance decreases. But if this observation is considered for source identification, then on collected information use rumor centrality measures to find source of rumor either in tree-like network or general network. In Ref. [49] proposed sensor nodes do not contain any textual information in the network to detect rumor source.

The above three observations are used to detect RS in social networks.

1.6.1.2   Query-Based Approach

This approach is proposed in Ref. [18] for source detection. It is purely based on queries and answers to find source. In general, asking queries gives information about rumor source. These queries like "Who shares you the rumor?" or "Are you the source of rumor?" and answers to these queries increases chance of rumor source identification. The authors considers two types of queries: 1) simple batch queries are simple queries as mentioned earlier, and 2) interactive queries are queries which may contain untruth queries and answers with some probability. To quantify the untruthfulness, they propose estimate algorithms for those queries. Author's uses centrality measures and SI diffusion model and they guarantee that quantifying untruth or truth from these queries and asking these kinds of queries significantly improve performance of source identification in tree-like structure and on Facebook network.

1.6.1.3   Anti-Rumor-Based Approach

It is based on anti-rumor diffusion over the network. To broaden anti-rumor knowledge in the network, monitor based observation is proposed in Ref. [19] for rumor source detection. They injected monitor or sensor nodes to diffuse "anti-rumor" messages inside the network, nodes are called as protectors. Initially, authors prove that injecting anti-rumors decreases performance for Maximum-Likelihood (ML) estimator in large-scale networks. If rumors receive anti-rumor find distance between rumor source and protector. To find this distance they propose two algorithms 1) learn distance distributor parameter under ML estimator and 2) Rumor source detector under Maximum-A-Posterior-Estimator (MAPE) based on the learnt parameters. These two learning algorithms give distance between rumor source and protector, based on the difference analyze the actual rumor source.

1.6.2   Multiple Source Detection

Many researchers believe that rumor diffusion occurs from only a single source in network, but in general people use several sources to boost the rumor diffusion quickly. Single source identification is comparatively easier and several approaches have already been developed, which are discussed in Section 1.6.1. In this section multiple source of rumor in network is discussed. Detection of multiple sources is proposed in Ref. [48]. They use BFS technique and give final tree after several observations. Following section explains some techniques to find multiple source of rumor. There are four methods: ranking-based, network partitioning, approximation-based and community-based.

In network partitioning rumor centrality is evaluated in two phases [20]. First phase, identify infected nodes and classify into groups, source in each group identified using rumor center method. Second phase, these recognized sources classified into two and in each again uses source estimator to identify source in that group.

Community-based is proposed in Ref. [21], by partitioning the community to identify several sources in every community. To recognize unseen and improved nodes use reverse diffusion approach through SIR model. Community detection method group all infected nodes into groups. Then apply single source detection approaches to find rumor source in each community. There are two more multiple source detection approaches such as ranking-based and approximation-based. For details see Ref. [10].

1.7 Conclusion

Social networks like Facebook, Twitter, and WhatsApp are generating huge amount of data from their user profiles. But generation of huge data creates real world problems like rumor diffusion in network. It is difficult to find that whether information spreading in network is rumor or not and as each network has many users, it is not possible to find who spread that rumor. So classification of rumors and facts and finding rumor source in network is an emerging challenge in society. This chapter surveys various social networks, their features, cyber-crime and its classifications, and how these cyber-crimes occur in social networks. This chapter is specifically purposeful on cyber-crime in social network i.e. rumor diffusion. There are some popular classification algorithms such as Naïve Bayes and support vector machine classifiers to distinguish between rumors and facts. Next, to find source of a rumor consider three factors such as network structure, diffusion models, and centrality measures. There are two kinds of sources: 1) single source and 2) multiple source. To find single source use three approaches such as anti-rumor-based, query-based, and network observation. For multiple sources of rumor use several approaches like approximation-based, ranking-based, network partitioning, and community-based. These approaches improve probability of rumor detection and its source identification in social networks. However, there are many classification techniques and still some are not easy to use in finding based on existing features. So there is a need to consider more features and much better classification techniques. In rumor source detection, current research mostly focused on single source identification. But nowadays, multiple users are spreading rumors for fast dissemination over the social networks. Thus, there is need of developing new techniques to detect multiple sources of rumor.

References

1. Bayleyegn, B. W., and Buta, D. B. The Effect of Social Media on Study Habits of Students:-A case study at Oda Bultum University, Oromia Regional State, Ethiopia. *Global Journal of Management And Business Research*, 2019.
2. Guille, A., Hacid, H., Favre, C., Zighed, D.A., Information diffusion in online social networks: A survey. *ACM Sigmod Rec.*, 42, 2, 17–28, 2013.
3. Kapoor, K. K., Tamilmani, K., Rana, N. P., Patil, P., Dwivedi, Y. K., & Nerur, S. Advances in social media research: Past, present and future. *Information Systems Frontiers*, 20(3), 531–558, 2018.
4. Bakshy, E., Rosenn, I., Marlow, C., & Adamic, L. (2012, April). The role of social networks in information diffusion. In *Proceedings of the 21st international conference on World Wide Web*, pp. 519–528, April 2012.
5. Moore, R. Cybercrime: Investigating high-technology computer crime. LexisNexis, 2005.
6. Smith, A. M. Protection of Children Online: Federal and State Laws Addressing Cyberstalking, Cyberharassment, and Cyberbulling. Congressional Research Service, 2009.
7. Cuşmaliuc, C. G., Coca, L. G., Iftene, A. Identifying Fake News on Twitter using Naive Bayes, SVM and Random Forest Distributed Algorithms. In Proceedings of The 13th Edition of the International Conference on Linguistic Resources and Tools for Processing Romanian Language (ConsILR-2018) pp. 177–188, 2018.
8. Cortes, C. and Vapnik, V., Support-vector networks. *Mach. Learn.*, 20, 3, 273–297, 1995.
9. Shah, D. and Zaman, T., Rumors in a network: Who's the culprit? *IEEE Trans. Inf. Theory*, 57, 8, 5163–5181, 2011.
10. Shelke, S. and Attar, V., Source detection of rumor in social network—A review. *Online Soc. Netw. Media*, 9, 30–42, 2019.
11. Jiang, J., Wen, S., Yu, S., Xiang, Y., Zhou, W., Identifying propagation sources in networks: State-of-the-art and comparative studies. *IEEE Commun. Surv. Tutorials*, 19, 1, 465–481, 2016.
12. Pastor-Satorras, R. and Vespignani, A., Epidemic spreading in scale-free networks. *Phys. Rev. Lett.*, 86, 14, 3200, 2001.
13. Newman, M.E.J., The structure and function of complex networks. *Soc. Ind. Appl. Math.*, 45, 167–256, 2003.
14. Newman, M.E., Threshold effects for two pathogens spreading on a network. *Phys. Rev. Lett.*, 95, 108701, 2005.
15. Liu, D., Yan, E.W., Song, M., Microblog information diffusion: Simulation based on sir model. *J. Beijing Univ. Posts Telecommun.*, 16, 28–33, 2014.
16. Jin, Y., Wang, W., Xiao, S., An SIRS model with a nonlinear incidence rate. *Chaos Solitons Fract.*, 34, 1482–1497, 2007.

17. Boudin, F., A comparison of centrality measures for graph-based keyphrase extraction. *Proceedings of the Sixth International Joint Conference on Natural Language Processing*, pp. 834–838, 2013.

18. Choi, J., Moon, S., Woo, J., Son, K., Shin, J., Yi, Y., Rumor source detection under querying with untruthful answers. *IEEE INFOCOM 2017-IEEE Conference on Computer Communications*, IEEE, pp. 1–9, 2017.

19. Choi, J., Moon, S., Shin, J., Yi, Y., Estimating the rumor source with anti-rumor in social networks. *2016 IEEE 24th International Conference on Network Protocols (ICNP)*, IEEE, pp. 1–6, 2016.

20. Luo, W., Tay, W.P., Leng, M., Identifying infection sources and regions in large networks. *IEEE Trans. Signal Process.*, 61, 11, 2850–2865, 2013.

21. Zang, W., Zhang, P., Zhou, C., Guo, L., Discovering multiple diffusion source nodes in social networks. *Procedia Comput. Sci.*, 29, 443–452, 2014.

22. Mustafa, S. E., & Hamzah, A. Online social networking: A new form of social interaction. *International Journal of Social Science and Humanity*, 1(2), 96, 2011.

23. Sofiya, G., Lesser known social media platforms you can use for marketing, 2019, April 2. Retrieved from http://fromdrive.com/blog/lesser-known-social-media-platforms-you-can-use-for-marketing/.

24. Clement, J., Social media—Statistics, 2019, Sep 4. https://www.statista.com/topics/1164/ social-networks/.

25. Azad, M. M., Mazid, K. N., & Sharmin, S. S. Cyber Crime Problem Areas, Legal Areas and the Cyber Crime Law. *International Journal of New Technology and Research*, 3(5), 2017.

26. Stopbullying.gov, What is Cyberbullying?, 2020. Retrieved from https://www.stopbullying.gov.

27. Halder, D. and Jaishankar, K., *Cyber-crime and the victimization of women: laws, rights and regulations*, Information Science Reference, Hershey, PA, 2012.

28. Moore, R., *Cybercrime: Investigating high-technology computer crime*, Routledge, CRC press, Taylor & Francis group 2014.

29. Kantarcıoglu, M., Vaidya, J., & Clifton, C. Privacy preserving naive bayes classifier for horizontally partitioned data. In IEEE ICDM workshop on privacy preserving data mining, pp. 3–9, 2003.

30. Murphy, K.P., *Naive Bayes classifiers*, vol. 18, p. 60, University of British Columbia, 2006.

31. Qazvinian, V., Rosengren, E., Radev, D., & Mei, Q. Rumor has it: Identifying misinformation in microblogs. In *Proceedings of the 2011 Conference on Empirical Methods in Natural Language Processing* pp. 1589–1599, 2011.

32. Hamidian, S. and Diab, M.T., Rumor detection and classification for twitter data, arXiv preprint arXiv:1912.08926, 2019.

33. Graves, Lucas; Amazeen, Michelle A., Fact-Checking as Idea and Practice in Journalism, Oxford Research Encyclopedia of Communication, Oxford University Press, 2019.

34. Fuchs, M. and Yu, P.D., Rumor source detection for rumor spreading on random increasing trees. *Electron. Commun. Probab.*, 20, 2015.

35. Shah, D. and Zaman, T., Finding rumor sources on random trees. *Oper. Res.*, 64, 3, 736–755, 2016.

36. Jiang, J., Wen, S., Yu, S., Xiang, Y., Zhou, W., Identifying propagation sources in networks: State-of-the-art and comparative studies. *IEEE Commun. Surv. Tutorials*, 19, 1, 465–481, 2016.

37. Wang, Z., Dong, W., Zhang, W., Tan, C.W., Rumor source detection with multiple observations: Fundamental limits and algorithms. *ACM SIGMETRICS Perform. Eval. Rev.*, 42, 1, 1–13, 2014.

38. Gross, T., D'Lima, C.J., Blasius, B., Epidemic dynamics on an adaptive network. *Phys. Rev. Lett.*, 96, 208701, 2006.

39. Watts, D.J. and Strogatz, S.H., Collective dynamics of 'small-world' networks. *Nature*, 393, 6684, 440, 1998.

40. Albert, R., Jeong, H., Barabási, A.L., Error and attack tolerance of complex networks. *Nature*, 406, 6794, 378–382, 2000.

41. Li, M., Wang, X., Gao, K., Zhang, S., A survey on information diffusion in online social networks: Models and methods. *Information*, 8, 4, 118, 2017.

42. Nguyen, D.T., Nguyen, N.P., Thai, M.T., Sources of misinformation in Online Social Networks: Who to suspect? *MILCOM 2012-2012 IEEE Military Communications Conference*, IEEE, pp. 1–6, October., 2012.

43. Klein, D.J., Centrality measure in graphs. *J. Math. Chem.*, 47, 4, 1209–1223, 2010.

44. Hage, P. and Harary, F., Eccentricity and centrality in networks. *Soc. Netw.*, 17, 1, 57–63, 1995.

45. Shah, D. and Zaman, T., Rumor centrality: a universal source detector. *Proceedings of the 12th ACM SIGMETRICS/PERFORMANCE joint international conference on Measurement and Modeling of Computer Systems*, pp. 199–210, 2012, June.

46. Freeman, L.C., Centrality in social networks conceptual clarification. *Soc. Netw.*, 1, 3, 215–239, 1978.

47. Louni, A. and Subbalakshmi, K.P., A two-stage algorithm to estimate the source of information diffusion in social media networks. *2014 IEEE Conference on Computer Communications Workshops (INFOCOM WKSHPS)*, IEEE, pp. 329–333, 2014, April.

48. Wang, Z., Dong, W., Zhang, W., Tan, C.W., Rooting our rumor sources in online social networks: The value of diversity from multiple observations. *IEEE J. Sel. Top. Signal Process.*, 9, 4, 663–677, 2015.

49. Xu, W. and Chen, H., Scalable rumor source detection under independent cascade model in online social networks. *2015 11th International Conference on Mobile Ad-hoc and Sensor Networks (MSN)*, IEEE, pp. 236–242, December, 2015.

2

Internet of Things (IoT) and Machine to Machine (M2M) Communication Techniques for Cyber Crime Prediction

Jaiprakash Narain Dwivedi

ECE, AU4, Chandigarh University, Mohali, Punjab, India

Abstract

Ambushes against adaptable structures have raised over the earlier decade. There have been additions of coercion, stage attacks, and malware. The Internet of Things (IoT) offers another ambush vector for Cybercriminals. M2M adds to the creating number of contraptions that usage remote structures for Internet affiliation. As new applications and stages are made, old vulnerabilities are moved to bleeding edge systems. There is an assessment gap that exists between the current systems for security structure improvement and the appreciation of how these new advancements are exceptional and how they are relative. This opening exists since structure fashioners, security modelers, and customers are not totally aware of security threats and how forefront devices can jeopardize prosperity and individual assurance. Current frameworks, for making security requirements, don't sufficiently consider the usage of new advances, and this cripples countermeasure executions. These frameworks rely upon security structures for necessities headway. These frameworks miss the mark on a methodology for perceiving front line security concerns and systems for taking a gander at, separating and surveying non-human device security protections. This Chapter presents a response for this issue by offering a novel security structure that is based on the examination of the "limits and capacities" of M2M devices and improves the structures headway life cycle for the general IoT natural framework.

Keywords: Internet of Things, M2M communication, security

Email: jaiprakash.e10013@cumail.in

Subhendu Kumar Pani, Sanjay Kumar Singh, Lalit Garg, Ram Bilas Pachori and Xiaobo Zhang (eds.) *Intelligent Data Analytics for Terror Threat Prediction: Architectures, Methodologies, Techniques and Applications*, (31–56) © 2021 Scrivener Publishing LLC

2.1   Introduction

The improvement of enmeshed things through Internet of Things (IoT) and Machine to Machine (M2M) Communication is unavoidable. The examiners have foreseen that by 2020, approximately 50 billion things all through the universe will be related with one another with the help of internetwork of adroit items. With the quantity of organized articles, develops the quantity of digital wrongdoing dangers. Anticipated fifth era of portable correspondence will be the met form of all the wired and remote systems administration administrations and advances. The heterogeneous systems administration approach offers ascend to different digital dangers. Structure of strong digital security answers for such diversified systems with savvy gadgets is a testing task.

The Internet of Things publicize grants of different mixes of sharp things/articles and sensor sort out developments. People using different and interoperable correspondence show comprehension that an incredible heterogeneous/multimodal framework can be sent in remote or out of reach (mines, oil stages, woodlands, funnels, tunnels, etc.) spaces or in cases of emergencies, for instance, shakes, floods, fire, radiation zones, and others. In IoT system, these things or objects will recognize and research each other and make sense of how to abuse each other's data by sharing resources and definitely redesigning the degree and dependability of the ensuing organizations.

Machine-to-Machine exchanges will be based more on the terminals and server ranches (for example, appropriated registering, home server ranches, others) than the center points, as in the current frameworks. Augmentation of limit at lower costs will achieve the local receptiveness of most information required by people or things/objects. This can be joined with improved taking care of capacities and reliably on accessibility. This will increase the activity of terminals in trades.

Internet of Things market and Machine-to-Machine correspondences will bring physical business focal points, for instance, significant standards the administrators of benefits and things, better joint exertion among endeavors, and improved life-cycle of the board. A significant parcel of these focal points are practiced through particular distinctive verification for solitary things/objects, which engage each other to team up self-sufficiently by stirring up an individual life history of cooperation and activities after some time. Among the business verticals, customer equipment, gathering and creation system, vehicle and transportation, and client and private verticals are depended upon to be the top verticals with the greatest salary over the period 2014–2019, trailed by present day and business structures, social protection, government, and others.

2.2   Advancement of Internet

Internet unique returns to 1970s where the Advanced Research Projects Agency Network (ARPANET) introduced first Internet affiliation which was customary for Military, Government and Educational Institutes in United States. Following that, America Online (AOL) second stage made which passed on fixed web that attracted email and web separating during 1990s. Current third stage that is 2010s is the hour of cutting edge cells with versatile Internet experience which is speedier and better. Direct the entire world is examining forward for the dynamic fifth timespan (5G) of gainful correspondence. Web of Things (IoT) and Machine to Machine (M2M) Communication are the essential piece of 5G. So the fourth time of Internet is named as Internet of Things or articles where most by a long shot of the traffic will be passed on by the relationship of striking objects of the physical world with the modernized world [1]. Figure 2.1 depicts

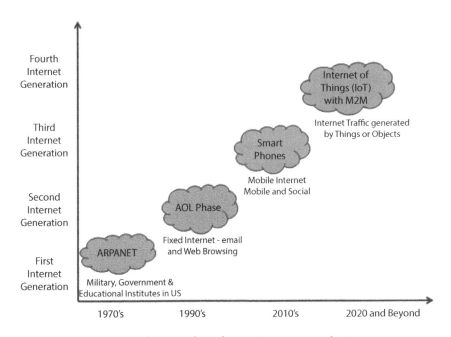

Figure 2.1 Advancement of Internet through ARPANET to IoT and M2M.

the improvement of Internet from ARPANET to IoT and M2M. On general condition, per individual in any event five contraptions are viewed as planned and taking everything into account, remembering about arranged articles that may go past fifty billion.

2.3 Internet of Things (IoT) and Machine to Machine (M2M) Communication

Machine to Machine goes under the goliath umbrella of IoT. There are various hypotheses among aces about IoT and M2M. It is changing into the referencing to be demolished deals like egg first or hen first. Regardless, these two musings are all around fascinating. M2M is the correspondence show for the co-assignments among machines with data, or machine to human interface. IoT is the net-working assistance which empowers interworking of all such vigilant machines. For instance, credit or charge card of the bank ATM is the circumstance of M2M considering the way that the ATM machine examines the data on the card and approaches as indicated by the necessities of client. Regardless, when client leaves the bank, along these lines the fans and lights are off, which is the circumstance of IoT wherein, the human closeness is seen and in like manner the electrical mechanical parties are turned on or off. From a general point of view, M2M is the channels for solid availability among plan objects for best structures association thought with IoT [2].

The Internet of Things is improvement of the current Internet relationship for every single thing which exists in this world or slanted to exist in the coming future. As IoT has become a working assessment zone, various frameworks from exchange perspectives have been investigated to move the new turn of events and notoriety of IoT [3]. One model is seeing IoT as Internet of Things where the open Web measures are kept up for data sharing and contraption interoperation. While bringing sharp things into existing web, the standard web affiliations should have been advanced and gotten together with the physical world [4]. The IoT is quickly extending an amazing bit of the idea in the condition of present day distant impart trades. The principal thought of the considerations, for example, Radio Frequency Identification (RFID) marks, sensors, actuators, telephones, and so on, which, through captivating tending to plans, can connect with one another and help out their neighbors to appear at shared targets [5].

Considering, many testing issues tended to on both inventive likewise as social groups must be discharged before the IoT thought is exhaustively perceived. Focal issues must undertake to help conceivable interoperability of interconnected contraptions, giving progressively critical degree of energy by drawing in their modification and self-regulating conduct, while ensuring trust, protection, and security. In addition, the IoT thought addresses two or three new issues concerning the systems association viewpoints. Truly, the things making the IoT will be portrayed by lesser basic of favorable circumstances the degree that calculation and essentialness limit. As necessities are, the proposed blueprints need to give remarkable idea to asset benefit other than the specific adaptability issues. The Internet of Things, a making in general Internet-based explicit structure engaging the trading of item and experiences in by and large systems impacts the security and protection of the included associates. Measures guaranteeing the structures for information check, get the chance to control and customer security should be set up.

M2M implies Machine to Machine correspondence which is the most mainstream interface for IoT in the current portable remote correspondence, whose information transmission is bolstered by link, remote, versatile and different advances, which may experience the ill effects of critical security vulnerabilities and dangers. M2M is broadly utilized in power, transportation, mechanical control, retail, open administrations the executives, wellbeing, water, security and different enterprises. M2M is ordinarily needed to be little, cheap and those ready to work unattended by people for stretched out timeframes and to impart over the remote territory organize. It can accomplish vehicle robbery security, wellbeing observing, automobile deals, mechanical support, and open vehicle the board, strategic and different capacities. The most significant part in IoT Internets is the association and interoperability between machines, which is called M2M. Security administrations, for example, information reconciliation, validation and key foundation are basic in M2M [6, 7]. Figure 2.2 shows different machine insight points of view fundamental for the IoT with the assistance of M2M.

There are mind boggling conceivable outcomes of progress and applications in IoT, which can be applied in essentially all aspects of human life, for instance, biological watching, clinical treatment and general prosperity, Intelligent Transportation System (ITS), clever cross section and various locales. Guideline enabling variable for promising perspective in the compromise of a couple of advances and correspondences plans is the IoT. Unmistakable evidence, distinguishing and checking propels, wired and far off sensor and actuator frameworks, overhauled correspondence shows and circulated insight for brilliant items are only the most significant.

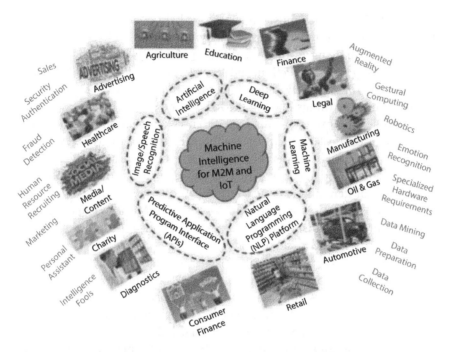

Figure 2.2 Machine knowledge points of view for IoT through M2M with Cyber Security.

The recent information regarding IoT and M2M communication are as follows:

Information	Detail	Source
The upcoming boom in smart buildings	Following quite a long while of more slow than anticipated development, the shrewd structure division is ready to soar. IDC anticipates that the market should significantly increase to $21.9 billion in only four years.	Fibocom Perfect Wireless Experience, "The Coming Boom in Smart Buildings", http://www.fibocom.com/news/2-4-4-2-44.html [8]

(Continued)

Information	Detail	Source
Progressing LTE relocation messengers monstrous change in worldwide M2M modules markets	A central part of exploration for this report included wide gatherings with 20 modules makers, flexible framework managers, M2M authority associations and M2M device creators to overview energy assessing designs for the 13 most standard varieties of M2M modules available in the overall market. News Date: 2013-12-22	Machina Research, M2M now—Latest Machine to Machine Industry News, Connected Car Report http://www. connectedcar.org.uk/ machinaltem2mnow/ 4586932250 [9]
Innovation relocation procedures of US bearers will trigger another time of LTE for the M2M business	The blend of falling module esteeming and the huge costs of superseding legacy modules will basically change the development orchestrating and cost examination of long stretch M2M associations. News Date: 2013-12-18	Machina Research, m2m now- Latest Machine to Machine Industry News http:// www.m2mnow. biz/2013/10/25/16033- technology- migration-strat egies-of-us-carriers- will-trigger-a-new- era-of-lte-for-the- m2m-industry/ [10]
The ascent of M2M/IoT Platforms features new advertisement elements, and new difficulties	Any likely provider of M2M/ IoT Application Platform game plans must move essentially past this middle capacity to pull in application creators and amass the situations imperative to build least sum. News Date: 2013-12-17	Machina Research, m2m now- Latest Machine to Machine Industry News http:// www.m2mnow. biz/2013/12/13/17392- the-rise-of-m2miot- platforms-highlights- new-commercial- dynamics-and-new- challenges/ [11]

(Continued)

Information	Detail	Source
M2M: The emphasis is still on individuals	Machines tending to machines makes a couple of individuals stress that there is a moving toward machine age. When in doubt, machine-to-machine (M2M) correspondence isn't science fiction, anyway science truth and, says Daryl Miller of Lantronix, individuals are as a rule unquestionably not left out. News Date: 2013-12-11	m2m now—latest machine to machine industry news http://www.m2mnow.biz/2013/06/17/12936-m2m-the-focus-is-still-on-people/ [12]
V2V infiltration in new vehicles to arrive at 62% by 2027, as per ABI Research	Vehicle-to-vehicle advancement subject to DSRC (Dedicated Short Range Communication) using the IEEE 802.11p vehicle Wi-Fi standard will a little bit at a time be introduced in new vehicles driven by orders just as vehicle industry exercises, realizing a passage pace of 61.8% by 2027. News Date: 2013-12-10	ABI Research, Technology Market Intelligence. https://www.abiresearch.com/press/v2v-penetration-in-new-vehicles-to-reach-62-by-202 [13]

2.4   A Definition of Security Frameworks

A security structure is an increasingly far reaching type of a data framework's system model. These models guarantee security by analyzing vulnerabilities and disposing of hazard. A total security structure remembers a few fundamental components for terms of innovative applications, individuals, utilizations, forms, arrangements, rules, business rationale and methodologies. To be of worth, a far reaching security system must include:

- Legitimate practices and execution of systems,
- Sound controls of people, methodology, and advancements,

- Analysis of risk,
- Acceptable decisions or choices,
- Have a direct utilization,
- Provide a procedure to test consistence against the structure.

The general assortment of research on M2M security isn't complete; actually, it is divided and to a great extent isolated into the distinctive basic foundation segments, as characterized by the U.S. Division of Homeland Security. Work has been practiced inside these parts, for instance, on the correspondences and security conventions for remote systems, shrewd lattices, savvy home observing frameworks, and social insurance frameworks.

M2M biological systems are inescapable in nature and found across numerous spaces (vitality divisions, fabricating, horticulture, vehicular telematics, data the board, clinical and wellbeing administrations, shrewd homes, and so forth.). They consider between area correspondence and slim systems administration for organization. Organization happens when M2M takes part in framework to-framework joint effort and interfaces together. These frameworks and their different parts collaborate with one another and perform works in the interest of people in the virtual and physical world. These motorized limits and the likely impact of their control or interference drive the prerequisite for new strategies and the headway of security development in M2M, to the extent device character the officials, security capacities for low controlled devices and security detectable quality mechanical assemblies. To this end, the composing review places an immense focus on understanding the openings in the composition and drawing relationship between current M2M shows and best practices in related progressions, for instance, Cellular Network Devices.

2.5 M2M Devices and Smartphone Technology

It is basic to appreciate the differences between machine-to-human and machine-to-machine devices in light of the fact that the contraptions have equivalent security concerns. A progressively unmistakable significance of exploration has happened in machine-to-human development than in machine-to-machine advancement, so it is for our potential benefit to fathom how much machine-to-human examination can be applied to security issues of M2M devices.

M2M gadgets [14] utilize a similar remote interchanges organizes as cell phones, yet additionally utilize short-go systems and entryways for shared informing. To this end, the turn of events and end-client gives that sway cell phone innovation and security additionally sway M2M gadget conventions.

Cell phones are machine-to-human interface gadgets that give contribution to correspondence and applications work. Machine-to-machine gadgets, then again, are little and cheap, and they are intended for robotized (instead of human-focused) wired or remote interchanges. The two gadgets depend on similar systems for interchanges, however M2M gadgets may offer more noteworthy security worries as for privacy, trustworthiness, and accessibility because of data transmission limitation, verification, get as far as possible, and the requirement for secure recognizable proof endorsements. Regardless, M2M conveyed gadgets will dwarf cell phones inside the following decade. In 2012, there were one billion cell phone clients around the world; before the finish of 2015, this number will arrive at 1.75 billion and, before the finish of 2020, the quantity of associated M2M gadgets will possibly arrive at 50 billion. While cell phones have explicit utilization and qualities from a client social point of view, M2M gadgets are intended for explicit undertakings and industry capacities. In any case various M2M contraptions by and by use 2G and 3G introduced modules, which lead to old and new vulnerabilities and security challenges that require new security instruments for countermeasures. Given these components, scientists have proposed different changes to verification so as to offer inherent confirmation and security for simpler arrangement and system improvement. Nonetheless, these progressions are untested and not normalized. Despite the fact that cell phones are able to do more mind boggling undertakings than most M2M gadgets, the usefulness of the two kinds of gadgets is fundamentally the equivalent. Both are alluring focuses for aggressors. The two kinds of gadgets can be influenced by information honesty issues and, accordingly, require information security confirmation. Cell phones hold client security information and M2M gadgets transport this equivalent information. For instance, cell phone worldwide situating framework (GPS) systems are attached to independent applications, but at the same time are progressively attached to internet based life administrations. The area put together programming with respect to a shopper's telephone might be occupied with gathering and distributing area data whether the buyer is really mindful of these procedures, and this information can be connected to brilliant city M2M gadgets too. GPS information would then be able to be utilized to stamp area data onto computerized photos so as to profile sightseers as they travel, which prompts a security infringement in the inspecting of the client's developments all through a city.

Information security best practices offer portrayal to the data to applying security controls to PDAs and the remote framework segments over which the contraptions work. In the M2M organic framework, on the other hand, robotized decisions and business reason make the standards on data transport, which requires the execution of increasingly raised degrees of security.

2.6   Explicit Hazards to M2M Devices Declared by Smartphone Challenges

There is proof that M2M gadgets have comparable regions of defenselessness to cell phones gadgets regarding information security. The various types of portable information are gathered and utilized by organizations in the accompanying three different ways.

Collect individual information and total it to offer to outsiders, use it inside, or both.

Collect individual information, staying with individual information inside the yet giving the chance to promoters to indicate a specific scope of attributes for target advertising.

Collect individual information with the expectation of selling the data, now and again including explicit profiles or names, to outsiders.

Buyers may not know about when and the methods by which this information is gathered through cell phones and M2M gadgets, nor of when it may be given to outsiders. This is on the grounds that most of clients don't peruse the protection and client understandings they sign when they buy or download programming. In any case, buyers don't see the association between these kinds of data and their utilization, particularly in a M2M environment where there probably won't be a client understanding. M2M organize proprietors have to turn out to be progressively mindful of how and why buyers decide to give them access to their own information, and whether there is a real decision occurring, particularly when a significant number of the information mining strategies are avoided the shopper's view every day. The entirety of this information is consequently liable to be available to outer investigation if the M2M or cell phone framework is undermined.

Security scientists have recognized approaches to sidestep gadget limitations and introduce modified firmware that makes pernicious vulnerabilities inside cell phones. In the event that these equivalent sorts of assaults were to happen inside the setting of a clinical M2M gadget rather than inside a cell phone condition, this could prompt the mischief or even passing of an emergency clinic tolerant.

M2M contraptions that transport clinical data are not secure in light of the fact that the memory of the devices is obliged. New approval and secure exchanges are required to guarantee the data and the contraption. Given these factors, both the possibly essential nature of the ventures required similarly as the likely risks to property and human prosperity center around M2M security.

The cell phone air interface danger is additionally critical to M2M gadgets since proof has demonstrated that cell phones and remote stages have been assaulted by various vectors that will bargain M2M gadgets. Models include: the "man-in-the-center" situation, where an assailant can put a gadget between the objective client and the system; the trading off of verification where an assault on the "challenge and reaction matches", the figure keys, supersedes the honesty keys of the confirmation vector; and spying, wherein the interloper tunes in to flagging and information associations related with clients and system components without the information on clients. Likewise, an assailant can mimic a client or a whole system by utilizing bogus signs, client information, or both through the system trying to cause the system to accept they begin from a "decent" client. Moreover, signals, client information, or both can be sent to an objective client to make that client accept they start from a certifiable system.

Regardless, the best danger to cell phones originates from malware installed in applications and the way that these gadgets are constantly associated with a system. Versatile application advancement has detonated, however the ability of sending portable malware to gadgets has detonated simultaneously. Malware has contaminated remote empowered gadgets and is equipped for engendering itself to different gadgets, including M2M gadgets. The remote business in general is poorly arranged to battle the issue.

Malware developed to pestilence extents from 2009 to 2011. Malware programs misused all versatile working frameworks, and their plans have arrived at a foremost degree of complexity. It is obscure how rapidly Malware will move in a M2M biological system. Information assaults have additionally been on the expansion. In the course of recent years, remote gadgets have become an ever increasing number of information empowered. M2M gadgets get and send information, and access applications and data rapidly. It has been analyzed the security benefits that are given at the gadget level and found that sellers and designers change security profiles for quicker information move over open systems. M2M gadgets need security tokens however move significant data and don't offer appropriate security rules for open remote systems, the absence of these rules builds security and protection concerns. Whenever contaminated with an infection, the put away data will be lost or even moved to an unapproved client. To advance better security, another structure approach is required that bolsters security plan at the part level and that characterizes best practices for cutting edge systems.

Gadget to-gadget assaults have additionally gotten progressively normal. These gadgets are fit for working as the two aggressors and survivors of an assault. Inspirations for such assaults run from basic vandalism to data robbery, cell phone spam, and disavowal of-administration assaults. In this type of malware, versatile bots work as proliferation applications that cause unnecessary charges to clients, weaken benefits, and even reason advertising debacles. The assaults need not be unpredictable and can serve to dispatch a validation assault on the working frameworks that sidesteps get to control instruments and powers a restart of the frameworks. An assault that utilized the cell phone as the vector and took into consideration access to records and system associations. Utilizing the M2M gadget as a vector will bargain applicable open data on different stages. The sheer increment of the quantities of M2M gadgets and their wide dispensing will introduce more open doors for gadgets to be utilized as vectors. The absence of security controls inside M2M makes the environment increasingly helpless to bargain, which could prompt inadvertent blow-back to the M2M biological system. Organization among M2M frameworks, including hairlike systems utilizing numerous correspondence conventions, offers much greater open door for bargain of validation, approval, and confirmation.

2.7   Security and Privacy Issues in IoT

With the closeness of IoT, clients will be fused and followed by incalculable sharp articles. Security and affirmation of the client is of most remarkable significance. There are different issues identified with these limits, for example, information request and trust dealings which are talked about underneath.

2.7.1   Dynamicity and Heterogeneity

IoT is the most uncommon framework where various contraptions shall be joined and ousted from the structure in a flood. Assurance and security plan for such remarkable and heterogeneous framework is the glorious test.

2.7.2 Security for Integrated Operational World with Digital World

Control planes filtered through till date have not thought about security moves close. In any case, the trade-off of physical and moved world with internetwork openness requests security.

2.7.3 Information Safety with Equipment Security

Bundle of investigation work has been contributed toward gadget security. Right now is an ideal open entryway for information security with gadget security. IoT and M2M bases on correspondence among objects which request information security.

2.7.4 Data Source Information

It is on a very basic level fundamental to comprehend that from where the information has begun. Information about information source is huge for control, review, manage and at long last secure the IoT and M2M correspondence [15].

2.7.5 Information Confidentiality

Information puzzle looks out for an essential issue in IoT conditions, indicating the verification that single got a handle on substances can get to and change information. This is especially huge in the business setting, whereby information may address an upheld condition for be ensured going to shield honesty and market respects. In the IoT setting clients, yet what's inexorably supported articles may get to information. This expects paying special mind to two crucial focuses: first, the centrality of a portion control part and second, the importance of a thing check process (with a related character the authorities structure).

2.7.6 Trust Arrangement

Trust is used in never-ending different settings and with evolving suggestions. Trust is an odd idea with respect to which no understanding exists in the PC and information science making, paying little psyche to the way that its imperativeness has been usually watched. Different definitions are possible depending on the got perspective. A standard issue with various techniques towards trust definition is that they don't push themselves to the establishment of estimations and assessment procedures.

For the most part used security approaches are for controlling gets to resources and capacities that are required to satisfy such outlines. Trust course of action construes the procedure of accreditation exchanges that allows a party requiring a help or a favored situation from another get-together to give the significant capacities to get the affiliation or the pre-ferred position. This criticalness of trust is ordinary for secure information the chairmen as structures may need to trade accreditations before sharing information. Thus, we base our assessment of trust issues in IoT upon it. Trust exchange depends upon appropriated joint endeavors, and includes the iterative disclosure of modernized capacities, tending to articulations ensured by given segments, for attesting properties of their holders so as to set up shared trust. In such a system, get to assets are conceivable basically after a gainful trust exchange has been developed [16].

Figure 2.3, speaks to the hypothetical model on present dangers accepted to undermine the IoT environment, trailed by a short portrayal of the sig-nificant classifications as depicted by the OWASP Internet of Things Top 10 Risks (2014). This model distinguishes dangers related over the IoT bio-logical systems spaces.

In Figure 2.4 underneath offers an improved model of the Top 5 dan-gers that undermine the M2M gadgets that will work inside the IoT. It sorts the five significant level hazard spaces identified with M2M gadgets and distinguishes shortcoming from the M2M gadget's point of view. This model gives an agenda of ideas that prompts more grounded securities for the M2M gadgets and procedures.

Featured are five key classifications where specialized vulnerabilities have been found and seen during the prototyping stage. These classes include:

The "Correspondences Network Risks" indicating that M2M gadgets are profoundly powerless against heritage remote system assaults. M2M gadgets must be fit for social event data and conveying that data depend-ably and safely. The current convention suite displays vulnerabilities that thwart execution, and system unwavering quality, these vulnerabilities incorporate the shortcoming of the vehicle layer and incorporate, RF sticking and listening in assaults. M2M gadgets are defenseless against a significant number of the equivalent "Applications Risks" that compro-mise Mobile and Smartphone gadgets.

In any case, the IoT design is reliant on numerous innovations from various spaces, this makes the M2M gadgets less secure in view of lacking distinguishing proof, verification and approval for interoperability across

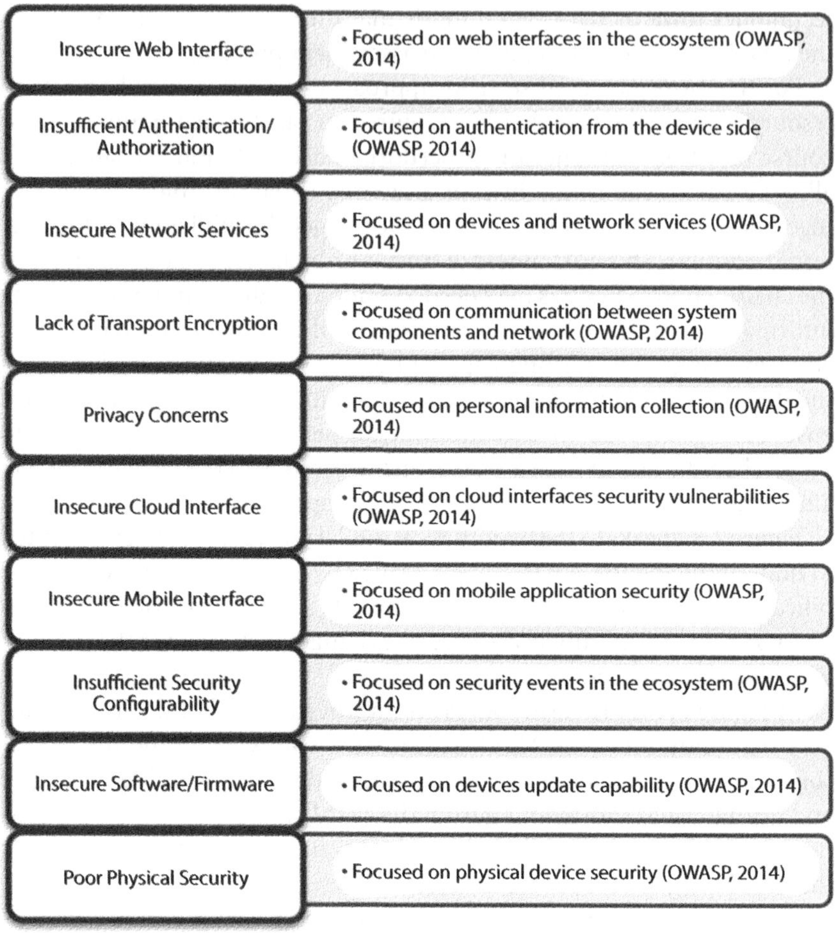

Insecure Web Interface	• Focused on web interfaces in the ecosystem (OWASP, 2014)
Insufficient Authentication/ Authorization	• Focused on authentication from the device side (OWASP, 2014)
Insecure Network Services	• Focused on devices and network services (OWASP, 2014)
Lack of Transport Encryption	• Focused on communication between system components and network (OWASP, 2014)
Privacy Concerns	• Focused on personal information collection (OWASP, 2014)
Insecure Cloud Interface	• Focused on cloud interfaces security vulnerabilities (OWASP, 2014)
Insecure Mobile Interface	• Focused on mobile application security (OWASP, 2014)
Insufficient Security Configurability	• Focused on security events in the ecosystem (OWASP, 2014)
Insecure Software/Firmware	• Focused on devices update capability (OWASP, 2014)
Poor Physical Security	• Focused on physical device security (OWASP, 2014)

Figure 2.3 IoT Theoretical Top 10 Risks.

slim systems inside the areas. Present advancements don't scale across united systems and different IoT environments due to lacking normalization endeavors and solid framework interfaces.

Some M2M gadgets are intended to perform solo to constrained errands making the gadgets helpless against "Gadgets Limitations Risks". These dangers incorporate low and constrained information stockpiling capacities, low handling capacity, restricted accessibility of intensity assets and little situational acknowledgment. In any case, these vulnerabilities likewise exist among gadgets and entryways in fine systems where numerous gadgets may speak with one another demonstrating again that lacking interoperability and the executives abilities, prompts significantly more

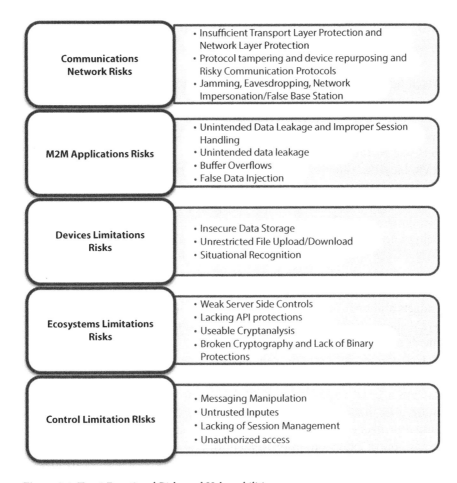

Figure 2.4 Top 5 Functional Risks and Vulnerabilities.

noteworthy restrictions and hazard. The very idea of the physical condition that numerous M2M gadgets are conveyed inside makes a critical danger to the gadget in light of the fact that cruel conditions lead to compounding assets, new bombing focuses and assault vectors. Additionally, conventions for cryptanalysis and API insurances in IoT are not sufficient and effectively tried from the gadget side.

M2M gadgets need solid "control" systems and assaults may prompt the malevolent takeover of the physical gadget. These incorporate informing control from untrusted inputs and unapproved access from secure meeting the executives. Absence of all around safeguarded necessities and principles arrangements cause an inadmissible framework plan and the executives arrangement.

2.8   Protection in Machine to Machine Communication

Machine-to-Machine (M2M) gadgets are involved reasonable sensors that are conveyed across a wide range of spaces. These incorporate brilliant force frameworks, vehicular telematics, data the executives, clinical and wellbeing administrations, and savvy home systems [17]. Since M2M gadgets will in the long run be remembered for all items, including books, TVs, bicycles, vehicles, and homes, the enormous measure of information is a security hazard in itself. The information gathered is put away in obscure areas inside the cloud and can unveil data about people, for example, purchasing behavior, areas, correspondence exercises, and even wellbeing information. M2M gadget costs fall in the area of $1 to $200. They have a wide scope of utilizations for various industry areas, which makes them a cheap alternative for business advances. M2M gadgets are solo and put in an assortment of areas, which gives programmers access to singular gadgets and opens them to burglary, reuse, and misrepresentation. As the M2M showcase develops, analysts expect that the quantity of fake employments of these gadgets will develop.

Cell phones, for example, cell phones, tablets, sensors, and PCs become devices for regular day to day existence. In any case, since clients of these gadgets are not completely mindful of security hazards, the gadgets are utilized in manners that may endanger the client's wellbeing and individual protection. Assaults against cell phones have risen because of an expansion of extortion, improvement of malware explicit to cell phones, and the elevated enthusiasm of digital law breakers. Cell phones are loaded with delicate data about clients and the organizations that utilize them; this crucial insight can be utilized to access inner business and individual systems and frameworks. Cell phones are not, at this point, just focused for low-level programmers, but on the other hand are the objectives of hoodlums looking to take individual and business interchanges and information. M2M systems and gadgets have almost no client cooperation, however similar vulnerabilities will compromise these frameworks. The key reason of this move in innovation isn't just to coordinate information for more noteworthy effectiveness, yet additionally to build up the methods by which to interface products and enterprises to purchasers and clients in vital advertising and commitment. Regardless of this principal premise, there are numerous extra aspects to the motivation behind M2M. Basically, the procedure separates the obstructions among advanced and physical articles. This can take into account more prominent associations and efficiencies in the offer of such items, in the utilization of instructive assets, in the advancement of human services targets, etc.

It is shown in Figure 2.5 that GSM-based modules associated over the remote system to the control place. The Control Center gives gadget initiation devices and permitted provisioning and moves up to be performed for the gadget strategy for testing and study. This took into account use investigation when security arrangements were changed and item execution, when capacities were expanded.

All the while, regardless, M2M presents the techniques by which additional challenges may occur. Issues of security, which is essentially the limit of the system to remain okay for customers and for affiliations, and of customer control, which is the limit of a customer to have command over the customer's own character and experience, are yet to be lit up. Plainly not the sum of the establishments for M2M systems have been romanticized to where people know, beyond a shadow of a doubt, that their private information is being made sure about. Clearly IoT condition and the aggregate of the new mechanical contraptions that they present make issues for both business and individual clients with respect to

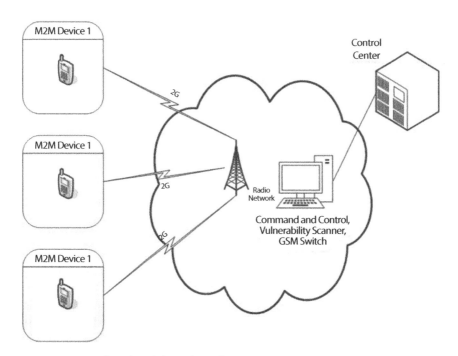

Figure 2.5 GSM-based modules with wireless connectivity.

security. This composing review charts the current challenges for M2M structures inside the setting of phone development. Since mobile phones share security shows and frameworks with the M2M natural framework, it is basic to draw on the wireless composition and its application to additional state-of-the-art M2M developments that have not been investigated as significantly in the momentum research. The composing overview in this way gives an examination of current troubles inside the M2M security structure and assesses the courses of action proposed by the composition and closes with an assessment and summary of the composition.

M2M gadgets will at long last interface with center system benefits through a course of action of means, from direct broadband or fine far off structures, to wired systems. Hairlike structures utilized by M2M frameworks are made of a course of action of affiliations, either far off or wired. System's fundamental duty is to give a powerfully extensive interconnection cutoff, abundancy and economy of association, correspondingly as solid nature of association. As a result of the huge number of focus focuses in M2M, it will accomplish revoking of association ambushes when information spread, since multitudinous machines sending information results into engineer block. In the association arrange, an attacker may tune in client information, hailing information and control information and unapproved access to deal with information inside the structure form parts, or do latent or dynamic spouting appraisal.

An assailant through the physical layer or show layer can meddle in the transmission of client information, hailing information or control information may utilize arrange associations to reflect real clients, or attempt acquainting access with confirmed clients by imagining associations structure to find the opportunity to sift through associations, to get unapproved engineer associations. To impede unapproved access to associations in Remote Validation outlines, the depending party truly evaluates the realness of the contraption dependent on the proof for the insistence got. Near to check are essentially inert, simply surveying validity estimations of the stacked and began parts.

Aggressors regularly get to, alter, embed, erase, or replay the client communication data by physical burglary, web based tuning in, acting like genuine clients and different methods, for example, the Man-in-the-Middle assaults, which can take or change the course of M2M correspondence of data between gadgets during the time spent "capture information alteration of information–sending information", bringing about the loss of authentic clients. Regularly, to get certain secret data, an aggressor will acquire interchanges information in any manners, for example, the utilization of web based tuning in, MITM assaults and other [18]. Thus the information correspondence between M2M gadgets should be uprightness and privacy security, and M2M gear ought to have proper components to achieve this capacity.

An aggressor may get to the applications programming and checking data for M2M by malware, Trojans or different strategies, and sometime later copy in other M2M contraptions to reestablish to fake utilization of M2M character of the client; he besides can change, supplement, and expel the client's correspondences information by a sullying or vindictive programming. Adversarial to sickness programming applications will decrease defilements and malware hurt on M2M apparatus, and M2M gear should have the option to routinely stimulate antivirus programming.

Data transmission is kept from arriving at the finish of administration, with the goal that the assailant can acquire client information, flagging information or control information however physical robbery or web based tuning in to accomplish the focus on unapproved get to. To gain the protected correspondence between heterogeneous framework systems, we can use the current development on introduced chip, which gives an independently security building that fills in as a security organization to any application. It is especially serialized during collecting. It is definitely not hard to realize and there are no confirmation servers to pass on, plan or keep up [19]. Protection is characterized in the region, for example [20],

i.   Storage
ii. Processing
iii. Communication
iv. Device

From safety perspective, characteristics referenced beneath are of prime significance [21].

Unwavering quality alludes to the way that the administration can be proceeded regardless of the framework getting defenseless. For disastrous frameworks, no security results are accessible there in nature. Viability represents the capacity of the typical framework to experience fixes and developments. Accessibility alludes to the way that information and frameworks can be gotten to approve people inside a proper time frame. Uprightness implies the information or/and programs have not been altered or annihilated inadvertently (for example transmission blunders) or with malignant expectation (for example harm). Privacy portrays the state wherein touchy data isn't uncovered to unapproved beneficiaries. Lost privacy happens when the substance of a correspondence or data are spilled.

2.9 Use Cases for M2M Portability

M2M correspondence plans to empower accomplice standard existing things and awards "nonhuman" content suppliers to manage the Internet with information in different structures a noteworthy piece of the time. The structures association world is meandering toward a completely arranged Future Internet, which fundamentally develops the need for bleeding edge cunning applications. Sharp city associations ought to be able to investigate information and offer second consistent reactions for specific applications to drive positive results. There are a great deal of zones and conditions wherein M2M correspondence is probably going to improve the possibility of our lives, for example, sharp conditions (home, office, and plant), transportation, and human organizations. Seeing the need for solid structure frameworks, different guidelines causing affiliations to have beginning late pushed normalization rehearses in the M2M space and began their work by isolating potential use cases and association necessities. The idea driving M2M has been in closeness for a long time; different correspondence structures in the propelled locale (e.g., maritime power the load up, cost collect structures, and item following) are operational utilizing the current systems association foundation, for example, SMS over GSM frameworks. The basic driver for the progression of M2M structures is the customary expansion in information volume and the measure of affiliations, got along with the craving to draw in interoperability on a general scale.

Use case	eHealth	Smart home	Transportation	Smart metering
Mobility	Low mobility	Low/no mobility	High-speed mobility	No Mobility
Latency tolerance	Milliseconds (emergency case) to hours (remote monitoring)	Minutes	Milliseconds to minutes	Seconds to hours
Traffic pattern	Random	Random	Random	Regular
Message size	Few bytes	Bytes to Kilo bytes	Bytes	Small

(Continued)

Use case	eHealth	Smart home	Transportation	Smart metering
Device density	Medium	Low	High	Medium
Required throughput	10 kbps (Blood Pressure Monitor) to 91 kbps (video-encoding streams)	Kbps to Mbps (depending on installed devices)	1–3 kbps	9.6–56 kbps

2.10   Conclusion

The Internet of Things speaks to a massive chance. Envision the intensity of opening the bits of knowledge and information in the accompanying situations:

- ✓ Retail location scanners on a retail floor are associated with stockroom frameworks and examination programming at home office, for industry-driving effectiveness in stock.
- ✓ Robots on a manufacturing plant floor send creation and upkeep data legitimately to the individuals who need it, for unmatched dependability and uptime.
- ✓ Indicative pictures from a CT-filter machine are partaken in close to continuous with radiologists at another clinical office and the family specialist, for improved patient consideration.
- ✓ Other industry pioneers aren't pausing. Microsoft is conveying the versatile and cloud administrations for the Internet of Things today, helping clients drive operational productivity, improve advancement and empower the making of new plans of action. Cooperating, we can change your business by beginning from your current resources and making new bits of knowledge.
- ✓ Microsoft anticipates seeing what we can assist you with making with the Internet of Things. The potential is as boundless as our creative mind and as special as our business.

Bleeding edge convenient correspondence will eyewitness coordination of various wired and remote correspondence frameworks or organizations. IoT and M2M are going to hold most outrageous piece of all these wired and remote correspondence frameworks since it has reached essentially every possible field of correspondence. There exist security shows for IoT and M2M correspondence yet new computerized ambushes are rising every day. So advanced security courses of action should similarly grow properly and this will remain as a tenacious methodology. Occupation based access control instruments will accept crucial employments in the healthiness of the computerized security course of action progression for these organizations. Trust level based check instruments may realize the incredible and secure correspondence.

References

1. Tselentis, G., *Towards the Future Internet: A European Research Perspective*, IOS Press, Netherlands, 2009.
2. CTIA IoT White Paper, *Mobile Cybersecurity and the Internet of Things—Empowering M2M Communication*, Riverpublisher, springer May 2014.
3. Atzori, L., Iera, A., Morabito, G., *The Internet of Things: A Survey*, Elsevier, 2010, Addleton Academic Publishers, https://dl.acm.org/doi/10.1016/j.comnet.2010.05.010
4. Fleisch, E., *What is the Internet of Things?—An Economic Perspective*, Auto-ID Labs White Paper WP-BIZAPP-053, January 2010.
5. Nagesh, S., Roll of Data Mining in Cyber Security. *J. Exclusive Manage. Sci.*, 2, 5, 2277–5684, May 2013.
6. Ansari, A.Q., Patki, T., Patki, A.B., Kumar, V., Integrating Fuzzy Logic and Data Mining: Impact on Cyber Security. *Fourth International Conference on Fuzzy Systems and Knowledge Discovery, FSKD*, 2007.
7. Hongsong, C., Security and Trust Research in M2M System. *IEEE International Conference on Vehicular Electronics and Safety (ICVES)*, 2011.
8. Fibocom Perfect Wireless Experience, The Coming Boom in Smart Buildings. *J. Cyber Secur. Mobility*, 4, 1, 23-40, 2015. http://www.fibocom.com/news/2-4-4-2-44.html.
9. Machina Research, M2M now—Latest Machine to Machine Industry News. Connected Car Report, *J. Cyber Secur.*, 4, 23–40, 2015. http://www.connectedcar.org.uk/machinaltem2mnow/4586932250.
10. Machina Research, M2M now—Latest Machine to Machine Industry News. IoT Now Magazine - October 25, 2013. http://www.m2mnow.biz/2013/10/25/16033-technology-migration-strategies-of-us-carriers-will-trigger-a-new-era-of-lte-for-the-m2m-industry/.

11. Machina Research, M2M now—Latest Machine to Machine Industry News. IoT Now Magazine - December 13, 2013. http://www.m2mnow. biz/2013/12/13/17392-the-rise-of-m2miot-platforms-highlights-new-commercial-dynamics-and-new-challenges/.

12. M2M now—Latest machine to machine industry news. Jeremy Cowan - June 17, 2013. http://www.m2mnow.biz/2013/06/17/12936-m2m-the-focus-is-still-on-people/.

13. ABI Research, Technology Market Intelligence. Oyster Bay, New York - 19 Mar 2013. https://www.abiresearch.com/press/v2v-penetration-in-new-vehicles-to-reach-62-by-202.

14. Demblewski, M., Security Frameworks for Machine-to-Machine Devices and Networks, Doctoral dissertation. Nova Southeastern University. Retrieved from NSUWorks, College of Engineering and Computing, 68, Security Frameworks for Machine-to-Machine Devices and Networks, 2015, https://nsuworks.nova.edu/gscis_etd/68.

15. Namboodiri, M., Thoughts on M2M and IoT security and privacy for 2015, Blog on Thoughts about M2M and Internet of Things as well as related worlds from the M2Mi team. https://www.linkedin.com/pulse/m2m-iot-security-privacy-thoughts-2015-manu-namboodiri

16. Asokan, N., Huth, M., Flechais, I., Capkun, S., Coles-Kemp, L. (Eds.), Trust and Trustworthy Computing. *6th International Conference, TRUST 2013, London, UK, Proceedings*, Springer, June 2013.

17. Gazis, V., Sasloglou, K., Frangiadakis, N., Kikiras, P., Wireless Sensor Networking, Automation Technologies and Machine to Machine Developments on the Path to the Internet of Things. *16th Panhellenic Conference on Informatics*, 2012.

18. Stojmenovic, I., Large Scale Cyber-Physical Systems: Distributed Actuation, In-Network Processing and Machine-to-Machine Communications. *Mediterranean Conference on Embedded Computing*, 2013.

19. Ghidini, G., Emmons, S.P., Kamangar, F.A., Smith, J.O., Advancing M2M Communications Management: A Cloud-based System for Cellular Traffic Analysis. *15th International IEEE Symposium on A World of Wireless, Mobile and Multimedia Networks (WoWMoM)*, 2014.

20. Chen, M. and Wan, J., A Survey of Recent Developments in Home M2M Networks. *IEEE Communications Surveys and Tutorials*, vol. 16, issue. 1, 2014.

21. Wang, H., Roy, S., Das, A., Paul, S., A Framework for Security Quantification of Networked Machines. *Second International IEEE Conference on Communication Systems and Networks (COMSNETS)*, 2010.

3

Crime Predictive Model Using Big Data Analytics

Hemanta Kumar Bhuyan[1]* and Subhendu Kumar Pani[2]

[1]Department of Information Technology, Vignan University (VFSTR), Guntur, Andhra Pradesh, India
[2]Department of Computer Science and Engineering, Odisha Engineering College, Bhubaneswar, Odisha, India

Abstract

Big data analytics (BDA) is systematized based on recognized diverse data group models, data family members, and movements within a huge amount of information. It considers BDA for criminal data where investigative data analysis is carried out for getting flow of activities on criminals. The rate of cyber-crime is growing in the internet to violate the digital access of public demand. The traditional data of crime can't be analysed to catch criminals. The different structure of criminal data needs analysing to detect criminal activities. Thus, it may be considered to take BDA for huge information of different criminal activities. The data collection and distribution over geographic location is important for data analytics with security.

Different kind of business and individual development are increased by internet as per public or private demand. In this scenario, cybercrime incidents are happened through several digital media. To identify crime characteristics is a big challenge, because criminals are smarter than investigation process. Thus, it needs to develop the technology to identify the criminal activities using Geographic Information System (GIS) and techniques of machine learning to develop different techniques to catch criminals based on their track of activities.

Keywords: Big data analytics, geographic information system, hadoop distributed file system, criminology

---

*Corresponding author: hmb.bhuyan@gmail.com

Subhendu Kumar Pani, Sanjay Kumar Singh, Lalit Garg, Ram Bilas Pachori and Xiaobo Zhang (eds.) *Intelligent Data Analytics for Terror Threat Prediction: Architectures, Methodologies, Techniques and Applications*, (57–78) © 2021 Scrivener Publishing LLC

3.1   Introduction

In few decades, Big Data Analytics (BDA) has been focused on up-and-coming techniques to utilize the proper data based on applicable areas [1]. The growth of population in urbanization creates important central roles in our society in different developmental activities. For developmental activities, advanced tool is needed. But criminals use these tools for making several problems and also incidents for society. It attempts to solve different kinds of difficulties through societal awareness on several illegal activities and use mining potential patterns and factors for public safety [2]. In addition, several challenges as per public policy are treated with huge amounts of accessible data. As per rapid effective practice, BDA can assist institutes to operate their data with novel opportunities. Moreover, BDA can be organized to assist bright commerce with effectual procedures, high turnovers and fulfilled customers. Subsequently, BDA becomes mounting critical for associations to deal with their developmental concerns [3].

Several criminal issues have been raised in human society. Criminal get advantages due to lack of alertness of public. Generally, Crime might be unplanned or planned where unplanned crime is unfortunate and unexpectedly occurs at any place that is harmful for public and planned crime occurs intentionally by criminal with proper plan. In crowded area or alert less area, criminals try to do their crime to avoid less chances of being caught [4]. Crime mapping is needed to get crime pattern based on their crime occurrences. Several technologies are also used in crime mapping to detect their activities based on criminal spatial data. Crime mapping is very much helpful to identify crime location where crime happened and it reduces the crime from the society.

The traditional database can't help to store different structure of criminal data where the model of data like structured, unstructured and semi structured data are designed to store any kind of data as demanded. This model of data can designed with help of BDA [5]. The model of data can be taken as digital data as above model. Generally, the digital data can be considered as a structured kind of data which is easy to predict criminal activities [5]. This kind of structured data identify different criminal instances with own corresponding features/attributes. Sometimes, several mining approaches are utilized to explain the criminal activities at different location. But it can't be considered the combination of all kinds of digital data for analysis.

For other kinds of data such as semi structured or unstructured data, usual mining approaches may not be considered. But it can be designed through BDA [6]. Generally, large data is a simply massive volume which is stored with model of structured or unstructured data. Traditional dealing out system [5] may not be successful in handing out such huge amount data. BDA uses widespread approaches and tools for analyzing huge amount data sets and generates successful conclusions based on data analysis. The role of Hadoop is important to take care of this kind of data in big data. MapReduce can also help to analyze these kinds of data and produce the result by using data mining methodology.

Further, R tool is utilized to utilize the data geographically based on geospatial representation of data. Data analysis with several image patterns of shared data can be achieved at this tool. For different distributed data processing, the techniques of Artificial Neural Network [ANN] can be considered where ANN is the collection of dissimilar processing neurons or nodes (processing elements) which gives the predicted information using obtainable data or clustered data. The prophecy correctness of ANN is normally exceptionally high measuring up to other approaches like Fuzzy system or Bayesian Network [7].

3.1.1   Geographic Information System (GIS)

Geographic Information System (GIS) is a system of large area of Geo-informatics [8]. The GIS is developed and intended for the purpose of several aspects of software activities on geo-data such as collection, stock up, change, distribute and explain all geo-referenced information for different human activities. It is an internet communicational information retrieval term through online engines. Such internet communication (e.g. Google Earth, Google Map, Microsoft's Virtual Earth, Wikimedia) identifies different geographical locations from earth. Users can use the above software communication tools to recover concerned data from the interactive online service through geographical map as their modification.

Another geographical information system called Volunteered Geographic Information (VGI) has raised the variety of geo-referenced data existing online [9]. It enhances the wide-range of Geo-informatics system. VGI can assist to congregate crime information using web, mobile and social network as per crime incident reporting application. Both VGI and GIS can facilitate to collect crime accident information from the local areas to global area to enrich the crime analysis process. The above system provides strategy of infrastructure related to crime data analysis such as collect, create, validate, share and analyze information based on geo-referenced technology with geo-database. The system also has several facilities to assemble data taken into custody by customer's devices like cellular phone camera and communal network.

From local level, users apply individual camera to collect footage captured data and send to corresponding proper receiver without disturbing the data. This original data use is for effective big data pattern analysis from the bottom level itself. VGI collects the information from local people that help to explain on variety of data analysis. Web 2.0 assist to post related to above concerns through web [10]. The role of social networking is important for posting of any information and incidents on small crimes. So it needs the help of network and large data for data collection and analysis. Several data like structured, unstructured, and semi-structured data are analyzed based on Hadoop framework on BDA. These kinds of data are analyzed officially by crime investigators team [11]. The role of Hadoop is considered to expect upcoming crimes and their locations are easily found based on crime patterns with effective manner.

Big data is always assisting to transform huge amount of raw data based on unstructured or structured data into vital and significant information. The law lords and government are always trying to impose rule and regulation against crimes for controlling criminal activities and making a safe society. Thus they create and update the situational rule for the safety of society with the help of healthy decision support system. Machine Learning takes steps to find out historical crime patterns based on Hadoop framework. Thus several parts of Hadoop such as MapReduce processing, Hive processing, Sqoop importing that are used for Predictive analysis of crimes. Software people develop different software products to detect crimes without more man power and save cost and time of government bureaucrats.

3.2   Crime Data Mining

In criminology, several crimes from a choice of factors are considered to be analyzed based on historical crime pattern discovery [12], road map development and unemployment rate [13], and crime scene analysis [14]. Based on statistical data mining approaches, numerous algorithms have been developed and utilized through appropriate taking data. The two important parts of data mining such as classification and statistical models are used for analyzing offense prototypes and crime forecast from corresponding data base [15] and also takes advantage of spatio-temporal patterns [16]. Wu et al. [17] built up a system for crime patterns by gathering of knowledgeably assembled crime-logged data with the intention of accomplishing more useful crime prevention. In Vineeth *et al.* [18], a random forest technique is implemented to find relationship among several crimes to categorize the circumstances of crime as per crime activities.

The role of unsupervised learning is considered for mining of crime activities data such as crime outlines and hotpots. For predicting criminal patterns, differential fuzzy cluster [19] is used and fuzzy C-means algorithm [20] is used for cluster criminal events in space. The association mining rules is used by Noor *et al.* [21] to establish connections among several crimes. Similarly, several data mining techniques are also implemented on social media by Injadat *et al.* [26]. The crime incidences are predicted using deep learning and neural networks techniques [22]. The BDA is applied in computer vision and predicted class using deep learning [23] and artificial intelligence [24].

The determination of power loss on grid system is developed through neural network by Kashef *et al.* [25]. The radio signals analysis is explained through big data processing architecture by Zheng *et al.* [27]. The prediction of travel time and effective speed model are analyzed through neural network and LSTM by Zhao *et al.* [28] and Niu *et al.* [29] respectively. Online medium data mining is explained by Peral *et al.* [30].

Crime means "act against the law" which is harmful for public to survive in daily life. To survive in human society, Government implements lawful powers that serve as law enforcement authority of government" for the public and constitute the amendment or article in constitution of India. The article of constitution was made for the different crimes such as illegal social activities: create wrong rumors in society, drugs mafia, murders, rape, theft and cyber-crime [31]. Most of the crime data are analyzed using several mining practices with appropriate software tools like WEKA, Language R, ORANGE and Tanagra, etc. Sometimes k-means clustering approach of data mining is utilized for crime data analysis [10]. The crime profile [9] is analyzed by the digital data.

Other techniques and tools are also used to determine crime activities from several geographically locations. Thus k-means clustering algorithm and Expectation maximizing algorithm are utilized for crime detection [10, 11, 32]. The role of R tool is important for crime detection over geographic areas. The technology is used for clustering of criminal data in Ref. [33]. GA (Genetic Algorithm) is also experimented for clustering of crime data in Big Data Analytics.

For amassing and analyzing the data through several clusters, the Apache Foundation offered the appropriate powerful tools such as MapReduce and HDFS (Hadoop File System) for successful performance. HDFS is used as a distributed nature for file system [34] and also utilizes two important servers such as NameNode and DataNode servers for distributed data applications [35]. MapReduce helps to practice the semi-structured as well as unstructured data. Thus, Hadoop platform is maintains a huge amount of data based on several data models. Further, the BDA is used solve many problems similar to updating data size, diversity of storing data design based on its multifaceted nature and time utilization.

The system basically uses two important tools such as HDFS and MapReduce to maintain database based on high throughput and low maintenance cost. Some techniques such as joins, partitions and bucketing are also used in Hadoop for better performance and R Tool is used for graphical representing of data. For crime type and the succeeding crime incident, the system is designed through proposal to counseling actions, matching measures and useful policies. Thus the system maintains improved security, monitoring, handling and deterrence of criminal proceed incidences.

Artificial Neural Networks (ANNs) are utilized to find out the prediction pattern from analyzed data or given data. Although other soft computing techniques such as fuzzy time series, Bayesian networks are bring into play for prediction intention but ANNs are more powerful based on comparison of accuracy. The parameters are used to select for Bayesian networks whereas the performance of Fuzzy Time Series is affected by different factors. But it is difficult to implement using Artificial Neural Networks [36, 37]. For predicting crime location with occurrences, the digital forensics is also considered to analyze the criminal activities. Digital forensics utilizes some data mining technique and big data analytics for crime mapping as per occurrences of crime locations. Digital forensics is used to analyze through digital nature of facts and tries to find out through different digital devices such as smart phones, computers, laptops, tablets, palmtops, etc. The major problem is handled with the existing infrastructure and is the reason for approaching big analytics [38].

3.2.1 Different Methods for Crime Data Analysis

The several techniques or tools such as R tool, BDA and ANNs are exercised to execute the crime mapping. There are three methods considered to analyze crime data such as (a) geographically data distribution, (b) Clustering on crime data and (c) forecast of crime activities.

  a. The crime data is shared out over several geographical locations where crime activities occurred. To find such data, it considered R tool to execute several crime data with the geographical data pack ups and generated the clusters among data. For creating clusters, it used the KDE (Kernel Density Estimation) technique to analysis mapped data.

b. The cluster analysis is considered for crime data using Hadoop platform. Parallel processing is performed for different clusters using Hadoop with fast processing compare to usual processing. The GAMMA Test is exercised for clustering over this method.

c. Hadoop made use of the ANN as an input for crime anticipating. The regression tree and classification are performed for prediction specification. The output of ANN identified the pattern of predicted crime rate at different locations with high occurrences of crime. ANN decided on predicting the pattern compare to other in terms of producing pattern.

3.3   Visual Data Analysis

Generally, crime data can be described as per software crime analysis with bureaucrat's investigation. But it needs several analyses on criminal activities which are mentioned below.

(A) Features Analysis

Different aspects of crimes are taken to analyze the criminal activities and make its data base as per the following features.

a. Incident Num: Every incident case has individual incident/ case number;

b. Dates: Date and time is very important for crime incident, because same criminal can make different crimes at several times on same date;

c. Category: Different kind of crimes with style of crimes. This data is important for the target/label crimes. This data helps to analyze and predict crimes through data classification;

d. Description: A brief description is maintained on history of criminal like how many times, style of crime, location of crime, etc.;

e. Day Of Week: Some time, crime occurred in particular day of the week;

f. Pd District: The crimes occurred under near to which Police Department (pd) with District ID;

    g. Resolution: The resolution is based on how criminal is caught out based on crimes and tries to get whole information of crimes through process;

    h. Address: The fairly accurate or particular location/address needs to be collected of the crime happening;

    i. X: Longitude of the location of a crime;

    j. Y: Latitude of the location of a crime;

    k. Coordinate: Coordination between Longitude and Latitude;

    l. Dome: This feature identifies for crime id domestic or non-domestic;

    m. Arrest: Culprit is arrested or not.

(B) Analysis of Data Processing

For executing procedures on datasets, a sequence of pre-processing steps are considered to perform the better result based on accuracy of dataset as follows:

    a. The discretized time is considered with combined columns to permit for sequential time predicting for whole movement inside the dataset.

    b. Attributed random values are collected from non-missing values and make computation for average and replaces in the missing ones in datasets [39].

    c. The timestamp is identified the date and time of each incidents of each crime. It reduced to five features: Year, Month, Day, Hour, and Minute.

    d. Few features are not necessary, so it removes some features based on that surplus data like incident—Num, coordinate.

(C) Visual analysis

Visual analysis is considered for the geographic location of the crimes. To find the exact map for location, Google map is exercised for video image data to define latitude/longitude information of the crime incidents and also generates cluster of the crime data. The marker cluster algorithm [40] assist to handle multiple markers based on zooming levels of equivalent a variety of spatial extents or decisions. For zooming out, a large geographic map is considered for coarser scale based on cluster of markers. At high zooming level of map, the accurate location of the incident can be viewed through individual markers. Through the interactive map, users can find out and see several crimes on precise dates and streets location. This helps to make basic guide of the associated incidents.

3.4   Technological Analysis

3.4.1   Hadoop and MapReduce

Hadoop framework facilitates to develop the volume data by clusters of productive hardware based on MapReduce [41]. Generally, two interior parts are involved in Hadoop such as (a) Hadoop Distributed File System (HDFS) and (b) MapReduce.

3.4.1.1   Hadoop Distributed File System (HDFS)

HDFS is designed as master-slave architecture with two standard elements which are explained as follows:

i.   Namenode: This node acts as a master node help to execute the job tracker and includes data about data at each datanode. It supervises the building blocks survive on the datanodes. Its nature is to collect data without storing the data as per namespaces and edit logs accordingly.

ii. Datanode: This node acts as slave node to organize each machine for cluster and assist to store the genuine data. Sending and receiving data is accountable to read and write the request of clients. Task responders are taken the responsibility for namenode that generate the message for all datanode as active or not. In datanode, fault-tolerance contains imitation of data and Rack awareness makes sure lesser latency with amplifying fault tolerance.

3.4.1.2   MapReduce

The role of MapReduce is important to analyze huge amount of data sets. It covers different stages for working as follows:

a.   Input splits: As per several configurations, many inputs are splitted from large cluster of datasets in Hadoop.

b.   Map: Map processes create key-value pair based on input splitting data.

c.   Sorter: Here, the data is sorted as per the key.

d.   Combiner: It reduces traffic between mapper and reducer.

e.   Shuffler: This stage shuffles data from mapper to reducer.

f. Partitioner: It takes decision for key move to which reducer.
g. Reducer: Reducer produces final output as per logical processes the data [42].

3.4.1.2.1 MapReduce-Based Data Analytic

MapReduce [46] is a programming method used for analysis of huge amount datasets. Generally Java language is used for writing MapReduce program. Different parallel and distributed algorithms are used for data processing in clusters. The MapReduce algorithm is involved with mapper, reducer and a driver [45].

Map Stage: The inputs are processed through the mapper's job that is gathered at HDFS. Similarly the input files are processed by the mapper function and generates various tiny portions of the data.

Reduce stage: After map stage, the Reducer exercises the data and provides fresh outputs to store at HDFS.

Map Reduce Process:

a. Splitting: The job splits into unchanging inputs using single map.
b. Mapping: The mapping function collects data from each split and provides output values. For example, to collect number of times of crimes from particular area/location, then calculate the different types of crimes with list.
c. Shuffling: The relevant records shuffles to get output of Mapping.
d. Reducing: This phase generates single output value by the combination of values from Shuffling phase. Map Reduce is very important for processing and analyzing efficiently using Hadoop.

3.4.1.2.2 Work Style of MapReduce

MapReduce work style is different than other programming model. It works for crime as follows:

a. MapReduce Pogram needs 3 classes to solve many crime problems such as: (a) Driver, (b) Mapper and (c) Reducer.
b. MapReduce analyzes the statistical calculation i.e., mean and total crime from different location of city, state or country.

   c.   It tries to find out the maximum occurrences of crimes.

   d.   Determines the occurrences of crimes per year.

In addition, the Apache Hadoop permits the distributed processing based on programming models for huge amount of data sets for clustering. It extends into numerous machines from solo servers with recommending limited working out and storage space. Apache Hadoop encompasses two most important parts such as (a) HDFS and (b) YARN.

   a.   HDFS: Hadoop File System [9] is developed by means of sharing file system, keeping huge number of data and easy services to access. Different machines stocks up several files for safety of data storage instead of any failure case occurs.

   b.   YARN (Yet Another Resource Negotiator): It is a cluster technology to manage the several resources. YARN is also an operating system for Hadoop to handle many resources such as the RAM, CPU of each node (machine) in the Hadoop cluster. Spark appeals YARN to assign resources to accomplish the jobs using Hive, MapReduce.

3.4.2   Hive

Hive is a part of Hadoop used for data warehouse based on querying and analysis of data. Hive uses especially SQL language called HiveQL, to analyze the structured data based on querying. It helps to develop scripts for language. It lessens efforts and plug in custom mapper/reducer code. Hive use embedded Apache Derby database for storing metadata. Meta-store is a storing place for schemas of tables using hive warehouse [43].

3.4.2.1   Analysis of Crime Data using Hive

Hive is also used to crime analysis as follows:

   a.   Crime data table is created in Hive using Sqoop.

   b.   Several crimes data are analyzed with occurrences of crimes in certain location using Hive Query Language (HQL).

   c.   Calculate total number of crimes for certain duration.

   d.   For better analysis of crime data, it divides table for crime attributes in Hive.

   e.   Based on bucket volume, clustering of dataset is generated in Hive.

3.4.2.2   Data Analytic Module With Hive

The role of Hive is important in Hadoop to create data warehouse software facility. HQL helps to analyse the crime data set based on several Hive operations such as Table creations, joins, Partition, Bucketing concept for better performance.

3.4.3   Sqoop

Sqoop helps to successfully transmit of huge amount of data between HDFS and relational data. Further transmit data is considered by Sqoop. It assists to trade in tables or whole databases to HDFS. Java classes are considered in Sqoop to cooperate with trade in data. Data is imported to HDFS in file format during importing data [44].

3.4.3.1   Pre-Processing and Sqoop

Before using data for Sqoop, data are required to pre-process as follows:

    a.   Initially, the crime data in excel format needs to convert into .csv file.
    b.   Next the .csv file needs to transfer into a table using MySql Query Browser.
    c.   Lastly, it exports the table to HDFS using the Sqoop tool.

3.4.3.2   Data Migration Module With Sqoop

Sqoop helps to transfer data between relational databases and HDFS. It performs several functions fetching the data using Sqoop tool.

3.4.3.3   Partitioning

Partitioning is generated through way of querying. It essentially divides the table into needed partitions based on querying process. Partitioning is applied for more than one column and compelling multi-dimensional arrangement on directory storage space.

3.4.3.4   Bucketing

The hash function helps to divide tables into number of partition called Buckets or Clusters. The Bucketing concept is considered as the kind of bucketing column which share outs the data in files or buckets. Each column has identical hash value that is in the right places to the matching bucket.

3.4.3.5   *R-Tool Analyse Crime Data*

R programming language is exercised for graphical investigation of data. R tool can carry out several data analysis such as data updating, data investigation, data visualization, etc. R-tool visualizes the data through graphical representation. It also is considered to do the following:

    a.   Create Bar Graph based on several crimes in each month in a year.
    b.   Ggplot-Diverse crimes in different location in city, country, out of country
    c.   Ggplot-Crimes in Hourly distribution, day-wise distribution, monthly distribution, Yearly distribution
    d.   Analysis on crime data using correlation matrix.

3.4.3.6   *Correlation Matrix*

This matrix is a relational data matrix establishes the family member among features from database. Based on correlation matrix, one can find strong correlation on pair of attributes. Several types of correlation matrices can be created for data base. But here, it considers several attributes on crime data to find correlation between pair of attributes which helps to get data analysis on crime data.

3.5   Big Data Framework

Although big data framework contains several components, here, Big Data framework contains 5 major components [47]:

    a.   Resource manager,
    b.   Clustering framework,
    c.   Data warehousing with computation,
    d.   Data storing management, and
    e.   Visual data analysis.

A. Resource Manager

Resource management is a significant part to analyze the information in Big data. It handles all needed resources, bringing together the resources with up/down mode as follows: (a) increase the following resource sub-components such as: utilization, performance, interoperability, reliability of the Big Data framework and (b) decrease management cost. Resource manager always manages live and dead nodes with detached storing at dealing out sections.

The wanted processing resources are covered to implement whole application to increase automated many items such as arrangement, coordination and management of computer complex system and services in environment. In general, resource management and scheduling platform are Mesos and Yarn in Big Data for utilization of resources as per needed application. Mesos and Yarn propose to enlarge the reserved clustering by distributing resources among several practicing frameworks like such as Hadoop, MPI, Spark, etc. [32, 33].

B. Cluster Frameworks

The framework is considered for working out on huge cluster of shared out data. It classified on computation as (a) group processing and (b) immediate processing [34]. It maintains the following technical supports for computation:

    a. The offline processing is developed by MapReduce,
    b. The batch processing is maintained by Hadoop,
    c. The iterative computing is developed by Spark,
    d. The batch-oriented processing is worked by Horton,
    e. The online processing is formed by Storm,
    f. The high performance is generated by MPI,
    g. The stream processing is assigned to Flume,

C. Data Warehousing with computation

The computation of data warehousing is developed by following techniques:

    a. The cluster of data is analyzed by Hive,
    b. For analyzing information, clustering framework like Shark use SQL through query processing,
    c. Several languages are used for computation like Pig reduces the development time based on writing queries,

    d.   Mahout is used for machine learning and

    e.   Drill is used for extended database.

Generally, the data warehouse is communicated through attached servers and work out framework maintains extendable NoSQL database such as Hbase [35].

D. Data storing management
Generally, the data are stored in big data with three categories such as:

    a.   Structured,

    b.   Semi-structured and

    c.   Unstructured data in database.

It maintains the supervision concerns such as extendable, imitation, high performance, etc. Thus it divides the data base into following two categories.

    a.   Relational Database Management System (RDBMS), and

    b.   NoSQL Database Management System [36].

    a.   RDBMS always maintains structured data in form rows and column of tables and it is easy to operate data base manipulation. RDBMS cooperate with data storing layer by connector called Sqoop. It is intended to relocate volume data in Hadoop. Sqoop uses the technique as import or export the data between RDBMS and HDFS (import from RDBMS to HDFS and export for reverse). It uses Hive table to directly import the data from RDBMS.

    b.   NoSQL supplies the most excellent frame on both structured and unstructured data. NoSQL Database Management System makes possible aspects such as: concurrent, attribute oriented, shred, extendable, strong, sparse and arranged data [37].

E. Visual data analysis
The data visualization and analysis is generated to assist in cooperative dashboards. Visual data analysis is developed by various tools such as D3.js [38], Tableau, RapidMiner or R Tool. The above tools assist to quickly capture the image, analyze the visual and distribute information [35]. Another

tool, Tableau, uses Apache Hive through ODBC connection for SQL access in Hadoop [10]. The above categories generate patterns of data based on data visualization and make prediction for future information.

3.6   Architecture for Crime Technical Model

The architecture for crime technical model is developed using several processes based on analyzing VGI and Web 2.0 captured data for successful crime analysis [48, 49]. So it needs different constructive layers to design architecture for above model which is mentioned below for crime activities.

A. Integration Layer
The different data collect by dissimilar sources like from social network where people help to post crime incidents, close friends, distributed information from known person and through chatting. All the data integrate in a single database for better analysis. It is easy to analyze the above data based on specific keyword for these activities all the time. Further, another way is considered to collect crime incident report based on the application of web and mobile. In this application user utilizes the web form to fill up the crime incident data and send to investigation department. Integration of the data gathers at web crime database and GIS online services warehouse [50, 51].

B. Security Layer
This layer is an important layer in crime analysis architecture where personal information is secured using secure algorithm. Here authentication is maintained by two factors (a) bio metric identification using password and (b) authorization considered for specific access [52].

C. Physical Infrastructure Layer
This layer supports Big Data horizontal and scalable environment for different kinds of data analyses and also makes extremely fault tolerant, high performance, appropriate to describe huge dataset and consistent [53].

D. Database Processing Layer
The other name of this layer is known as Hadoop layer that permits to process volume data sets across cluster based on programming framework such as HDFS and MapReduce. These two frameworks are utilized for storing and exercising of data separately as: (a) HDFS is used for storing data

and (b) MapReduce is used for exercising of huge datasets. The several manipulations are considered to update data set such as scalable, sorted, etc. The distributed database is created using several database management systems like Hbase, Cassandra and MongoDB [54].

E. Analysis Layer

The role of Hadoop is very important in this layer by using several components of Hadoop such as Hive, Pig, Shark and MLlib for type of data collection. Data are imported from HDFS through connector and Sqoop and also analysis by Hive. Flume is a reliable tool that helps to collect data from social networks and sharing services for several manipulations such as collection of data, forwarding of data, and cumulating huge amount of log data with effectively. Subsequent to collecting of all data, data are stocked up in HDFS and these data are used for processing by MapReduce simple programming model. This programming model is used to write either in Java or in any convenient supportive language like Python to fulfil the processing of data. The crime data collect from investigation office to generate effective crime patterns. Here JOIN operation is used to gather several data from different storing resources to generate huge amount of crime data set.

3.7   Challenges

The architecture for crime technical model has explained a helpful and vigorous approach on crime occurrences by incorporating of visual data with offense issues. The crime evidences from bureaucrats department is used to analyze several crimes as per crime levels such as lowest level, middle level and highest level. But it needs to take several challenges to achieve such analysis as per the following list:

A. Security

The security is important part of data for sharing, storing from any database system. For proposed architecture on crime analysis, data security is important part of data base which need to maintain secrecy of data during sharing information to avoid death threats by criminals. Thus, several authenticated identification is needed to make secrecy of data during sharing of data. For example Individual Information can be considered as safety data based on validated proof such as (a) safety servers and (b) encrypted communications. Another important checking is needed of Logs regularly for any kind of hacking activities.

B. Infrastructure Cost

The several benefits are involved for analyzing information with Big Data. But the design cost is high for stocking up huge amount of data in cluster, to obtain replication in Big Data, data visualization. Big Data technology always tries to choose with less cost with Max-Benefits ratio.

C. Spam or Refuted Data

Many times, the unauthorized message/information comes by unauthorized users to misguide or trouble to police department. This is happening through spam data and is generated automatically. These spam information create several ambiguity situation for public. Thus it needs to verify regularly up to strong conformation of right information.

D. RapidMiner

RapidMiner is a tool used for several visual data analyses with forecast. It creates an interactive and shareable dashboard to imagine the movement, dissimilarities, prototype and amount of data with graphical representation of above concerns. Hive creates the result by itself from database and imports to RapidMiner for additional data visualization.

RapidMiner is also utilized to see the Hive output easily with the help of Naïve Bayes algorithm. Further RapidMiner provides several algorithms based on machine learning and deep learning techniques.

3.8 Conclusions

The role of VGI is important to collect crime data from social network such as web data or mobile data on crimes, from tags of Twitter handles and availability on CrimeInfo repository. Several attributes of the crime data assist to analyze the incidents and predict the future crime with locations using Big Data and Machine learning framework. Thus architecture proposed to lessen cost and endeavors of bureaucrats department to control the sensitive crime areas. The model assists to reduce crime on the security authorities and enquiry of crimes. Based on Big Data Analytics with clustering approach, it lessens the search time and find out secrete information through correlation and categorization.

Thus the role of Big data Analytics is important for making over unrefined data with the help of legislature and judiciary steps to control day-wise crimes. As per growth of population, crimes are increased. Thus legislative and judiciary rule need to implement strongly without compromise with criminals to make more safety of public life.

The several challenges need to implement through software as well as hardware technology to control crimes from different location throughout globe. Thus it can build the generic big data analytics platform to process of diversity data for broad range of applications. Several strategies can be considered to integrate multivariate visualization with data mining techniques to create potential patterns of data. Several case studies can be taken to test different crime data to predict for future crimes as per the model.

References

1. Gandomi, A. and Haider, M., Beyond the hype: Big data concepts, methods, and analytics. *Int. J. Inf. Manage.*, 35, 2, 137–144, Apr. 2015.

2. Hassani, H., Huang, X., Ghodsi, M., Silva, E.S., A review of data mining applications in crime. *Stat. Anal. Data Mining, ASA Data Sci. J.*, 9, 3, 139–154, Apr. 2016.

3. Wang, Y., Kung, L., Wang, W.Y.C., Cegielski, C.G., An integrated big data analytics-enabled transformation model: Application to health care. *Inf. Manage.*, 55, 1, 64–79, Jan. 2018.

4. Saoumya, and Baghel, A.S., A Predictive Model For Mapping Crime Using Big Data Analytics. *IJRET*, 04, 04, 344–348, 2015.

5. Nagpal, R. and Sehgal, R., Crime Analysis using K-Means Clustering. *Int. J. Comput. Appl.*, 83, 4, 0975–8887, December 2013.

6. Jain, M. and Varma, C., Adapting K-means for Clustering in Big Data. *Int. J. Comput. Appl.*, 101, 1, 19–24, 2014.

7. Sanse, K. and Sharma, M., Clustering methods for Big data analysis. *IJARCET*, 4, 3, 642–648, 2015.

8. Herrera, F., Sosa, R., Delgado, T., GeoBI and Big VGI for Crime Analysis and Report. *IEEE Conference Publication, [Online]*. Available: https://ieeexplore. ieee.org/abstract/document/7300856. [Accessed: 15-Apr-2019].

9. Bakillah, M. and J.L., Exploiting Big VGI to Improve Routing and Navigation Services, in: *Big Data*, 18-Feb-2014, [Online]. Available: https://www. taylorfrancis.com/. [Accessed: 15-Apr-2019].

10. Broadhurst, R., Grabosky, P., Alazab, M., Bouhours, B., Chon, S., *An Analysis of the Nature of Groups Engaged in Cyber Crime, Social Science Research Network*, SSRN Scholarly Paper ID 2461983, Rochester, NY, Feb. 2014.

11. Nandimath, J., Banerjee, E., Patil, A., Kakade, P., Vaidya, S., Chaturvedi, D., Big data analysis using Apache Hadoop. *2013 IEEE 14th International Conference on Information Reuse Integration (IRI)*, pp. 700–703, 2013.

12. Yu, C.H., Morabito, M., Chen, P., Ding, W., Hierarchical spatiotemporal pattern discovery and predictive modeling. *IEEE Trans. Knowl. Data Eng.*, 28, 4, 979–993, Apr. 2016.
13. Musa, S., Smart cities: A road map for development. *IEEE Potentials*, 37, 2, 19–23, Apr. 2018.
14. Wang, S., Wang, X., Ye, P., Yuan, Y., Liu, S., Wang, F.Y., Parallel crime scene analysis based on ACP approach. *IEEE Trans. Computat. Social Syst.*, 5, 1, 244–255, Mar. 2018.
15. Yadav, S., Yadav, A., Vishwakarma, R., Yadav, N., Timbadia, M., Crime pattern detection, analysis & prediction. *Proc. IEEE Int. Conf. Electron., Commun. Aerosp. Technol.*, Coimbatore, India, pp. 225–230, Apr. 2017.
16. Zhao, X. and Tang, J., Exploring transfer learning for crime prediction. *Proc. IEEE Int. Conf. Data Mining Workshops*, New Orleans, LA, USA, pp. 1158–1159, Nov. 2017.
17. Wu, S., Male, J., Dragut, E., Spatial–temporal campus crime pattern mining from historical alert messages. *Proc. Int. Conf. Comput., Netw. Commun.*, Santa Clara, CA, USA, pp. 778–782, 2017.
18. Vineeth, K.R.S., Pradhan, T., Pandey, A., A novel approach for intelligent crime pattern discovery and prediction. *Proc. Int. Conf. Adv. Commun. Control Comput. Technol*, Ramanathapuram, India, pp. 531–538, 2016.
19. Rodríguez, C.R., Gomez, D.M., Rey, M.A.M., Forecasting time series from clustering by a memetic differential fuzzy approach: An application to crime prediction. *Proc. IEEE Symp. Ser. Comput. Intell.*, Honolulu, HI, USA, pp. 1–8, Nov./Dec. 2017.
20. Joshi, A., Sabitha, A.S., Choudhury, T., Crime analysis using K-means clustering. *Proc. 3rd Int. Conf. Comput. Intell. Netw.*, Odisha, India, pp. 33–39, 2017.
21. Noor, N.M.M., Nawawi, W.M.F.W., Ghazali, A.F., Supporting decision making in situational crime prevention using fuzzy association rule. *Proc. Int. Conf. Comput., Control, Informat. Appl. (IC3INA)*, Jakarta, Indonesia, pp. 225–229, 2013.
22. Wang, M., Zhang, F., Guan, H., Li, X., Chen, G., Li, T., Xi, X., Hybrid neural network mixed with random forests and Perlin noise. *Proc. 2nd IEEE Int. Conf. Comput. Commun. (ICCC)*, Chengdu, China, pp. 1937–1941, Oct. 2016.
23. Wang, Z., Zhang, D., Sun, M., Jiang, J., Ren, J., A deep-learning based feature hybrid framework for spatiotemporal saliency detection inside videos. *Neurocomputing*, 287, 68–83, Apr. 2018.
24. Yan, Y., Ren, J., Zhao, H., Sun, G., Wang, Z., Zheng, J., Marshall, S., Soraghan, J., Cognitive fusion of thermal and visible imagery for effective detection and tracking of pedestrians in videos. *Cognit. Comput.*, 10, 1, 94–104, Feb. 2018.
25. Kashef, H., Abdel-Nasser, M., Mahmoud, K., Power loss estimation in smart grids using a neural network model. *Proc. Int. Conf. Innov. Trends Comput. Eng. (ITCE)*, Aswan, Egypt, pp. 258–263, 2018.

26. Injadat, M., Salo, F., Nassif, A.B., Data mining techniques in social media: A survey. *Neurocomputing*, 214, 654–670, Nov. 2016.
27. Zheng, S., Chen, S., Yang, L., Zhu, J., Luo, Z., Hu, J., Yang, X., Big data processing architecture for radio signals empowered by deep learning: Concept, experiment, applications and challenges. *IEEE Access*, 6, 55907–55922, 2018.
28. Zhao, J., Gao, Y., Qu, Y., Yin, H., Liu, Y., Sun, H., Travel time prediction: Based on gated recurrent unit method and data fusion. *IEEE Access*, 6, 70463–70472, 2018.
29. Niu, K., Zhang, H., Cheng, C., Wang, C., Zhou, T., A novel spatiotemporal model for city-scale traf_c speed prediction. *IEEE Access*, 7, 30050–30057, 2019.
30. Peral, J., Ferrández, A., Gil, D., Kauffmann, E., Mora, H., A review of the analytics techniques for an efficient management of online forums: An architecture proposal. *IEEE Access*, 7, 12220–12240, 2019.
31. Crime Statistics, *data.gov.in*. [Online]. Available: https://data.gov.in/dataset-group-name/crime-statistics. [Accessed: 07-May-2019].
32. Electron: Towards Efficient Resource Management on Heterogeneous Clusters with Apache Mesos. *IEEE Conference Publication*, [Online]. Available: https://ieeexplore.ieee.org/abstract/document/8030597. [Accessed: 15-Apr-2019].
33. Apache Hadoop 2.7.4—MapReduce NextGen aka YARN aka MRv2. [Online]. Available: https://hadoop.apache.org/docs/r2.7.4/hadoop-yarn/hadoop-yarn-site/. [Accessed: 15-Apr-2019].
34. Singh, D. and Reddy, C.K., A survey on platforms for big data analytics. *J. Big Data*, 2, 1, 8, Oct. 2014.
35. Big data emerging technologies: A case study with analyzing Twitter data using apache hive. *IEEE Conference Publication.*, [Online]. Available: https://ieeexplore.ieee.org/abstract/document/7453400. [Accessed: 07-May-2019].
36. Agrawal, R., Borgida, A., Jagadish, H.V., Efficient Management of Transitive Relationships in Large Data and Knowledge Bases. *Proceedings of the 1989 ACM SIGMOD International Conference on Management of Data*, New York, NY, USA, pp. 253–262, 1989.
37. Gudivada, V.N., Rao, D., Raghavan, V.V., NoSQL Systems for Big Data Management. *2014 IEEE World Congress on Services*, pp. 190–197, 2014.
38. Keim, D., Qu, H., Ma, K., Big-Data Visualization. *IEEE Comput. Graph. Appl.*, 33, 4, 20–21, Jul. 2013.
39. Viswanathan, V. and Viswanathan, S.R., *Data Analysis Cookbook*, 2nd ed., pp. 30–39, Packt Publishing Ltd, Birmingham, U.K, 2015.
40. Boix, R., De Miguel-Molina, B., Hervás-Oliver, J.L., Microgeographies of creative industries clusters in Europe: From hot spots to assemblages. *Papers Regional Sci.*, 94, 4, 753–772, Jan. 2015.
41. Jain, A. and Bhatnagar, V., Crime Data Analysis Using Pig with Hadoop. *Procedia Comput. Sci.*, 78, 571–578, Jan. 2016.
42. Dittrich, J. and Quiané-Ruiz, J.A., Efficient Big Data Processing in Hadoop MapReduce. *Proc. VLDB Endow*, 5, 12, 2014–2015, Aug. 2012.

43. Menon, A., Big Data @ Facebook. *Proceedings of the 2012 Workshop on Management of Big Data Systems*, New York, NY, USA, pp. 31–32, 2012.
44. Casado, R. and Younas, M., Emerging trends and technologies in big data processing. *Concurr. Comput. Pract. Exp.*, 27, 8, 2078–2091, 2015.
45. Yun, C., An improvement apriori arithmetic based on rough set theory. *Circuits, Communications and System (PACCS), 2011 Third Pacific-Asia Conference on*, pp. 1–3, July 2011.
46. Kaza, S., Wang, T., Gowda, H., Chen, H., Target vehicle identificationfor border safety using mutual information. *Intelligent Transportation Systems, 2005. Proceedings. 2005 IEEE*, pp. 1141–1146, Sept 2005.
47. Shwarappa, I. and Anuradha, J., A Brief Introduction on Big Data 5Vs Characteristics and Hadoop Technology. *Procedia Comput. Sci.*, 48, 319–324, Jan. 2015.
48. Sawant, N. and Shah, H., Big Data Application Architecture, in: *Big Data Application Architecture Q & A: A Problem-Solution Approach*, N. Sawant and H. Shah (Eds.), pp. 9–28, Apress, Berkeley, CA, 2013.
49. Ghosh, D., Chun, S.A., Shafiq, B., Adam, N.R., Big Data-based Smart City Platform: Real-Time Crime Analysis. *Proceedings of the 17th International Digital Government Research Conference on Digital Government Research*, New York, NY, USA, pp. 58–66, 2016.
50. Hoffman, S., *Apache Flume: Distributed Log Collection for Hadoop*, Packt Publishing Ltd, Birmingham, UK, 2013.
51. Combining Qualitative and Quantitative Sampling, Data Collection, and Analysis Techniques in Mixed-Method Studies, Sandelowski—2000— Research in Nursing & Health, Wiley Online Library. [Online]. Available: https://onlinelibrary.wiley.com/doi/abs/10.1002/1098-240X(200006)23: 3%3C246::AID-NUR9%3E3.0.CO;2-H. [Accessed: 07-May-2019].
52. Big Data and Hadoop—a Study in Security Perspective, ScienceDirect. [Online]. Available: https://www.sciencedirect.com/science/article/pii/ S187705091500592X. [Accessed: 07-May-2019].
53. Jha, P., Sharma, D.A., Jha, R., Kaur, S., How can your IT Infrastructure Withstand the Pressure of Digitalization? *IJRECE*, 7, 1, 1099–1104, 2019.
54. O'Driscoll, A., Daugelaite, J., Sleator, R.D., Big data, Hadoop and cloud computing in genomics. *J. Biomed. Inform.*, 46, 5, 774–781, Oct. 2013.

4

The Role of Remote Sensing and GIS in Military Strategy to Prevent Terror Attacks

Sushobhan Majumdar

Department of Geography, Jadavpur University, Kolkata, India

Abstract

Remote Sensing (RS) and Geographic Information System (GIS) play a pivotal role in military operations as these are very much dynamic in nature and the concepts of Command, Control, Communication and Coordination in military operations are largely dependent on the availability of accurate information in order to arrive at quick decisions for operational orders. In the present digital era, both Remote Sensing and GIS is an excellent tool for Military commanders in the operations because of the easy availability of the high resolution satellite images. The use of RS-GIS and its applications in defense purposes has revolutionized the way in which these forces operate and function. Military forces use GIS in a variety of applications including cartography, intelligence, battlefield management, terrain analysis, military installation management and monitoring of possible terrorist activity. In this paper an attempt has been made to scrutinize the role of Remote Sensing and GIS for defense purposes especially in case of land based operation. Side by side effort has been made to find out the problems of using these techniques and how it can be minimized. This study represents useful information about the role of RS and GIS in defense purposes. It may also help the planners and decision makers to understand the usefulness of these techniques in military operations to prevent terror activity.

Keywords: Remote sensing, geographic information system, terrain analysis, battlefield management, intelligence

Email: sushobhan91@gmail.com

Subhendu Kumar Pani, Sanjay Kumar Singh, Lalit Garg, Ram Bilas Pachori and Xiaobo Zhang (eds.) *Intelligent Data Analytics for Terror Threat Prediction: Architectures, Methodologies, Techniques and Applications*, (79–94) © 2021 Scrivener Publishing LLC

4.1 Introduction

Remote sensing process means to acquire the information without any physical contact with the object. It may be of two types i.e. analog remote sensing and digital remote sensing. According to Jensen [1], remote sensing is the technique of capturing the data without touching it. Cameras, scanners, X-rays, magnetometer are essential elements of remote sensing which have been used extensively to capture the data or information.

The term Geographical Information System (GIS) is a combination of two different subsystems i.e. geography and information systems. GIS helps to convert various kinds of data into information. GIS is basically a system of information mainly used for the capturing of the data and analyzing the information. GIS is a facility for preparing, presenting and interpreting facts about the surface of the earth [2]. From the ancient period military forces or defense forces have played an important role for the development of the country. Over time different technologies have been innovated in military science for defense purposes which have enhanced the defense strategy and defense techniques. Because of this changing technology the dominance of military power in the war front has also been significantly increased. The war finishes when military forces occupy the land of the enemies. In this sense, GIS is also helpful to occupy the land of the enemies. As GIS is associated with the spatial extension of an area, so it is very much important.

Remote sensing and GIS or Geo-informatics have plenty of applications in the various disciplines of science. Application of this tool is increasing rapidly day by day. Remote Sensing and GIS as tools have been used in the natural resource management, wildlife habitat protection, baseline mapping for the GIS input, urban planning field, planning for seismic, fire and terrorist activities, land use survey, etc. Spatial information about the location is very much useful for the army officers, commanders for understanding the topography of the area. So, it has been considered as one of the important skills in defense strategy. Strategy making map has played an important role for gathering of knowledge for the essence of understanding. GIS has played a key role for querying and displaying the geographical data for the army officials for the completion of their mission.

Use of map in the battlefield is not a modern concept rather it is an old one. In the ancient period hardcopy maps or mental maps were mainly used in the battlefield. But in modern era mainly digital maps have been used like surveyed map, topographic map, cadastral map, etc. By these maps user can easily identify their location with in-depth information like latitude, longitude, height (from mean sea level), etc. Change in the orientation of the maps may be termed as paradigm shift i.e. changes in map form i.e. from old hardcopy maps to newer digital form.

From the last quarter of the century, geospatial information has been used by the commanders for defense purpose and in that time hardcopy maps played an important role in battlefield management system [3–6]. Geospatial data has been used firstly in Grenada in 1983 [7]. Presently GIS has been used effectively for military base [8]. The uses of Global Positioning System (GPS) and microelectronics are playing a pivotal role for authentic worldwide navigation and positioning system [9]. Different system devices and GPS aided weapons have been extensively used for navigation, positioning, battlefield management, search and rescue operation, etc. [10]. In the mid-nineteenth century mainly aerial photograph had been used for defense purpose. But at present, digital or online maps are used instead of old hardcopy maps [11]. The applications of remote sensing and GIS have been changed in recent decades. Now different high resolution satellite images have been used for the defense purposes [12] and according to Welch [13], the spatial resolutions of 0.5 to 10 m diameter have been categorized as high resolution satellite.

Here an attempt has been made to find out the uses of RS and GIS for making defense strategy to prevent terror attacks. The objective of this study is to find out the role of RS and GIS in constructing defense strategy to prevent terror attacks. Side by side emphasis has also been done to investigate the problem of using this technology. Few measures have also been suggested how it can be minimized.

4.2   Database and Methods

This study has been done on the basis of various applications of remote sensing and GIS in different disciplines. For this study the concept about various approaches of remote sensing and GIS has been collected on the basis of researcher's real-time experience. For study purpose different maps have been collected from the various online sources like UGGS server, Glovis, etc. For the mapping purposes different softwares have been used. For the processing of the satellite images various softwares (like Erdas v 14,

Envi 5.3, etc.) have been used. For the vectorization process or for the polygon mapping, various GIS softwares like Arc GIS 10.3, Arc Scene 10.3 version, Q GIS software have been used. For the analysis purposes various 3D mapping methods have been used (like Digital Elevation Model, Triangulated Network Model, Digital Terrain Model, etc.).

4.3   Discussion and Analysis

Remote sensing and GIS play an important role in defense strategy to prevent terror attacks. As the core concepts of defense strategy strongly depends on the command, control, communication and coordination which largely depend on the positional accuracy of the user's location. GIS has extended its applications in the various fields like cartography, intelligence, topographic analysis, battlefield management, etc. In GIS, there are four types of functions i.e. query about data, overlay operations, neighborhood analysis and connectivity operations [14–17]. In the field of geosciences, spatial data and its management played a vital role as in the battlefield for the positional accuracy of each of an area which is very much significant. Figure 4.1 shows the relationship between military science with the Geographical Information Systems.

GIS presents a combining area for mobilizing logistics, combining different sources and setting strong communication for successful operations

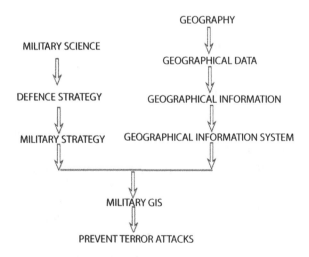

Figure 4.1 Frame work of military GIS.

in the battlefield. From the real time it is so much necessary for success-ful military operations in the battlefield. GIS technology is also helpful for armed forces for various levels of information. Air borne satellites like spy cameras play a vital role for making strategy in the warfield. It also helps for the battlefield intelligence making and its management. As the spy camera or airborne sensor gives high resolution data, it is very much useful to the user. It is also helpful for maintaining the monitor for the warfare gad-gets. The image capturing from the camera is relatively much coarser in the developed countries rather than the developing countries because of high technological development. For the nuclear attack or for missile attack to any enemies user has to integrate both the GIS technology with the mil-itary science. Different international agencies have coordinated both the GIS technology with the defense technology for the destructive purposes.

4.4   Role of Remote Sensing and GIS

The earth is constantly under observation from the various satellites which are revolving outside the earth's surface. There are mainly two types of sat-ellite, i.e. Sun Synchronous Satellite and Geostationary Satellite. The works of those satellite systems are different. There are also various types of plat-forms in remote sensing like air borne platform, space borne platform and ground based platform. In the military science, data from all three plat-forms have been used. The uses of remote sensing and GIS for the defense purpose have flourished so rapidly that at present it is an effective tool for defense strategy construction and its management. Role of remote sensing and GIS in military science can be explained in this way. Figure 4.2 shows various applications of GIS in defense strategy.

4.5   Cartographic Model

Cartography is a very old branch of science which mainly may be termed as a science of map making and the term cartography refers to the art and science of map making. In the old days maps were drawn by the use of pen and pencil on a paper but nowadays computer has been used for the purpose of map making. This change can be referred as a shift of para-digm in map making. Cartography mainly intends to science of map making by maintaining its properties like shape, size, area, azimuth and direction. Now cartography has been used widely for the construction of various models of the earth's surface. Those models can be used easily for

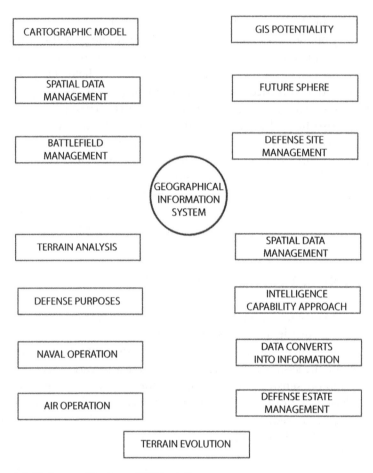

Figure 4.2 Various applications of GIS in defense strategy.

making or constructing defense strategy. Digital Elevation Model (DEM), Triangulated Irregular Network (TIN) Model, etc. are the examples of cartographic models (Figure 4.5) which have been used for defense purposes.

Digital Elevation Model (DEM) is mainly used for geometric modeling of the earth's surface using satellite images. It is also used for the 3D modeling of the earth's surface using the contour lines, bench mark or spot height of an area. This model is mainly used for the positional accuracy and for the topographic modeling. From this model the user can easily identify the slope, aspect, terrain, topography of that area. Recently this model has been used extensively in the military applications. For some cases stereo images have been used for DEM [18, 19].

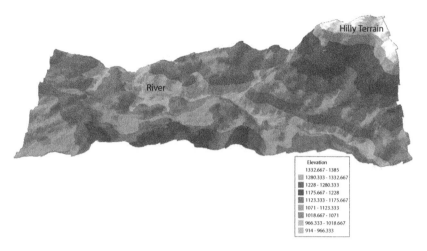

Figure 4.3 Cartographic model for land management in hilly area.

GIS has been used by the army commanders for topographic evolution [20]. Figure 4.3 and 4.4 shows sample of cartographic model and demographic model of a hilly terrain respectively.

4.5.1   Spatial Data Management

Spatial data management is a process of capturing or management of the database of the real world. This has been used widely in the field of geosciences, military science, earth sciences, etc. Management of the database can be flexible according to the user. By this spatial management system, user can easily capture, store and analyze the data as per requirement. Spatial data management is related with the spatial data modeling which includes field view and object view.

4.5.2   Battlefield Management

Battlefield Management System (BMS) is a management system for integration of information, to enhance works of command and control prompt in the defense system. For the management of the battlefield the applications of GIS are new. Different analyses like Digital Elevation Model (DEM), Digital Terrain Model (DTM), and Triangulated Irregular Network (TIN) Model, etc. can be applied for the purpose of defense management. For topographic modeling user can create a 3D Model of the earth's surface which will be acted as a replica of the earth's surface.

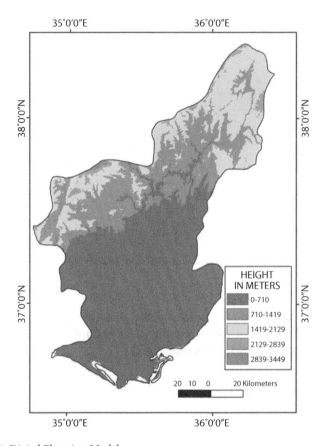

Figure 4.4 Digital Elevation Model.

4.5.3   Terrain Analysis

Terrain Analysis is the representation of the topographic features using Geographical Information System. Terrain analysis includes slope, aspect, viewshed, hillshade, elevation, contour lines, etc. of the earth's surface. For some cases it has been used to build correlation between the physical and social aspects. The uses of terrain analysis are very high in the field of military mainly to construct the defense strategy. COTS software can be used for this terrain evolution purpose [21].

Hillshade analysis is a model which shows the curvature of the earth surface based on height of each reference point. In this model each pixel of this raster image contains a specific z values which indicates the heights of that area. Hillshade analysis is mainly used for the visual purpose for the analysis purposes. It mainly provides an attractive and realistic outlook

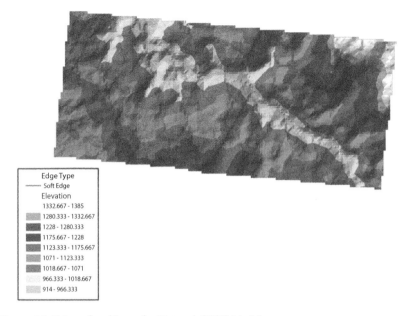

Edge Type
——— Soft Edge
Elevation
1332.667 - 1385
1280.333 - 1332.667
1228 - 1280.333
1175.667 - 1228
1123.333 - 1175.667
1071 - 1123.333
1018.667 - 1071
966.333 - 1018.667
914 - 966.333

Figure 4.5 Triangulated Irregular Network (TIN) Model.

about the surface features. In the boundary area, these types of model are really helpful for battlefield management. Figure 4.6 shows a hillshade analysis model of a hilly area.

Like hillshade, viewshed analysis is also helpful to prevent terror attacks. Viewshed is basically a visual area of the earth surface from a fixed point. Normally this fixed point is a higher area from the surrounding area. By this analysis, the views of the observer can be easily adjusted over or under the land surface. Now viewshed has been used extensively in the field of military science. This analysis is useful for battlefield planning during war like accurate position of an area where whole region can cover, height of the towers of army, etc.

4.6   Mapping Techniques Used for Defense Purposes

For the defense purposes different remote sensing and GIS techniques may be used to prevent terror attacks. Among the RS-GIS techniques mosaicking, subsetting, etc. of the satellite image is very much import-ant. Mosaicking has been mainly used for stitching of the two or more images of an area having same geo-referencing system using GIS. By these

HILLSHADE
Value
High : 180
Low : 0

Figure 4.6 Hillshade analysis model for terrain analysis.

mosaicking techniques user can easily create a large size image by stitching numerous number of small images and from that image the user can easily identify the zone or areas of terror attacks. User can create a buffer zone from the neighboring countries to construct various defense strategy. On the other hand subsetting is one of the useful strategies often used for mapping purposes. Subsetting means clipping of an area using a target file. Both the file must be same projection system. Through subsetting techniques user can easily focus on target area from an entire region. Subsetting is also helpful for the landscape designing as the error increases with the size of the area. Presently in most cases 3D images of the smaller area has been used for the defense purposes for clearer understanding about the dispute area.

4.7   Naval Operations

Remote sensing and GIS can also be applied for naval operations in sea surface. If any commercial vessel enters into the countries jurisdiction without any permission then it will be a punishable offense. By tracking through the satellite image the user can easily identify those impermissible vehicles. Except this researcher can easily identify the oil spill incident in sea surface as it is harmful for marine organisms. Through the satellite image the user can easily identify the submerged ship in the sea. To identify these issues different airborne sensors are playing an active role as it gives user the images of inaccessible areas of the ocean. To identify the areas of oil spill in the sea surface, laser fluorocensors and SAR sensors mainly used. Remote sensing and GIS are also helpful for predicting the weather condition of the sea surface. If any accident takes place in the ship then the damage can easily be identified through this technology. If any ship faces serious problem (like physical damage, problem of engines, etc.) then the captain of that ship can easily contact with the other nearest ship by the radar sensor for rescuing from that problem.

4.7.1   Air Operations

Geo-informatics is also helpful for air operations for the security purposes. Using radar sensor the user can easily identify the aircraft of the other countries that have entered into the countries jurisdiction without legal permission. By the airborne sensors the user can easily track each one of the aircraft in the country. At the time of war or any serious problem by the air operations any country can easily send food, secret news or information using satellite images. By the images user can easily differentiate the changes in the army aircraft of the other countries. New technology and high resolution satellite vehicles like Pléiades Neo, etc. will play a major role for making defense strategy and national security also.

4.7.2   GIS Potential in Military

Computer generated automated systems through the combination of GIS technology and information systems can provide assistance to military forces for terrain analysis and evolution. But there are also few complexities for using GIS. With the uses of technology the costs for using GIS will get minimized. Now GIS has been used in the various fields of science and the sphere of application has been increasing day by day.

4.8   Future Sphere of GIS in Military Science

Future sphere of GIS depends upon about in what way military has attached with this information system. Different types of mapping are used in the military science like terrain evolution, digital elevation modeling, etc. Mainly the positive side of using GIS is it is attached with the communication systems, different navigation techniques and real time data imagery. Terrain evolution and accuracy of ground location are the essential tools in remote sensing and GIS. Precise location of the target will minimize the percentage of errors. Most of the military leaders and commanders use this technology to enter into the enemy's area within a shorter time period. It also helps the other members to know the topographic condition of the area with the lithological characteristics. GIS gives the user real-time data about the battlefield with the ongoing situation of the war to build up new strategy.

4.8.1   Defense Site Management

Defense Site Management in military operations is very much useful. It is one of the methods operated by GIS systems. GIS helps by the management of military base facilities, maintenance costs, enhancing the effectiveness of the mission, etc.

4.8.2   Spatial Data Management

The data about any specific location in earth surface can be termed as spatial data of an area. These are the confidential matter which is mainly handled by the army officers or field commanders. For this issue the officers or field commanders have to know all types of pictures, maps, figures, etc. In earlier days the uses of data are restricted because of confined specifications. For the maintenance of this database integration among the users are highly needed.

4.8.3   Intelligence Capability Approach

GIS is one such platform that can hold, capture and analyze the data. In the intelligence building approach GIS helps in many ways like terrorist targets in accurate location, battlefield management, target areas in the Warfield, hitting the target with minimal impact on the environment, decision making to build up defense strategy, etc. GIS software plays a vital role for making success these types of activities.

4.8.4   Data Converts Into Information

As GIS has the capability of data holding, data capturing and data analyzing, using this power GIS can turn numerous number of data into information. As a consequence the application of data will be increased in various disciplines including military science also. It also provides various tools to unlock and reveal the data in a meaningful form for all types of maps, diagrams, pictures, etc. It also helps for 3D modeling of an area.

4.8.5   Defense Estate Management

Uses of GIS in the defense management have played a vital role. It also allows military land management by reducing secret operation time, maintenance costs; improve the effectiveness of the war. It is also helpful by providing the alternative strategies of war, enhances the effectiveness of communication and also by gaining knowledge.

4.9   Terrain Evolution

Terrain evolution is also helpful for land based military operations. For this purpose GIS has been played a vital role. GIS helps the user to know or to measure the elevations of the target area, the uses of weapons, carrier, etc. Except these it is also helpful to identify different land covers including vegetation, transportation networks, spatial location of target area, etc. Detailed map of an area with types of land, terrain modeling is also helpful for essential military operations. Spatial location is crucial in military science as accuracy of location is very much important. Any types of error can create huge problem to the users. Different reasons like magnetic inclination and declination, wrong positional information are the major reasons behind the error in military operations.

4.9.1   Problems Regarding the Uses of Remote Sensing and GIS

Remote Sensing and GIS are new technologies which have flourished mainly in recent decades. These have already experienced extensive uses in the field military GIS. Though the sphere of application of GIS has been increased recently but there are also some problems regarding the uses of remote sensing and GIS in the field of military GIS.

Most important problems in the area of military GIS are the data which are used are mostly expensive. For purchasing, processing and analyzing of the data requires lots of money. So, expensive data are one of the major problems faced by the users for using this technology. Another problem is that in few cases previous data are not available; if it is available then the data found having very low resolution. This creates huge problems to the users. The analyzing, processing and analysis of the data are very time consuming which is also a serious problem faced by the user. Another problem is that it is techno-centric approach in the field of military GIS. It is only operated by efficient user which is also another problem faced by the authorities. To efficiently use RS–GIS needs lots of efficient user for the processing and analyzing of the data which is totally unavailable. This data is weather dependent. The data are sometimes unusable because of the huge cloud coverage. Unavailability of the data in rainy season is another problem. It is not understandable to lay user. Only user can understand it, after processing and analyzing it is understandable to the viewers.

4.9.2   Recommendations

The uses of new technologies have flourished in recent decades for defense purposes. But the sphere of remote sensing and GIS should be more enhanced. To enhance the uses of RS and GIS for the defense purposes needs more funding from the national level or from the international level. User training is very much required for the properly uses of the data in a shorter time limit. If possible then the user can take training from abroad also. More research and development programs are required as the spheres of uses are very small. More awareness program is needed among the people about its advantages. The high resolution data are very much expensive. The authorities who are providing data (like USGS, ISRO, etc.) should give subsidy for the uses of the data for defense purposes. For the downloading, purchasing of the data requires high networking facility (Like local area connection networking system, etc.). So, in-sufficient network facility is also a problem faced by the user.

4.10   Conclusion

Remote sensing and GIS has plenty of application in the various disciplines of science. Among them its applications in the military science have flourished recently. Presently the orientation of map in the battlefield has also changed from the old hardcopy to modern digital form. The extents of using GIS have been increased in recent decades. Now it has been used in cartographic modeling, defense management, naval operations, air operations, battlefield management, etc. Though it has lots of advantages but there are some serious problems of using this tool. Uses of this technology are very much expensive and it requires high network connection which is totally unavailable in hilly region due to remote location. Except these insufficient no of user, weather dependency also creates lots of problem. To minimize this problem few strategies may be taken like allocation of funds (both national level and international level) special training for the user to increase the controlling power may be taken. This work will extend new light over the military science for constructing defense strategy to prevent terror attacks. By minimizing the problems the sphere of geosciences can be increased extensively. This study represents useful information about the role of RS and GIS in defense purposes. It may also help the planners and decision makers to understand the usefulness of these techniques in military operations to prevent terror activity.

References

1. Jensen, J.R., *Remote Sensing of the Environment: An Earth Resource Perspective*, p. 544, Pearson Education, New Delhi, 2004.
2. Tomlin, C.D., *Geographic Information Systems and Cartographic Modeling*, p. 249, Prentice-Hall, New Jersey, 1990.
3. Greiss, T.E., *The Second World War*, Department of History, United States Military Academy, New York: West Point, 1984.
4. Ballendorf, D.A.,The Battle for Tarawa: A Validation of the U.S. Marines. The Patriot Files. http://www.tiggertags.com/patriotfiles/forum/showthread.php?t=24504, Accessed 17 November 2019, 2003.
5. Conry, T. and Goldberg, J., Integrating facility, comprehensive planning, and environmental management at a large Air Force Base using GIS, in: *URISA Proceedings.*, pp. 542–53, Washington DC, 1994.
6. Lamb, W.R., Evans, B.J., Perry, M.I., McKimley, M.I., Petrie, G.M., Wessels, D.P., *The base-wide environmental analysis and restoration (BEAR) system for Eielson Air Force Base, Alaska*, vol. 2, pp. 196–199, Technical Papers of ACSM/ASPRS Convention and Exposition, Washington DC, ACSM, 1994.
7. Cole, R.H., Grenada, Panama and Haiti: Joint operational reform, in: *Joint Forces Quarterly Autumn/Winter Edition*, pp. 57–64, 1998.
8. GISO (Geographic Information Systems Office), Integrated Geographic Information Repository (IGIR), in: *US Marine Corps Report*, p. 386, Camp Lejeune, NC, 2001.
9. Huybrechts, S., *The High Ground*, National Defense University, National War College, Washington, D.C, 2004.
10. NAVSTAR (GPS Program Office), *Global Positioning Systems Wings*. Los Angeles, Calif. <http://gps.losangeles.af.mil/> Accessed 07 November 2019, 2001.
11. NOAA, *Airline photography and shoreline mapping*. Washington, D.C. <http://www.oceanservice.noaa.gov/topics/navops/mapping/welcome.html> Accessed 01 November 2019, 1997.
12. Behling, T. and McGruther, K., Satellite reconnaissance of the future, in: *Joint Forces Quarterly, Spring Edition*, pp. 23–30, 1998.
13. Welch, R., Spatial resolution requirements for urban studies. *Int. J. Remote Sens.*, 3, 2, 139–146, 1982.
14. Aronoff, S., *Geographic Information Systems: A Management Perspective*, WDL Publications, Ottawa,Canada, 1991.

15. Maguire, D.J., Goodchild, M.F., Rhind, D.W., *Geographical Information Systems: Principles and Applications*, vol. 2, London: Longman, 1991.
16. Lo, C.P. and Yeung, A., *Concepts and Techniques of Geographic Information Systems*, Prentice Hall, Upper Saddle River, New Jersey, 2002.
17. Fleming, S., Jordan, T., Madden, M., Usery, E.L., Welch, R., GIS applications for military operations in coastal zones. *Int. J. Photogramm. Remote Sens.*, 64, 2, 15–21, 2008.
18. Dial, G. and Grodecki, J., Applications of Ikonos imagery. *Proceedings of the ASPRS 2003 Annual Convention, 5–9 May.* Anchorage, Alaska, Bethesda. Md., American Society for Photogrammetry and Remote Sensing, unpaginated, CD-ROM, 2003.
19. Haverkamp, D. and Poulsen, R., Change detection using Ikonos imagery. *Proceedings of the ASPRS 2003 Annual Convention, 5–9 May.* Anchorage, Alaska. Bethesda, Md., American Society for Photogrammetry and Remote Sensing, unpaginated CD-ROM, 2003.
20. Peuquet., D.J. and Bacastow, T., Organizational issues in the development of geographical information systems: a case study of US Army topographic information automation. *Int. J. Geogr. Inf. Syst.*, 5, 303–319, 1991.
21. Graff, L.H. and Visone, D.L., The seamless integration of commercial-off-the-shelf (COTS) and government-off-the-shelf (GOTS) products to meet the Army's terrain analysis requirements. *Proceedings, Sixteenth Annual ESRI User Conference*, Redlands, pp. 4–5, 1996.

5

Text Mining for Secure Cyber Space

Supriya Raheja* and Geetika Munjal

Amity University, Noida, Uttar Pradesh, India

Abstract

Natural language processing techniques can be used to automatically classify sentences from input texts to the potential cyber-attack events. This work presents an expert system for extracting similarity score of cyber-attack related keywords among various resources. The proposed work uses Text Mining approach for making a secure cyber space. To achieve this, an integrated model of lower upper triangular decomposition along with Cholskey decomposition has proposed, further the output is executed in Singular Value Decomposition. The approach is evaluated on accuracy parameter in finding similarity and MRR score of vulnerable keywords. Such studies provide us valuable inputs and insights regarding possible cyber-attacks.

Keywords: Cyberspace, natural language processing, text mining, matrix decomposition

5.1 Introduction

In digital era, the rapid inclusion of evolving technologies significantly increases not only the growth and efficiency of organizations but also opens the door for the cyber-attacks. Cyber-attacks threaten the code-assisted cyber space. "Cyber" notion is used to relate the concepts of computer networks specifically in the area of security. Now, the term "cyber" becomes a standard for industrialists as well as for researchers and academicians. It is linked with all words like cyber-attack, cyber-crime, cyber-defense, offensive cyber, etc. and they all make an environment which is called as

---

*Corresponding author: supriya.raheja@gmail.com

Subhendu Kumar Pani, Sanjay Kumar Singh, Lalit Garg, Ram Bilas Pachori and Xiaobo Zhang (eds.) *Intelligent Data Analytics for Terror Threat Prediction: Architectures, Methodologies, Techniques and Applications*, (95–118) © 2021 Scrivener Publishing LLC

cyberspace. Cyberspace can refer to several matters of the society. No single definition exists for cyberspace; different authors defined it in their own way. Ottis and Lorents have indicated about these issues and defines cyberspace as "cyberspace is a time dependent set of interconnected information systems and the human users that interact with these systems" [32, 33]. Interconnected information systems may comprise the different components for interaction information, software, hardware and means which links them.

Cyber-attack is an issue from cyberspace that refers to careful activities in contrast to data, software, or hardware in interconnected systems. It has generated a worldwide threat for both local and global interconnected systems. Moreover, these attacks possess the capability of spreading themselves in few seconds. The frequency of Cyber-attacks has amplified over the years [29]. For an exploitation of a Cyber-attack, few important things are required by an attacker like access to an interconnected system or network, presence of vulnerabilities in the systems, and a payload. Vulnerabilities may exist in hardware, software, communication interfaces, configuration tables, etc. whereas payload is a code which executes specific assigned task whenever vulnerability has been detected by an attacker [14].

As per the report [34] around 73% attacks occur in Microsoft office products in the year 2019. All these attacks occurred related to vulnerabilities that exist in office applications. These applications include equation editor, zero day issue, etc. All the vulnerabilities are identified by their CVE numbers. These vulnerabilities can be very costly for companies, thus some measures are required to avoid or overcome these issues.

The existence of vulnerabilities in the software also makes the system prone for exploitation on the network or even on a standalone machine. Therefore, the ability to find vulnerabilities is a key metric that organizations and customers use to scale the inclination of a software security [25]. This is one of the inside drivers that sets up the good structure in the zone of how one methodologies divulging vulnerabilities once they have been found. The best in class web lists give a flexible response for versatile and capable chase of web records, getting total web "adroitness" to rank recouped reports [11]. Along these lines to manage request depended upon to work for documents identifying with particular spaces where certain learning and vocabulary can be abused to improve the exactness of the recuperated results [2].

The aim of this work is to develop an expert system which performs text mining of vulnerable keywords especially in Microsoft Office by reusing and integrating mature software components such as Lucene APIs, LSA techniques, and NLP. This work also performs web scrapping to fetch the data from various sites which are further used as the dataset for text mining.

The rest of the chapter is as follows: Section 5.2 discusses the research present till date on text mining for cyber space. Section 5.3 discusses the text mining with Latent Semantic Analysis. Section 5.4 introduces the suggested work followed by results an analysis in Section 5.5. Chapter ends with conclusion in last section.

5.2 Literature Review

The research area in text mining for finding out some pattern in texts includes searching and retrieval, document navigation and retrieval, exploration, text analysis, knowledge management, extraction of topics from text or collection of text and analysis of the topic trending in text stream. All these text mining mechanisms help in finding bugs in various online databases that can lead to possible cyber-attacks [12]. In various studies text mining methods have been applied to get significant information through cyber documents. Text mining in form of Natural language processing techniques help in finding similarity among documents and identifying vulnerable keywords [28, 30]. The broad steps followed in text mining are depicted in Figure 5.1.

Both text mining and data mining technologies have different concepts because textual data is to be converted into structured form. Text data is to be processed so that we can extract binary terms, term frequency or term frequency inverse documents to form document term matrix [27]. In text mining simply mapping words to documents does not provide much help. Latent Semantic Indexing (LSI) is a data recovery strategy and is generally used to quantify the level of likeness between arrangements of content based reports. This technique play as it attempts to leverage the context around the words to capture the hidden concepts, also known

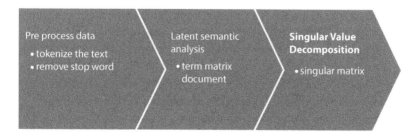

Figure 5.1 Broad steps followed in text mining.

as topics. LSA is also used for dimension reduction. LSA is followed by Singular value decomposition (SVD) to further refine the output of LSA [3]. Various studies have used the concept of text mining in extracting useful information from existing repositories.

One such study was conducted by Wang *et al.*, in which authors have exploited NLP techniques similarity reports [9]. The match rates achieved are 67–93%. In this study Firefox data is used with 77 duplicate bug reports for four months [18]. Similar approached when applied on larger dataset achieved a recall rate reduced in the range 535–69% [19]. The larger dataset has some 5-year Firefox data.

Mokhov *et al.* have made use of same approach with Firefox repository and succeeded with a 50% recall rate [4]. In Ref. [5], BM25F textual similarity function and the results are improved substantially. Chue *et al.* [3] have proposed that most clients regularly express their data requirements by means of short questions to web search tools and they regularly need to physically filter through the query items in light of significance positioning, making the procedure of importance judgment tedious. The structure of the Web increases the complexity to fetch information from web. Semantic Virtual Documents (SVD) techniques have been very much helpful in mining and recovering this web content. In another approach [5] Bayesian learning and text categorization yielded a 30% prediction rate. This paper displays a review that utilizes broad investigation of genuine security vulnerabilities to drive the improvement of: i) runtime procedures for location/covering of security assaults and ii) formal source code investigation techniques to empower ID and evacuation of potential security vulnerabilities. A finite state machine (FSM) approach is utilized to deteriorate programs into different basic exercises, making it conceivable to concentrate basic predicates to be guaranteed for security. The FSM examination pinpoints normal attributes among an expansive scope of security vulnerabilities: unsurprising memory format, unprotected control information, and pointer twistedness. They proposed memory format randomization and control information randomization to cover the vulnerabilities at runtime. They proposed a static examination to deal with distinguish potential security vulnerabilities by utilizing the idea of pointer twistedness.

Corregidor *et al.* [6] state that the malware issue has been around for a long time but still there is no arrangement for avoiding it. Results show that hostility to malware items, noticeably more progressed, because of the new malware tests being found every day. In this authors have identified security vulnerabilities that could be abused by malware of Microsoft Windows 8. Mehta *et al.* [7] have proposed a dominant part of assaults on PC frameworks. An Attack Graph is used for every single conceivable succession of endeavors which can be used to accomplish a particular objective. For genuine frameworks, the size and multifaceted nature of attack graphs significantly surpass human capacity to picture, comprehend and break down.

Kotsiantis *et al.* [8] have enlisted Regulated grouping as one of the substantial number of methods which have been created based on Artificial Intelligence (Logic-based systems, Perceptron-based procedures) and Statistics (Bayesian Networks, Instance-based systems). The objective of directed learning is to assemble a succinct model of the conveyance of class names regarding indicator highlights. Classifier obtained is then used to allot names of class to the testing occurrences here qualities of the indicator elements are known, yet the estimation of the class name is obscure. Wang *et al.* [9] have proposed and actualized a tool Rebug-Indicator, which identifies linked bugs utilizing bug data and code elements. Right off the bat, it separates bug highlights from bug data in bug stores; also, indicator finds bug strategies in code of program, and afterward removes code elements of bug techniques; it also figures similitudes between every abrogated or over-burden strategy & bug techniques; in conclusion, it figures out which technique possibly creating potential linked or comparable bugs. This tool thoroughly identified sixty one linked bugs, which includes 21 genuine bugs & ten presumed bugs and took approx. 15 min.

Shi *et al.* [10] have proposed a prevalent nonlinear element extraction technique called Part foremost segment investigation (KPCA). Its most part utilizes Eigen-deterioration procedure to remove the chief parts. But the technique is infeasible for huge scale information set as a result of the capacity and computational issue. To overcome these inconveniences, an effective iterative technique of registering bit important parts is proposed. To begin with, the Gram grid is changed into the two triangular grids utilizing fragmented Cholesky disintegration. At that point each segment of the triangular lattice is dealt with as the info test for the sans covariance calculation. Hence, the chief segments can be iteratively figured without the Eigen decomposition.

Xu *et al.* [12] have worked on building secure programming which is an overwhelming objective in programming advancement. This paper presents a static examination structure to identify programming vulnerabilities; authors have executed an investigation instrument called Melon based on the Microsoft Phoenix. They assessed the adequacy of Melon through various testing, and successfully investigated programming vulnerabilities.

Kazemi *et al.* [13] have developed High attachment administration service oriented architecture (SOA) which benefitted on single business usefulness. Current measurements for measuring administration attachment reflect most part as the auxiliary part of attachment and in this manner can't be used to gauge theoretical attachment of administrations. Latent Semantic Indexing (LSI) is a data recovery strategy and is generally used to quantify the level of likeness between arrangements of content based reports. In current work we have adopted this approach.

Identifying duplicate words and finding similarity among report uses techniques to measure word frequency [26]. These techniques can be further applied for detection of common usage patterns in logs which may be helpful in detection of cyber-attacks.

5.2.1 Text Mining With Latent Semantic Analysis

Text Mining is a procedure to identify and analyze large amount of unstructured text data to derive quality information. It becomes more popular among data scientists due to the development of big data and deep learning algorithms which helps them to analyze huge amount of unstructured data [16]. Moreover, it helps organizations to find potential information from customer emails, logs, blogs, medical records of employee, documents and other foundations of text data. It facilitates analysis of words or cluster of words present in documents. Text mining process follows a series of steps to extract the information from a text as illustrated in Figure 5.2 [31].

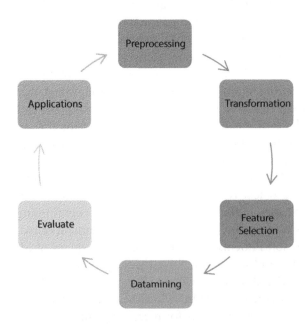

Figure 5.2 Process of text mining.

Different techniques which are used in text mining are as follows:

- Information Extraction (IE):

IE technique is used to analyze the unstructured text. It finds the important words as well as the relationships among them. It works on the method of pattern matching. The IE technique incorporates language processing units. This technique is mainly preferred in case of large amount of data.

- Categorization:

This technique is used to classify the text document into different categories. It follows multiple steps namely preprocessing, indexing, reduction in dimension and then classification.

- Clustering:

Clustering technique is used to make the group or clusters of text documents based on similar content. This technique also presents comparison and relationship among different clusters.

- Visualization:

This technique makes use of text flags and colors to refer documents and their compactness. It represents the information in a more attractive way.

- Summarization:

It is used to highlight the important points as it summarizes the entire document in brief. This technique also reduces the size of the document.

5.3   Latent Semantic Analysis

Latent semantic analysis (LSA) is a concept of knowledge procurement, initiation and representation [3]. It basically converts a document into a vector. It is an automatic mathematical learning approach which analyzes the relationships and similar structures among documents based on the distance between vectors. The main motive of LSA is to reduce the dimension which can be noticed via a matrix/lattice operation named SVD (Singular Value Decomposition) [17]. In a matrix, each row refers to a key word and each column as a document where this keyword appears. Frequency of a key word can be computed using the entry of that keyword in matrix. SVD is the key factor of LSA which is applied on the matrix to reduce the dimensionality.

LSA is an effective factual method for ordering, recovery and investigation of literary data utilized as a part of various fields of the human perception amid the most recent decade. The strategy is completely programmed and does not utilize any preparatory developed word references, semantic systems, information bases, theoretical chains of command, linguistic, not even the acceptable analyzer [20, 22]. The overall thought is that we have an existing arrangement of inactive conditions between the words and their respective contexts. Their recognizable proof & appropriate treatment licenses LSA to bargain effectively with the synonymy and incompletely with the synonymy. LSA is a two-organize handle and incorporates instruction and investigation of the ordered information. Amid the instruction stage LSA plays out a programmed archive ordering. The procedure begins when a grid X is developed whose sections were related with archives, & lines with terms. The cell (a, b) holds the event recurrence of terms in report b. The network X is then give in to a particular esteem decay which provides thus 3 frameworks D, T (orthonormal) and S (askew), to such level that X = DSTt. Vast majority of the lines & segments of D, S and T were evacuated in such a manner that the lattice $X' = D'S'T'$ is the slightest squares best fit estimate of X. This results in pressure of the foundation space in considerably littler one where we have just a set no. of huge components. Accordingly, each term or record is related to a vector of diminished measurements, e.g. 100. It is conceivable to play out complex SVD that accelerates procedure after specifically finding the shortened lattices D', S' & T'. The 2nd stage is examination stage. Regularly this incorporates the investigation of the nearness between a few records, a few words or between a word and a report. A basic numerical change licenses to acquire the vector for a non-indexed content. This allows the plan of a LSA based web index handling characteristic dialect questions. The nearness degree between two records will be figured as speck item between standardized LSA vectors. Use of different actions is additionally conceivable, e.g.: Euclidean & Manhattan separations, Minkowski events, Pearson's coefficient and so on [15].

5.4   Proposed Work

In this work, authors are designing an expert system that will work as a tool to search the cyber-attack related keywords from the text files. After that, it performs indexing and ranking of the text documents in decreasing order. The resultant rank-1 document is having the maximum similarity index w.r.t. the query to be searched whereas the last document is having the least similarity index. To achieve this goal, authors have proposed hybrid approach. Firstly, we applied the Lower Upper Triangular decomposition and Cholesky decomposition techniques. Later, we have combined both the approaches and executed on SVD.

SVD algorithm constructs the matrices for both term–term and document–document. This further decomposes them in to other sub-matrices by the help of Eigen values and Eigen vectors. Finally cosine similarity formula is used to calculate the similarity score. It defines similarity of searched query in the documents for further analyses. The work flow of text mining is illustrated through Figure 5.3.

Dataset is generated dynamically from different websites using web scrapping [1]. Our expert system, first perform the web scrapping so that the user always get an updated dataset [4].

Input summarization automatically works on a collection of dataset. Singular Value Decomposition (SVD) smooth the frequency of data and after that expert system will generate synonyms that are used to search the word pairs with similar terms [23, 24].

The calculation requires an inquiry with a vast corpus of content, a wide scope thesaurus of equivalent words, and a proficient usage of SVD. LSI takes as information about an arrangement of word combinations, and builds a framework that can be utilized to locate the social similitude between any two word sets. We proposed a consecutive grouping of words based on calculation that scales directly with the quantity of exemplary words thus by effectively bunching a larger number of specimens [4]. We have depicted general steps followed in text mining with the help of Algorithm 1.

Algorithm 1:

> *Input:* q: query word pair; X: set of answer word pairs; clusters (wp): function which returns the clusters for a given word pair; *Num_Clusters*: number of clusters
>
> *Output:* choice: An answer choice which attains the highest score.
>
> cq = group(q);
>
> We apply a for loop with group = 0; group <Num_Clusters; group + +

Figure 5.3 Work flow of text mining.

```
do
n = 0; /* Number of unique answers in the same group as the
question */
        for each x belong to X do
                ca = group(x);
                if cq[group] == ca[group] then
                n88
                end
        end
        for each x belong to X do
                ca = group (x);
                if cq[group] == ca[group] then
                score[x] = score[x] + Num_Clusters[group]/n;
                end
        end
end
choice = max(score);
```

In present work, weighing the score on the basis of numbers of clusters, grouping of clusters is done for cyber-attack related keywords.

5.5   Detailed Work Flow of Proposed Approach

Working of the proposed system is shown with the help of Figure 5.4. Since, text mining is content and semantic based searching. It takes a document and parameters specified through configuration files and carries out the mentioned steps in Figure 5.4.

A matrix decomposition or matrix factorization is a factorization of a matrix into a product of matrices. There are various fundamental matrix decomposition algorithms, which are useful in this proposed flow to decompose the matrix for the terms and documents. The algorithms used are as follows:

i)   *Cholesky Decomposition* is a kind of factorization or method of decomposing the matrix that uses hermitian framework. Cholesky decomposition is used to avoid the non-orthogonality problem in the non-integer matrix factorization (NMF). This decomposition can be improved with help of conjugate gradient to obtain feature space [35].

$$A = LL^*$$ (5.1)

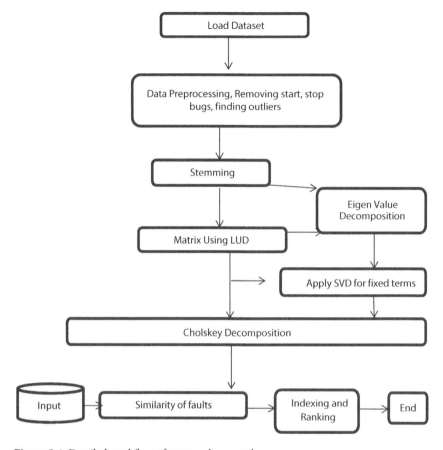

Figure 5.4 Detailed workflow of proposed approach.

This method is expressed using equation (1)where L refers to the lower triangular matrix with real and explicit point to point text, and L* means the conjugate transpose of L.

$$A = \begin{bmatrix} a_{11} & a_{12} & a_{13} \\ a_{21} & a_{22} & a_{23} \\ a_{31} & a_{32} & a_{33} \end{bmatrix} \qquad L = \begin{bmatrix} l_{11} & 0 & 0 \\ l_{21} & l_{22} & 0 \\ l_{31} & l_{32} & l_{33} \end{bmatrix}$$

ii)   *Lower upper* (LU) Decomposition is an algorithm in which numerical investigation and straight variable based math, LU decay (where "LU" remains for 'lower upper', and furthermore called LU factorization) considers a network as the result of a lower triangular framework and an upper triangular lattice

$$A = LU \qquad (5.2)$$

Above mentioned Equation (5.2) states the LU decomposition algorithm where L is lower triangular matrix and U refers to Upper triangular matrix. Problem with this technique is that sometimes it is impossible to write a matrix in the form "lower triangular" × "upper triangular" which limits its use.

iii) *QR Decomposition* putrefies grid into an item A = QR of an orthogonal network Q and an upper triangular lattice R. QR decomposition is frequently used to solve direct minimum squares issue, and this is the reason that it is used for a specific eigenvalue calculation. Any genuine square grid A might be decomposed as Equation (5.3). QR method is effective in terms of classification error rate on the reduced dimensional space [36].

$$A = QR \qquad (5.3)$$

iv) Singular Value Decomposition *(SVD)* is an algorithm of factorizing the complex and real matrix. This method is preferred to handle very large and sparse matrix *A*. For large singular values this method gives high accuracy and smaller singular values it gives low accuracy, which are typically of little interest for the analyses [3].

5.5.1 Defining the Stop Words

As we word on content mining applications, "stop words" is the commonly used expression. Stop words are a collection of commonly used words in any language not English words. Stop words helps to concentrate on the vital words.

For example, if we search a query on search engine like "how to implement secure applications" then the search engine returns the web pages with terms "how", "to" "implement", "secure ", "applications". In addition to that, the search engine also returns the pages which contains the terms "how", "to" as these are so often used words in the English. However, buy considering these as stop words (ignoring these terms), we can make the search engine to focus only on those web pages which are containing the keywords: "implement" "secure" "applications". It brings only those pages that are of user's interest [13]. These words can be used as a part of assignments. Some of them are:

- *Supervised machine learning*—It removes stop words from the feature space.
- *Clustering*—clustering stop words can be used to remove the info related to clusters.
- *Information retrieval*—This prevents the stop words to get indexed.
- *Text summarization*—This won't allow stop words to participate in summarization scores i.e. why it deletes the stop words.

The Stop words are mainly known to be "solitary arrangement of words". They are truly varied from application to applications. In a few requests expelling the terms like determiners (for e.g. a, an, the), relational words (for e.g. before, over, above), descriptors (e.g. great, pleasant) can be a fitting stop word list. For example, in opinion investigation expelling descriptive word terms, like "great", "decent" with nullifications "not" can divert the calculations. In such cases, one can utilize this stop list comprising of just determiners or determiners with relational words [15]. Few examples of Stop words are:

- *Determiners*—Determiners mark nouns. In general the determiner is followed by a noun. E.g.: a, an, another
- *Coordinating conjunctions*—These conjunctions connect words, phrase, and clauses. E.g.: but, or, yet, so, for, an, nor.
- *Prepositions*—preposition expresses relations in terms of time and space.
  E.g.: under, in, before, towards.

5.5.2   Stemming

Stemming is used to truncate the words into common base. Present work uses the Porter Stemmer algorithm for stemming.

The postfix stripping calculations require a couple of terms like.

- A consonant in a word is a letter other than *a, e, i, o, u* and other than y gone before a consonant. So in a word "*toy*" the consonants are *t* and *y*, and in *syzygy* they are *s, z* and *g*.

- A consonant is referred by *y, c, a* vowel by *v*. A series of *ccc...* of length more than 0 will be meant by *C*, and a series of *vvv...* of length more than 0 will be signified by *V*.

Word can be in four forms:

- *cvcv.....c*
- *cvcv.....v*
- *vcvc....v*
- *vcvc....v*

These all above forms can be represented by the single expression: "[c] vcvc ... [v]", here these square brackets denote the arbitrary presence of the content.

- There is another way of writing this expression using (vc) {m}: [c](vc){m}[v], here vc repeats m times. *m* is the measure of any word or part of the word.

In this particular case, when m = 0 it covers the words which have null values. Some of the examples are:

At m=0   tr, ee, tree, y, by.
At m=1   trouble, trees, oats, ivy.
At m=2   private, oaten, troubles, orrery.

- There are some rules which are set to remove or delete the suffix from a word like:

(con) s1 -> s2

If a word is ending with a suffix s1 and the stem before the s1 is satisfying the given condition the s1 will be replaced by s2. The condition to be satisfied will be given in the terms of m [19].

If s1 is "ement" and s2 is null,it will map "replacement" to "replac", as "replac" is a part of word in which m = 2.

- There could be one another way of putting conditions which is as follows:

*s—this states that when the stem ends with s.

v—this stem consist of a vowel.

*d—the stem ends with a double consonant (e.g. -tt, -ss).

*o—the stem ends with the series in form cvc in which the second c cannot be w, x or   (e.g. -hop, -wil).

- Also the condition part could be in this way containing "and, or, not" [19]
  E.g: (m>1 and (*s or *t)): It verifies for a stem with m >1 and ending in s or t,
  (*d and not (*l or *s or *z)): It will pass for the stem which is ending with the double consonant but not "l, s, or z".

5.5.3 Proposed Algorithm: A Hybrid Approach

This work proposed a hybrid approach which merges lower upper triangular decomposition and Cholesky decomposition algorithm and both are run on singular value decomposition algorithm. The proposed algorithms gives a flow of searching a cyber-attack related keywords in number of documents and matching them exactly and does indexing by finding similarity score. It then finally rank the documents according to the higher similarity score.

There will be multiple document IDs created from the dataset. The documents are in .txt format. There are 20 document Ids from which the keyword is searched. Whenever a keyword is searched then searching performs in all 20 document IDs. Every keyword will have different similarity score for every document ID.

The outcome of Algorithm 2 will be a matrix that is approximated using Equation (5.4) to some rank.

$$A_k = S_k \Sigma_k U^T_K \tag{5.4}$$

Algorithm 2:

Input: A, m, n where A is $m * n$ matrix.
Output: Σ, U, V and Σ is diagonal matrix.

1. Given a matrix A which is $m * n$. The matrix is term*document. Compose a matrix B which is n * n such that $B = A^T A$. This matrix is document*document.
2. Calculate the Eigen values and Eigen vectors for the matrix B.
3. Now, Perform SVD on matrix A using B and C where B and C are the matrices such that $B = A^T A$ and $C = AA^T$. C is term*term matrix.

   $A = S\Sigma U^T$ where U is matrix of Eigen vectors of B

S is matrix of Eigen vectors of *C*,

$$\Sigma \text{ is diagonal matrix of singular value}$$

Now, implement rank-2 approximation by keeping the first two columns of *S* and *U* and first two columns and rows of Σ and U^T.

4. By reducing the matrix Σ to Σ_T in which k * k matrix contains only the singular values k (that are kept) and also reduce *S* and U^T into S_k and U^Tk.

After matrix approximation, distance/similarity measure is applied to find the similarity score, one of similarity score is *cosine similarity*. The cosine similitude measure utilizes two limited dimensional vectors of a similar measurement where every vector speaks to an archive. The document is then transformed to as a n-dimensional vector $\overrightarrow{v_D}$. Let *tf(D,t)* mean the recurrence of term $t \in D$ in the document *D*. We can compute the closeness by utilizing below mentioned cosine similitude measure given in Equation (5.5) where g is a query matrix

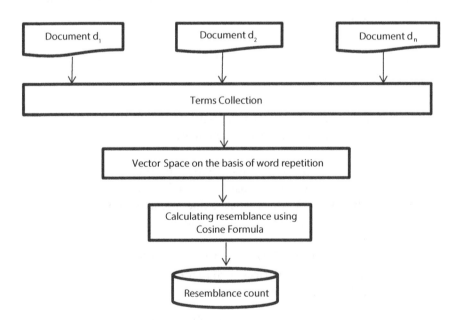

Figure 5.5 Process followed to obtain similarity score.

$$\text{Sim}(g, d) = \frac{g \cdot c}{|q||d|} \qquad (5.5)$$

And c is a document matrix. If the value of *sim (g,c)* is closer to 1 then that document is considered to be more similar to that query. Figure 5.5 shows how cosine similarity can be helpful in the overall process.

5.6   Results and Discussion

Individually when LUD is implemented this gives the offset values and frequency of the keyword when it is searched. On the basis of the keyword frequency similarity score is found. The Cholesky decomposition algorithm finds the keyword exactly in the document and highlights that line which has similarity in the document. So, Cholesky and LUD algorithm show their accuracy by MRR.

The accuracy of the keyword 'Authentication' is shown in Figure 5.6 and the similarity score of authentication is given in Table 5.1.

5.6.1   Analysis Using Hybrid Approach

The performance evaluation in the work is being carried out by standard calculation of rank and precision for every keyword. Firstly, the similarity index comes out when the hybrid approach is implemented. On the basis of searching a keyword in the documents, different readings were taken. Let us assume the searching for a keyword "SQL Injection" [21]. The respective readings are mentioned in Table 5.2.

The graphical representation for keyword "SQL Injection" is shown in Figure 5.7.

Table 5.1 Similarity score of keyword 'Authentication' in various Document ID.

Document ID	Similarity by LUD	Similarity by Cholskey	MRR
1	0.57	0.8	0.41
2	0.65	0.67	0.37
3	0.52	0.9	0.42
4	0.69	0.84	0.34
5	0.64	0.72	0.28

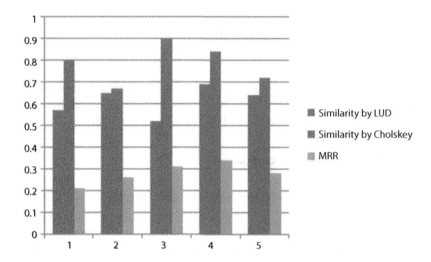

Figure 5.6 Similarity and accuracy for the keyword 'Authentication'.

Table 5.2 Similarity score of keyword 'SQL injection' in various documents.

Document ID	Similarity
7	80.2
8	79.9
3	78.01
6	77.45
9	77.1
5	76.4
1	75.4
2	74.3
9	70.1
10	69.7
11	68.1
12	57.79
13	42.1

(*Continued*)

Table 5.2 Similarity score of keyword 'SQL injection' in various documents. (*Continued*)

Document ID	Similarity
14	41.6
18	37.6
16	33.1
17	28.1
15	25.9
19	20.6
20	19.5

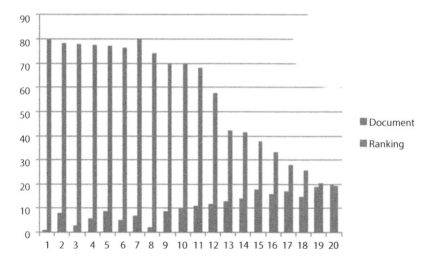

Figure 5.7 Ranking graph of document and similarity for keyword 'SQL Injection'.

Figure 5.7 clearly shows how a query has performed for a method with respect to the other. The ranking is done by LSI Indexing which is depicted in the results. When "SQL Injection" query is searched then document number 1 has higher similarity score i.e. 80.2 followed by document 1 which has 79.9 similarity score and many more documents as follows.

To check the accuracy and to validate proposed work, the performance measure MRR (Mean reciprocal rank) is used. The closeness of MRR value to 1 depicts the more accuracy of results. So, different cyber-attack related keywords are searched to test the proposed work and then their MRR is calculated with respect to the similarity index results.

Table 5.3 Accuracy for searching cyber-attack related keywords using hybrid approach.

Keyword	Document	Similarity	MRR
Buffer Overflow	2	0.94	0.81
SQL Injection	7	0.80	0.67
Web server	8	0.91	0.53
Denial of Service	1	0.94	0.71
Cryptanalysis	8	0.68	0.61
Confidentiality	4	0.73	0.44
Port scanning	8	0.81	0.49
Flash memory Attack	7	0.74	0.47
Memory Corruption	6	0.41	0.37
XSS Attack	8	0.85	0.67

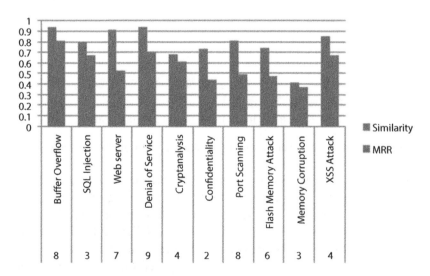

Figure 5.8 Accuracy for searching vulnerable keywords.

Table 5.3 shows the results of some of the cyber-attack related keywords which are tested.

Graphical representation for the same is shown in Figure 5.8.

For every query, the resultant value of MRR which is close to 1 proves the accuracy of proposed hybrid approach. Whenever a keyword is searched with proposed approach it results higher MRR values in comparison to those in existing work. This validates the performance of proposed text mining approach.

5.7   Conclusion

This work discusses how text mining approach can be used for building rich models for cybersecurity analytics. Some of the most interesting approach which are described and used LSI, NLP, SVD and LUD. These techniques have helped us in understanding the content of document and easily identify the user needs. By all this, relationship between the query and data is found and indexing is done on that basis only. We have also observed that available data in text form and word alone may not be applicable while predicting all types of attacks on the organization whereas updation of vulnerable keywords in database may help.

Further we can extend the approach so that it can be identified, how such system can contribute in gathering cyber attack's information automatically from the web. As per our understanding the accuracy of such systems can help in working towards future threats tailored to a particular organization.

When large amount of data faces threats it needs to be served with strong base for intelligent analysis using the discussed approach.

References

1. National Vulnerability Database, URL: https://nvd.nist.gov/.
2. Vulnerabilities Security Information, "www.frhack.org".
3. Chue, W.L. and Chen, L.H., SVD: A Novel content- based representation technique for web documents. *Fourth International Conference on Information, Communications and Signal Processing, IEEE 2003, Singapore*, pp. 1840–1844, 2003.
4. Mokhov, S.A., Laverdière, M.A., Benredjem, D., Taxonomy of Linux Kernel Vulnerability Solutions, in: *Innovative Techniques in Instruction Technology, E-learning, E-assessment, and Education*, M. Iskander (Ed.), pp. 485–493, Springer, Dordrecht, 2008.

5. Chen, S., Jun, X.U., Kalbarczyk, Z.T., Iyer, R.K., Security Vulnerabilities: From Analysis to Detection and Masking Techniques. *Proc. IEEE*, 94, 2, 407–418, Feb 2006.

6. Corregedor, M. and Von Solms, S., *Windows 8 32bit-Improved Security?*, 2006, Publisher IEEE, https://ieeexplore.ieee.org/document/6757678?reload=true&arnumber=6757678.

7. Mehta, V., Bartzis, C., Zhu, H., Clarke, E., Wing, J., Ranking Attack Graphs, in: *International Workshop on Recent Advances in Intrusion Detection (RAID-2006)*, pp. 127–144, Springer, Berlin Heidelberg, LNCS 4219, 2006.

8. Kotsiantis, S.B., Zaharakis, I.D., Pintelas, P.E., Machine learning: A Review of Classification and Combining Techniques. *Artif. Intell. Rev.*, 26, 159–190, 2007.

9. Wang, D., Lin, M., Zang, H., Hu, H., Detect Related Bugs from Source Code using Bug Information. *34th Annual Conference on Computer Software and Applications (COMPSAC)*, pp. 328–336, 2010.

10. Shi, W. and Guo, Y., Incomplete Cholesky Decomposition based Kernel Principal Component Analysis for Large-scale Data Set. *The 2010 International Joint Conference on Neural Networks (IJCNN), IEEE*, pp. 1–6, 2010.

11. Wang, J.A., Wang, H., Guo, M., Zhou, L., Camargo, J., Ranking Attacks Based on Vulnerability Analysis. *2010 43rd Hawaii International Conference on System Sciences*, pp. 1–10, 2010.

12. Xu, J., Cheng, S., Wang, J., Li, Z., Jiang, F., Software Vulnerability Analysis Framework Based on Uniform Intermediate Representation. *2nd International Conference on Software Technology and Engineering (ICSTE)*, vol. 1, IEEE, pp. 357–361, 2010.

13. Kazemi, A., Rostampour, A., Zamiri, A., Jamshidi, P., Haghighi, H., Shams, F., An Information Retrieval Based Approach for Measuring Service Conceptual Cohesion. *11th International Conference on Quality Software, Madrid, 2011*, pp. 102–111, 2011.

14. Chen, H., Yandong, M., Xi, W., Dong, Z., Nickolai, Z., Kaashoek, M., Linux Kernel Vulnerabilities: State-of-the-Art Defenses and Open Problems, in: *Proceedings of the 2nd Asia-Pacific Workshop on Systems, APSys'11*, 2011.

15. Lucia, A.D., Penta, M.D., Oliveto, R., Panichella, A., Panichella, S., Improving IR-based Traceability Recovery Using Smoothing Filters. *2011 IEEE 19th International Conference on Program Comprehension, Kingston, ON, 2011*, pp. 21–30, 2011.

16. Gharehchopogh, F.S. and Khalifelu, Z.A., Analysis and Evaluation of Unstructured Data: Text Mining versus Natural Language Processing. *2011 5th International Conference on Application of Information and Communication Technologies (AICT)*, Baku, pp. 1–4, 2011.

17. Lu, H., Vaidya, J., Atluri, V., Hong, Y., Constraint-Aware Role Mining via Extended Boolean Matrix Decomposition. *IEEE Trans. Dependable Secure Comput.*, 9, 5, 655–669, Sept.–Oct. 2012.

18. Banerjee, S., Cukic, B., Adjeroh, D., Automated Duplicate Bug Report Classification Using Subsequence Matching. *2012 IEEE 14th International Symposium on High-Assurance Systems Engineering*, Omaha, NE, pp. 74–81, 2012.

19. Saha, R.K., Lease, M., Khurshid, S., Perry, D.E., Improving bug localization using structured information retrieval. *28th IEEE/ACM International Conference on Automated Software Engineering (ASE)*, Silicon Valley, CA, pp. 345–355, 2013.

20. Dhanya, R., Krishnaprasad, T., Trivikram, I., A Modular Approach to Document Indexing and Semantic Search. *IASTED International Conference on Web Technologies, Applications, and Services, Calgary, Alberta, Canada, July 4–6, 2005*, pp. 165–170, 2005.

21. Bojken, S. and Xhuvani, A., A Literature Review and Comparative Analyses on SQL Injection: Vulnerabilities, Attacks and their Prevention and Detection Techniques. *Int. J. Comput. Sci. Issues (IJCSI)*, 11, 4, 28–37, 2014.

22. Wong, C., Xiong, Y., Zhang, H., Hao, D., Zhang, L., Mei, H., Boosting Bug-Report-Oriented Fault Localization with Segmentation and Stack-Trace Analysis. *IEEE International Conference on Software Maintenance and Evolution, Victoria, BC*, vol. 2014, pp. 181–190, 2014.

23. Sohsah, G., Akkurt, E., Safarli, I., Unal, M., Guzey, O., Automatically Filtering Irrelevant Words for Applications in Language Acquisition. *13th International Conference on Machine Learning and Applications, Detroit, MI, 2014*, pp. 557–561, 2014.

24. Tung, K.T., Hung, D., Hanh, L.T.M., A Comparison of Algorithms used to measure the Similarity between two documents. *Int. J. Adv. Res. Comput. Eng. Technol.*, 4, 4, 1117–1121, 2015.

25. Raheja, S., Munjal, G., Shagun, Analysis of Linux Kernel Vulnerabilities. *Indian J. Sci. Technol.*, 9, 48, 12–29, 2016.

26. Benedetti, F., Beneventano, D., Bergamaschi, S., Simonin, G., Computing inter-document similarity with Context Semantic Analysis, in: *Information Systems*, vol. 80, pp. 136–147, Elsevier, 2018.

27. Radovanovic, M. and Ivanovic, M., Text Mining: Approaches and Applications. *Novi Sad J. Math.*, 38, 3, 227–234, 2008.

28. Rashid, A., Danezis, G., Chivers, H., Lupu, E., Martin, A., Lewis, M., Peersman, C., Scoping the Cyber security body of knowledge. *IEEE Secur. Priv.*, 16, 96–102, 2018.

29. Sohrabi, B., Mohsen, V.R., Shineh, B., Topic Modeling and Classification of Cyberspace Papers Using Text Mining. *J. Cyberspace Stud.*, 2, 1, 103–125, 2018.

30. Arimura, H., Abe, H., Fujino, R., Sakamoto, H., Shimozono, S., Arikawa, S., Text Data Mining: Discovery of Important Keywords in the Cyberspace. *International Conference on Digital Libraries: Research and Practice, Kyoto, Japan, 2000*, pp. 220–226, 2000.

31. Mhamdi, C., Al-Emran, M., Salloum, S.A., Text Mining and Analytics: A Case Study from News Channels Posts on Facebook, in: *Intelligent Natural Language Processing: Trends and Applications. Studies in Computational Intelligence*, vol. 740, K. Shaalan, A. Hassanien, F. Tolba (Eds.), Springer, Cham, 2018.

32. Ottis, R. and Lorents, P., Cyberspace: Definition and Implications. *Proceedings of the 5th International Conference on Information Warfare and Security, Dayton, OH*, USA Academic Publishing Limited, pp. 267–270, 2010.

33. Ottis, R.A., Sonning Common: Academic Conferences International Limited. *International Conference on Cyber Warfare and Security*, p. 267, 2010.

34. https://ciso.economictimes.indiatimes.com/news/73-cyberattacks-occur-on-microsoft-office-products-report/72882928.

35. Alostad, J.M., Reducing Dimensionality Using NMF Based Cholesky Decomposition. *International Conference on Research in Adaptive and Convergent*, p. 49, 2017.

36. Jieping, Y., Li, Q., Xiong, H., Park, H., Janardan, R., Kumar, V., IDR/QR: an incremental dimension reduction algorithm via QR decomposition. *IEEE Trans. Knowl. Data Eng.*, 1208, 17, 9, 1208–1222, 2005.

6

Analyses on Artificial Intelligence Framework to Detect Crime Pattern

R. Arshath Raja[1], N. Yuvaraj[1] and N.V. Kousik[2]*

[1]*Research and Development, ICT Academy, Chennai, India*
[2]*School of Computing Science and Engineering, Galgotias University, Greater Noida, Uttarpradesh, India*

Abstract

In this paper, an Artificial Intelligence (AI)-based crime scene detection method is designed to improve the identification of crime scene in real-time basis. The design focuses entirely on improving the processing speed by suitably analyzing the data at each stage. The study uses a series of operation that includes pre-processing, feature extraction, classification, crime pattern identification and clustering. The pre-processing eliminates the unstructured data, feature extraction using an object oriented model, classification using multi-class multi-level machine learning (MCML) classifier, crime pattern identification using Genetic Apriori Algorithm (GAA) and finally clustering using consensus clustering. The experimental validation is carried out on unstructured data collected from past criminal records. The performance of the proposed clustering model for crime pattern investigation is compared with time series analysis, support vector machine, artificial neural network. The analysis is carried out against various performance metrics that includes: accuracy, specificity, sensitivity and f-measure. The performance evaluation shows that the proposed method obtains improved accuracy in finding the crime patterns than the existing methods with higher accuracy of 98.73%.

Keywords: Artificial Intelligence, crime pattern analysis, classification, feature extraction, Genetic Apriori Algorithm (GAA), Multi-Class Multi-Level Machine Learning (MCML) classifier

Corresponding author: nvkousik@galgotiasuniversity.edu.in; nvkousik@gmail.com

Subhendu Kumar Pani, Sanjay Kumar Singh, Lalit Garg, Ram Bilas Pachori and Xiaobo Zhang (eds.) *Intelligent Data Analytics for Terror Threat Prediction: Architectures, Methodologies, Techniques and Applications*, (119–132) © 2021 Scrivener Publishing LLC

6.1   Introduction

The criminal sector was chosen as an area of study for this work due to its growing social significance. In the tradition of crime monitoring and prevention, a vast number of professionals and specialists in criminal justice and law enforcement have naturally been fortunate in this important field. Throughout recent times, computer data analytics has taken practical steps to help law enforcement officials and police to improve the process of criminal detection and increase the efficiency due to rapid technological advances including growing use of the computerized tools to monitor and document crime [2].

In recent times, criminal cases are increasing with varying intensity levels and adaptability. This has increased the life threat to individuals in terms of social and monitory loss. The artificial intelligence era may work greatly to reduce the crime by predicting it. This may reduce the loss of life and property using intelligence learning. The utilization of artificial intelligence-based framework examines the datasets to find the patterns of error at a specific location. With such aim, the proposed study models a prediction system that analyses the data collected from past police records.

However, the major challenge that lies with AI-based learning is the versatile nature of the crime data makes the system predict with less prediction accuracy. Further, the accuracy of the system tends to degrade as the nature of the data is versatile. Various existing researches are carried out under AI-based learning to predict the crime patterns in future using valuable input parameters. These approaches include time series analysis, support vector machine, artificial neural network, etc. These models detect the crime pattern but it suffers mostly from the redundant data collected from several sources.

Document clustering is known as one of the most common forms of identification and data clustering for topics or events or categories of criminal records. The first step is to file documentation and remove terms and phrases from the criminal record. The second process is to describe the offenses in documents in order to collect the most important information from the criminal record and explain the similarities between those records. The final method for clustering the documents consists of implementing an algorithm based on similarities between the documents in classes of the documents with subjects/events or types of crime [5].

The present study is designed in such a way that it increases the processing speed and effectively analyzing the datasets. This involves the extraction of relevant data from the historical datasets using a clustering algorithm, where a consensus clustering algorithm finds the similarity between the crime patterns from the existing database.

In order to perform suitable clustering, the present system adopts a series of methods prior to clustering that eliminates the redundant data, where the contributions of the paper are aligned.

- It initially involves the data pre-processing that removes the noise and null items present in the datasets. This reduces the number of unstructured items from the datasets with different size and types. An object oriented model is developed to extract the relevant data for setting it as an input to the next stage.
- The classification is the next phase, which uses multi-class multi-level machine learning classifier to classify the datasets into various classes. Here, probability of class belonging to a relevant crime pattern is considered to be highest than the other classes of crime.
- The next step is the identification of pattern that finds the crime sequences that are similar in nature and these sequences belongs to the same class of crime. The patterns are identified using Genetic Algorithm-based [1] Apriori algorithm [10] that mines the frequent itemsets of the same class with highest probability, and it highlights the nature of the crime or the crime pattern and its location.
- Finally, the clustering is carried out to predict the crime and that provides the outcome as yes or no.
- The experimental validation on crime pattern investigation is analyzed in terms of various performance metrics like accuracy, specificity, sensitivity and f-measure.

The outline of the paper is given below: Section 6.2 provides the related works. Section 6.3 discusses the proposed clustering model. Section 6.4 evaluates the entire work with other machine learning classification models. Finally, Section 6.5 concludes the entire work.

6.2 Related Works

Three different methods related to AI-based learning for crime pattern analysis are seen in this section. We have gone through several literatures;

however, we found the closest relevant literatures to the present study as given below:

A document unsupervised clustering technique that groups automatically the similar documents [2]. This method operates on two tasks namely feature extraction and clustering to improve the clustering of crime documents and to speed up the crime solving process.

A attempted a group incremental adaptive clustering technique that integrates the rough set theory and neural network [3]. The crime reports are clustered for investigating the crime reports, where the reports are classified based on the phrases in the document. The phrases are represented in the form of a binary vector of equi-dimensional phase and helps in generation of new clusters.

A investigates the analysis of text and classification technique to improve the crime report analysis [4]. A decision support system is developed with natural language processing techniques and further it includes similarity measures and Naïve Bayes classifier. This framework supports mainly the analysis of crimes and classifying it based on the incidents occurred.

6.3   Proposed Clustering for Detecting Crimes

Step 1: The first step is the data pre-processing that removes the null or unstructured items present in the document phrase.

Step 2: An object oriented model extracts the relevant data from the document phrase.

Step 3: Classification using MCML classifier helps in classification of crime instances present in the document phrase into different classes. Here, probability of class belonging to a relevant crime pattern is considered to be highest than the other classes of crime.

Step 4: Crime patterns are identified using GAA that mines the frequent itemsets based on the nature of the crime and location.

Step 5: Finally, the consensus clustering is carried out to predict the crime and that provides the outcome as yes or no.

The overall architecture of the Proposed clustering for Detecting crimes has been discussed and shown in the Figure 6.1.

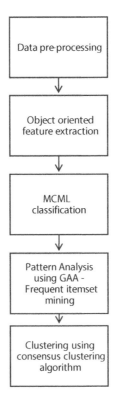

Figure 6.1 Overall architecture of the proposed method.

6.3.1 Data Pre-Processing

The method to clean up the data and organize the document for classification is the pre-processing phase. Online texts usually contain lots of noise and information, like HTML tags, scripts and publicity. Therefore, other terms in the document have no impact on the general context of this text at word stage.

Having such terms makes it much more difficult to consider the aspect of the question, and therefore, to define each term in the text as a single dimension. This is the theory that the data were accurately preprocessed: to eliminate the text noise, the classifier's output should be enhanced and the classification process speeds up, thereby aiding in the interpretation of the real-time feelings.

The whole process includes various steps: electronic cleaning of document, elimination of white space, addition, stemming, replacement of terms, managing of negation and eventually the option of functionality. All but the last stages are labeled transformations, while the last stage with some functions is called filters.

The names, terms or phrases which strongly express an opinion are either positive or negative in the sense of opinion mining. It implies that the direction of the document is greater than that of the same language. In the collection of functions many approaches are used where some are syntactic on the basis of the syntactic location of the term or on subsets of functions [7].

6.3.2 Object-Oriented Model

High-level retrieval of features involves the identification of text images types. Throughout feature extraction, the analysis usually looks for invariance characteristics so that the outcome does not differ depending on the conditions selected. It implies that artifacts can be identified, regardless of their position, orientation or height. This analysis deals with the types of each letter, which can be deformed. This uses criteria to find the object detection. Only if light and lighting can be managed, can this provide a remedy and two methods can be taken to extract the ingredients, the other to remove the element types [6].

6.3.3 MCML Classification

A Multi-Class Multi-Level (MCML) classification [7] uses divide and conquer rule to classify the instances or features obtained from the previous steps. Depending on the features, the texts are classified into classes.

6.3.4 GAA

This method uses an association rule using Genetic Apriori algorithm [8] analyses the patterns of classes from the previous classification step and provides the required crime pattern based on the classes obtained.

6.3.5 Consensus Clustering

Finally, consensus clustering [9] is used to cluster the patterns obtained and present the results as the crime to be occurred or not.

6.4 Performance Evaluation

In this section, we collect a corpora from Bernama news and the test datasets include six categories that includes Canny Ong with 5 events, Fandy,

Samsudin, and Jazlin with 8 events, MohdNashar, and Sosilawati articles (as shown in Table 6.2). A total of 247 documents from various topics are used as training and testing datasets, which are represented in Tables 6.1 and 6.2.

The proposed method is tested against the existing methods in terms of various performance measures that include precision, recall, sensitivity, specificity and accuracy. The proposed method is compared with Unsupervised Clustering, Group incremental adaptive clustering and Decision Support System.

6.4.1   Precision

Precision is defined as the ration of correctly obtained labeled TPs with entire TP labeled. It is defined as follows

$$Precision = TP/(TP + FP) \qquad (6.1)$$

Table 6.3 shows the results of precision between the proposed and existing methods with different topics that varies between 1 and 30. The result shows that the proposed method achieves higher precision than the existing methods.

6.4.2   Sensitivity

Sensitivity is defined as the ration of correctly labeled crime topics with entire true crime records. It is defined as follows

$$Sensitivity = TP/(TP + FN) \qquad (6.2)$$

Table 6.1 Topics in the dataset.

Topics	Documents
Canny Ong	48
Jazlin	59
Mohd-nashar	35
Samsudin	35
Fandy	35
Sosilawati	35

Table 6.2 Events present in the topics.

Topics	Description	Number of documents
Canny Ong	Investigation into	1
	Canny Ong case include medical report and trial	7
	Evidence into	1
	Canny Ong case	3
	DNA test	6
	Family reacts into Canny Ong and negligence suit	3
	Court Sentence, plead guilty	9
Jazlin	Investigation into	1
	Jazlin case include trial	3
	Evidence/Suspect into	1
	Jazlin case	3
	DNA test	3
	Reward for the public	3
	Family react to Jazlin investigation	8
	Public reacts to Jazlin investigation	5
	Investigation into	1
	Jazimin suit	2
	Suit to the court	2

Table 6.4 shows the results of sensitivity between the proposed and existing methods with different topics that varies between 1 and 30. The result shows that the proposed method achieves higher sensitivity than the existing methods.

Table 6.3 Precision.

Topics	Unsupervised clustering	Group incremental adaptive clustering	Decision support system	Supervised clustering using SVM	Time series analysis	Machine learning using artificial neural network	Proposed consensus clustering
1	80.36	82.42	85.51	85.71	86.17	86.62	87.57
5	81.39	83.45	86.54	86.74	87.20	87.67	88.60
10	82.42	84.48	87.57	87.77	88.24	88.71	89.63
15	83.45	85.51	88.60	88.81	89.28	89.76	90.66
20	84.48	86.54	89.63	89.84	90.32	90.80	91.69
25	85.51	87.57	90.66	90.87	91.36	91.84	92.72
30	86.54	88.60	91.69	91.90	92.39	92.89	93.75

Table 6.4 Sensitivity.

Topics	Unsupervised clustering	Group incremental adaptive clustering	Decision support system	Supervised clustering using SVM	Time series analysis	Machine learning using artificial neural network	Proposed consensus clustering
1	77.72	80.58	84.13	84.33	84.78	85.23	87.22
5	78.06	81.38	85.29	85.49	85.94	86.40	87.35
10	78.65	82.18	85.88	86.08	86.54	87.00	87.94
15	80.02	83.11	87.48	87.68	88.15	88.62	89.54
20	80.33	84.46	87.73	87.93	88.40	88.87	89.79
25	80.92	85.04	89.28	89.49	89.96	90.03	90.31
30	81.05	86.20	90.48	90.01	90.27	90.66	91.51

Table 6.5 Specificity.

Topics	Unsupervised clustering	Group incremental adaptive clustering	Decision support system	Supervised clustering using SVM	Time series analysis	Machine learning using artificial neural network	Proposed consensus clustering
1	81.90	83.45	87.57	87.77	87.82	87.85	88.80
5	82.62	84.48	88.60	88.81	88.85	88.88	90.55
10	84.27	85.51	89.63	89.84	89.89	89.92	91.48
15	85.40	86.54	90.66	90.87	90.92	90.95	92.61
20	86.23	87.57	91.69	91.90	91.95	91.98	92.82
25	87.15	88.60	92.72	92.94	92.99	93.02	93.03
30	87.77	89.63	93.75	93.97	94.02	94.05	94.06

Table 6.6 Accuracy.

Topics	Unsupervised clustering	Group incremental adaptive clustering	Decision support system	Supervised clustering using SVM	Time series analysis	Machine learning using artificial neural network	Proposed consensus clustering
1	87.27	94.30	95.15	95.37	95.42	95.45	97.20
5	88.07	95.54	96.90	97.13	97.18	97.21	97.92
10	89.59	96.27	97.30	97.53	97.58	97.61	98.32
15	90.28	97.54	98.04	98.27	98.32	98.35	99.06
20	91.13	98.16	98.40	98.63	98.68	98.71	99.12
25	92.26	98.77	99.03	99.26	99.31	99.35	99.65
30	93.05	99.05	99.07	99.30	99.35	99.39	99.84

6.4.3   Specificity

Specificity is defined as the ratio of incorrectly labeled crime topics with entire true crime records. It is defined as follows

$$\text{Specificity} = TN/(TN + FP) \qquad (6.3)$$

Table 6.5 shows the results of specificity between the proposed and existing methods with different topics that varies between 1 and 30. The result shows that the proposed method achieves higher specificity than the existing methods.

6.4.4   Accuracy

Accuracy defines the overall correctness of the proposed method and it is the ratio of correctly labeled records with the whole pool of records.

$$Accuracy = (TP + TN)/(TP + TN + FP + FN) \qquad (6.4)$$

Table 6.6 shows the results of accuracy between the proposed and existing methods with different topics that varies between 1 and 30. The result shows that the proposed method achieves higher clustering accuracy than the existing methods.

6.5   Conclusions

In this paper, we use an AI-based learning approach to predict the crimes patterns, which is designed to improve the prediction accuracy. This study avoids the data redundancy prior clustering using its suitable pre-processing and cleaning operations. The extraction of suitable features by OOM helps in classifying the datasets into classes using MCML classifier. After segregation of classes, the crime scene patterns are analyzed using GAA frequent itemset mining. Finally, the consensus clustering predicts whether the crime has occurred or not. Such effective operations improves its processing speed by utilizes well the given datasets. The simulation results shows that the improved detection of crime scenes by the clustering model than the existing methods in terms of improved accuracy (98.73%), specificity (91.9%), sensitivity (89.1%) and precision (90.7%). The major limitation of the study is the limited dataset documents are used for evaluating the efficacy of proposed study, however, in future the study tends to operate on big datasets to prove its effectiveness.

References

1. Mirjalili, S., Genetic algorithm, in: *Evolutionary Algorithms and Neural Networks*, pp. 43–55, Springer, Cham, 2019.
2. Bsoul, Q., Salim, J., Zakaria, L.Q., An intelligent document clustering approach to detect crime patterns. *Procedia Technol.*, 11, 1, 1181–1187, 2013.
3. Kang, Z., Peng, C., Cheng, Q., Kernel-driven similarity learning. *Neurocomputing*, 267, 210–219, 2017.
4. Ku, C.H. and Leroy, G., A decision support system: Automated crime report analysis and classification for e-government. *Gov. Inf. Q.*, 31, 4, 534–544, 2014.
5. Haddi, E., Liu, X., Shi, Y., The role of text pre-processing in sentiment analysis. *Procedia Comput. Sci.*, 17, 26–32, 2013.
6. Nixon, M.S. and Aguado, A.S., High-level feature extraction: Fixed shape matching, in: *Feature Extraction and Image Processing for Computer Vision (Fourth Edition)*, pp. 223–290, 2020.
7. Hameed, N., Shabut, A.M., Ghosh, M.K., Hossain, M.A., Multi-class multi-level classification algorithm for skin lesions classification using machine learning techniques. *Expert Syst. Appl.*, 141, 1–18, 2020.
8. Chadokar, S.K., Singh, D., Singh, A., Optimizing network traffic by generating association rules using hybrid apriori-genetic algorithm. *2013 Tenth International Conference on Wireless and Optical Communications Networks (WOCN)*, IEEE, pp. 1–5, 2013.
9. Tandon, A., Albeshri, A., Thayananthan, V., Alhalabi, W., Fortunato, S., Fast consensus clustering in complex networks. *Phys. Rev. E*, 99, 4, 1–6, 2019.
10. Krishna, B. and Amarawat, G., Data mining in frequent pattern matching using improved apriori algorithm, in: *Emerging Technologies in Data Mining and Information Security*, pp. 699–709, Springer, Singapore, 2019.

7

A Biometric Technology-Based Framework for Tackling and Preventing Crimes

Ebrahim A.M. Alrahawe¹, Vikas T. Humbe² and G.N. Shinde³*

¹School of Computational Sciences, S.R.T.M. University, Nanded, India
² School of Technology, S.R.T.M. University, Sub-Center, Latur, India
³Yeshwant College, Nanded, India

Abstract

Biometric recognition is defined as an automated recognition for individuals based on their own biological characteristics such as fingerprint, iris, face, veins, etc. or behavioral characteristics such as voice, signature, walking. In the past, some biometric traits like fingerprint, palm print, and DNA techniques have been used as evidence tools for identifying the criminal [1]. Nowadays, one can use a biometric technology-based crime prediction, through detecting some collectable biometric traits of offender (such as a gait, eyes, face, etc.), and/or detect crime tools which may be carried by criminal (such as gun, knife, etc.) to obtain the required data, like CCTV videos, iris sensors, etc. This chapter aims at investigating the ability to use biometric systems to prevent crimes before happening.

This chapter is organized in five sections are as follows: First section introduces biometric traits in an overview; second section explores surveillance systems; third section discusses the legality of surveillance and its relationship to privacy and rights; theoretically, the fourth section provides an insight into the possibility of integrating surveillance systems with biometric systems at a single system in order to predict crime by identifying criminals and crime tools. The last section will be devoted for the conclusion.

Keywords: CCTV, crime prevention, biometric technology, tracking, soft biometric

*Corresponding author: shindegn@yahoo.co.in

Subhendu Kumar Pani, Sanjay Kumar Singh, Lalit Garg, Ram Bilas Pachori and Xiaobo Zhang (eds.)
Intelligent Data Analytics for Terror Threat Prediction: Architectures, Methodologies, Techniques and Applications, (133–160) © 2021 Scrivener Publishing LLC

7.1   Introduction

A person is born with a common sense that does not know harm or criminality, and the environment surrounding him contributes to shaping his personality and influences him, and some people may be exposed to a negative impact by the environment surrounding them, which causes them to deviate towards doing abnormal behavior and committing unacceptable practices to a normal person, which leads to crimes.

A crime is considered an unlawful act, and it is condemned by law since it is called a breach of all legal requirements. It is also defined as an aberration from the accepted activities, ethical and religious axioms in consideration of accomplishing a goal that does not comply with the codification and provisions in the law, which leads to negative effects on individuals and society. Crime is one of the old social phenomena. It happens when all the elements of its occurrence are available, so, as long as the factors contributing to the occurrence of the crime are combined, every person is at risk of the crime. The adverse effect of the crime depends on the circumstances of its execution, the means and the instruments associated with it, and the nature of the punishment applied. The perpetrator must be of the gravity of the severity, which ranges from a few days imprisonment to whole life imprisonment, and sometimes it reaches to the extent of death penalty.

Although humans enjoy the advantages that have followed the advancement of scientific techniques in modern society, deviations from traditional standards and pathology that are unknown in the past begin to emerge. Most citizens agree that CCTV (closed-circuit television) is the solution for crime prevention and criminal prosecutions, and advocate for it to be repaired and expanded. Independent folks communities support this request and do not wish to incur any investment costs [2]. Nowadays, video cameras, video recorder in digital storage devices, and the installation costs are falling down, especially with extra facilities like using wireless networks, and online management. It will encourage for more development for surveillance systems with new techniques which may help for crime prevent, or prediction [3].

One of biometrics' most impressive uses is crime solving. While real-life practices do not really coincide with the television visualizations of using biometrics in crime laboratories, crimes-fighting organizations and crime laboratories have some fantastic technology available to them. The FBI has been moving over the past few years into a new framework that enhances both the accuracy and efficiency of its current settings while incorporating more biometrics, including enhanced fingerprints, palm scans, facial recognition, and iris scans. It will take a bit of time for both federal, state and local police to upgrade their programs to work with the FBI in tandem, but that day is coming [4].

Basically, biometrics is considered as a statistical analysis tool to measure the people based on their biological such as face, finger; and/or behavioral such as speech, gait traits, in order, to recognize or identify an individuals. From the three security levels: 1) what you have? (E.g. ID card), 2) what you know? (E.g. PIN), and 3) who are you? (E.g. face), the last level is the strongest, and called as a biometric [5].

However, logically, biometric systems have two stages of enrollment where the system established the individuals traits have to collect and processed to store in the system, in order to facilitate another stage which called as authentication/identification stage where the traits of subject captured to match with stored traits that was recorded at enrollment stage [6].

Surveillance systems are the most appropriate tool to detect crime and track criminals, and biometric systems are the only solution for identifying criminals through their biometric characteristics.

Theoretically, this chapter attempts to provide an integrated view by combining surveillance and biometric systems. The first part will deal with a general background on biometrics. The general background on surveillance systems is covered in the second part. With some abbreviation, the legality of surveillance and its relationship to privacy and rights will be covered in Part Three. The fourth part will present the proposed vision for a multi-biometric system. The chapter ends with a summary.

7.2   Biometrics

As it is known, biometric is a combination of two Greek words, "bio" = life, and "metric" = measures. It is to say that, it includes two different fields: biological and measurements. The former is a natural science that studies life and living organisms, including physical structure, chemical processes, molecular interactions, physiological mechanisms, and development and evolution, the latter the process of associating numbers with physical quantities and phenomena.

Moreover, it is a field of studying the human life measures to make each person unique and has an ability to be distinguished from others forever. Those measures can be categorized in to such sets of traits as physiological, behavioral, and/or soft biometric [7].

Biometric or so-called biometric recognition tends to refer to persons being automatically recognized depending on their behavioral and/or biological attributes. The quality of fingerprint technologies in law enforcement and forensic applications, as well as increasing concerns regarding border control, financial fraud and cyber security, have aroused great interest in using fingerprints, along with other features, to auto-identify persons. It's not shocking, therefore, that biometrics circulate various segments of our community.

In the past, 14th century chines used fingerprint as a biometric systems for identification purposes [7]. Nowadays, biometric systems has been become an interest area for authentication, and identification purposes. The laws and regulations of biometric are in progress, and standard biometric industry are being tested [7]. In addition, cognitive biometric systems are currently being investigated to use facial recognition, brain response to odor stimuli, and mentally output in searching ports and strong-security places. Many biometric techniques, such as gait (walking motion), retina, hand veins, ear canal, facial thermogram, DNA, odor and palm prints are being created. Such biometric techniques may be the solution in the coming years to the emerging threats in the field of data systems and security [7].

As a matter of fact, although biometrics is related to identification/recognition and authentication/verification, many got confused on these two issues. As shown in Figure 7.1, through enrollment stage, biometric data collected from individual and preprocessed, and then stored in database as template. In a *verification system*, a person's identity authenticates by comparing the captured biometric features/trait with the stored person's own biometric template(s) in the database. Here, a claim of identity can be submitted through a magnetic-stripe card, login name, or smartcard to the system so as to be rejected or accepted. In a *recognition system*, the subject's identity matches with entire database subjects without of the subject having a claim identity. The decision of acceptance is built on the basis of matching similarity ratio taking into account that it fails to if the subject is not enrolled in the system database.

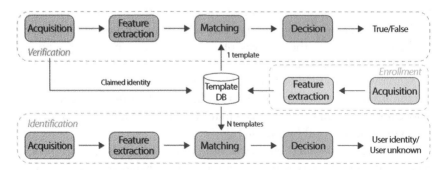

Figure 7.1 General flow of biometric systems.

Furthermore, *personal identification* is the task that is particularly associated with an individual's identity, whereas, biometric identification indicates to the identification of an individual depends on its distinctive physiological and/or behavioral traits/features. It associates/disassociates an individual based on how one is or what one does with established identity/identities previously. In fact, each individual has many physiological or behavioral characteristics and several of them can differentiate each individual. Due to that, biometrics identifiers are natively more accurate and have capability to distinguish between different individuals [6].

7.2.1   Biometric Systems Technologies

Biometric identification technologies are growing now to include many parts of human body known as physical biometric traits (Figure 7.2) such as fingerprint, face, eyes, etc. Also a lot of person actions are known as behaviors biometric traits such as signature, speech, walk, etc. [6]. Biometric systems are used one or more on the human traits that can be described as follows [7]:

1. Fingerprint: Considered as the oldest of all biometrics techniques. The fingerprint readers/sensors are the most common nowadays. It is based on variations in reflections at places where the papilla lines touch the reader's surface. Fingerprint matching techniques are Minutiae-based which firstly determine the minutiae point then match and Correlation-based techniques where translation and rotation processes are used.

2. Face recognition technology is a computer application for automatically identifying or verifying a person from a digital photo or vide. This is considered as the most common form of identity. Recently, there are two major fields in facial recognition which are face Eigen and facial metric. For automated personal identification, facial imaging has been widely discussed in a variety of different settings. Furthermore, when the selection requirements are unconstrained, automatic face recognition becomes challenges of today researches [8].

    Normally, it is a simple task to recognize each other, even with different environment and facial expressions. But in case of the automatic systems, face recognition systems need controlled capture process or constrained environment in capturing image task. So, several challenges have to address for unconstrained face recognition [8].

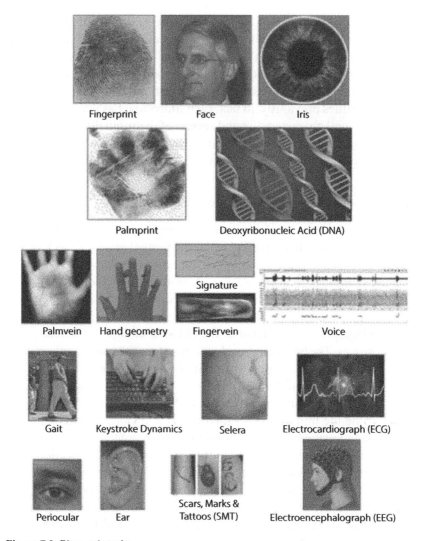

Figure 7.2 Biometric traits.

Surveillance search considered as an important application for face recognition under unconstrained scenario. Nowadays, by increasing of videos cameras installed to cover huge of places, face recognition is certainly an effective tool in the fighting on crime [8].

Automatic facial recognition technology would, therefore, perform an extremely important role in improving efficiency and productivity in contents retrieval [8].

3. Iris Technology: It is an identification method that uses the iris of the eye, a colored area that surrounds the pupil. Iris patterns are unique and can be collected from a video-based image acquisition system. Each iris structure features a complex pattern. This can be a set of features known as corona, crypts, capillaries, crypts, filaments, freckles, pits, furrows, striations and rings.

4. Hand Geometry Technology: This depends onto the truth which the hand of almost everyone is formed identically. Therefore the hand of the individual over a certain age may not keep changing. Such strategies involve estimation of the hand's length, width, thickness and surface area. A different approach is employed to calculate the optical hands principle.

5. Retina Geometry Technology: Depends on the shape of the blood vessel in the retina because there is a particular pattern in the veins at the back of the eye, this is mostly differentiating among eyes as well as individuals. The retinal acquisition requires people to take off their goggles, position their eyes close to the sensor, look at a certain spot, keep rising and concentrate on a specific position for around 10–15 s whereas the scanning is done.

6. Speech Recognition Technique: All of us have different sound tone, and yet speech recognition relies largely on learning a person's way of speaking, that is generally known as a behavioral trait.

7. Signature Verification Technique: Understanding the patterns of a signature depends on the composition of creating a signature, rather than a subsequent straight comparison of the signature itself. Mechanics are calculated as the curve dynamics form of strain, direction, acceleration, stroke length, number, and duration.

8. Palmprint: A somewhat different use of fingerprint technology is the Palmprint authentication. But the scanner size is considerably bigger, which is a crucial factor for use in desktop machines or handheld devices.

9. Hand vein: The structure of veins adopts the idea that a vein pattern is a typical form for various people. The subcutaneous veins absorb the infrared light and therefore have a darkened texture on the infrared camera's picture.

10. DNA: DNA sampling is requires some form of tissue, blood, or other physical sample. This capture method has yet to be improved. Until now, DNA analysis was not automatic enough to classify DNA analysis as a biotechnology. Human DNA can now be analyzed within 10 min.

11. Thermal imaging: it is a similar technique to geometry of hand vein. It also uses an infrared light source and/or camera to capture a vein pattern on the face or wrist.

12. Ear shape: Individuals are identified by the shape of the ear in law enforcement applications where ear signs are present at the crime scene.

13. Body odor: Biometrics for body odor is based on the fact that every human scent is unique. The odor is captured by sensors that are able to obtain odor from non-perforated parts of the body such as the back of the hand.

14. Keystroke Dynamics: behavioral trait which is a method of verifying an individual's identity through a writing rhythm that can handle both trained typists as well as amateur two-finger typing.

15. Nail Mattress (Fingernail Bed): The American AIMS Company is developing a system that scan the skin texture under the fingernail. The structure of the tongue and groove consists of almost parallel rows of vascular-rich skin. Between these parallel dermal structures are narrow channels and this is the distance between these measured by the AIMS.

Generally, to high recognition accuracy biometric traits should have set of properties such as [6, 9]:

- *Collectable* where the trait easily presentable to collected by a sensor,
- *Universal* where everyone possess himself trait,
- *Unique* which means dissimilarity between every two subjects, and
- *Permanent* where the trait should neither changeable nor be alterable.
- *Distinctiveness* when the trait has a special appearance such that make it a different and easy to recognize.
- *System performance.*

- *Ergonomics* which work better and more quickly.
- *Vulnerability to attacks.*
- Usability.

7.2.2   Biometric Recognition Framework

As a matter of fact, the framework of biometric recognition system includes two stages which is shown in Figure 7.3 and described as follows:

1. ***Enrolment Stage*:**

    o   Acquiring the subject.
    o   Feature extracting, i.e., salient have to be extracted.
    o   Storing these features in the database.

2. ***Recognition stage***

    o   Acquiring the subject (biometric trait) from the person.
    o   Feature extracting (with the use of the same extractor in the enrollment stage).
    o   Matching, which compare the feature set against the features of every individual on the database (in order to determine the matching rate or to verify a claimed identity).

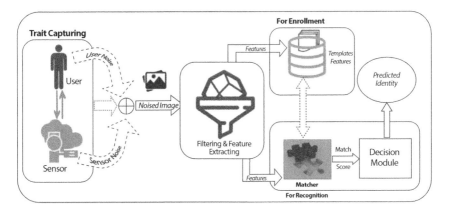

Figure 7.3 Biometric framework.

7.2.3   Biometric Applications/Usages

In the 21st century, biometrics is a part of daily life. Biometrics has been used in numerous fields such as corporate and school health, government departments, crossing borders and airports, hospital and blood bank for identification of patients; voice control of mobile devices; and investigations of criminal. Although several people may consider biometrics in forms of facial recognition, sound and iris, there are still other forms of biometrics that are being used or even under implementation [4].

Anyway, here are several forms biometrics can then be used to support solving of crimes, today and in the very upcoming years [10].

1. Finger print, which provide 99% of accuracy.
2. Palmprint, it can be considered as a helpful technique to the fingerprint.
3. Face recognition, which has 80% of accuracy.
4. DNA, it seems to be the effective method for investigating crimes.
5. Identification of iris, gait identification and detection of the smell. While many of the biometric measures are of specific use in criminal investigations, such new methods will help law enforcement identify offenders and terrorists worldwide quickly.

(a) National ID card   (b) Smartcard

(c) ATM transaction   (d) Computer login

Figure 7.4 Biometric applications.

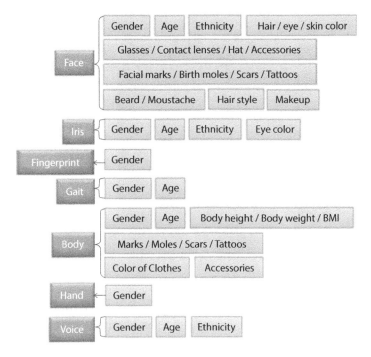

Figure 7.5 Soft biometric classification.

Applications include smart phone security, payment using mobile, cross-border, the National-Civil-Registry and entrance to prohibited services [11]. Such applications represented in Figure 7.4 as an example.

To identify such repeat offenders, set of anthropometric measurements and some soft biometric systems such as eye color, body geometry, etc. [11].

Soft biometric characteristics are physical, behavioral, or material features that are correlated with an person and that can be helpful for a subject's identification. These characteristics are classified in Figure 7.5, usually obtained from secondary and principal biometric information, can be grouped into predefined person comprehensible categories, and can be automated [12].

For the purpose out of identification, a human has several traits that make him different from another and share some traits with another. These traits are called as soft biometric traits. In other words, traits that may divide people into set of groups are called as soft biometric traits. E.g. gender will divide people into two groups, age will divide people into three or more, and color, etc. However, by increasing number of traits, the differentiation will increase. So, soft biometrics traits can be help to increase the accuracy of identification in biometric systems [12]. Likewise, soft biometric systems collect many information about people through capturing their photos, so, integrate these

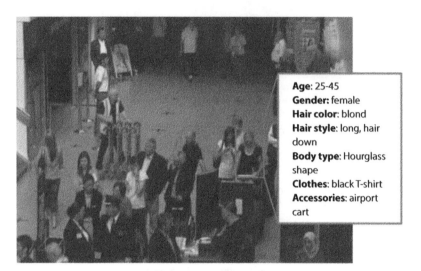

Age: 25-45
Gender: female
Hair color: blond
Hair style: long, hair down
Body type: Hourglass shape
Clothes: black T-shirt
Accessories: airport cart

Figure 7.6 Soft Biometric System Interface.

systems with CCTV will help for tracking any individual using his soft biometric traits. Figure 7.6 as an example of a soft biometric system interface.

7.3   Surveillance Systems (CCTV)

A Closed-Circuit Television (CCTV) is a system where a set of video cameras connected together into limited set of monitors are used in order to surveillance such places, Figure 7.7 shows a view of such systems.

Similarly, indoor or outdoor places prefer to install visual surveillance systems that are becoming a part of the organization infrastructure.

Figure 7.7 Surveillance system.

Therefore, there is a dire need for intelligent systems that can recognize human actions, and differentiate between normal and abnormal behaviors. In turn, it become high interesting topic and attract the attentions of many researchers as well as manufacturers [13].

The main objectives of intelligent video surveillance systems can be represented in an effective detection for interesting event that included in a large amount of videos and to predict or prevent some dangerous situation that is expected to happen. Therefore, there are many techniques used for such systems, in order to automatically rise an alarm when such abnormal behaviors are detected [13].

In dynamic scenes, visual surveillance aims to detect, recognize and track particular objects via series of images, and more generally to appreciate and explain some behaviors of objects. In order to implement smart visual monitoring there is a need to accomplish the task of surveillance automatically. With its many of applications, visual surveillance involves so many usages such as security guard for some important building, places, shops, traffic, borders, etc. [14].

To track people or vehicle, surveillance applications can be classified as:

1. Access control to specific zones: high sensitive to security for places/buildings, admissible people have special identity for entering. Using biometric techniques, database contains the legal visitors' biometric features, the system automatically collect the features of the current visitor once facing the cameras of the system. Then, the visitor will be permitted in case his records are confirmed in the database. The idea behind designing the database is that it is intended to obtain a set of human features such as gait, face, height, etc., of the legal visitors. Thus, directly, system captures the visitor features and matches them in the database in order to decide the admissibility.

2. Person-specific identification in certain scenes: smart surveillance system could be used for personal identification at a distance. This would help the police to catch the suspects by building a biometric suspects database that can be placed within visual surveillance system at different locations where they are likely to be.

3. Crowd flux statistics and congestion analysis: visual surveillance systems can use human detection techniques, and place it at interesting places to determine people flux. This is useful to safeguard people by avoiding congestions at shopping places, holy places, enjoyment places, beaches, etc.

4. Anomaly detection and alarming: behavioral of people is much important under some circumstances. Techniques of behavior recognizing can be used in the visual surveillance systems to differentiate between abnormal and normal behaviors. It may use for theft indicators at shops.
5. Interactive surveillance using multiple cameras: Cooperative visual surveillance systems by multiple cameras could be used for social security purposes to ensure the safety of an entire city. For example, tracking criminals across a wide area using multiple cameras.

Furthermore, Human Identification at a Distance (HID) is a program sponsored by DARPA based on multimodal technologies of surveillance systems, which aims to successfully detecting, classifying, and identifying people at a different distance and improve protection from terrorist attacks [14].

7.3.1   CCTV Goals

The goals of the surveillance cameras systems are listed below [15]:

- To reduce crime
- To reduce fear of crime
- Improving public safety
- To improve property security
- To create a safe and vital place to spend free time and fun people from and visitors to public places.
- Ensure that persons such as the elderly, the handicapped, women and indigenous peoples can safely use public space.

7.3.2   CCTV Processes

For more accurate system, the main processes of an intelligent surveillance system are:

1. Motion Detection
   A process of fragmenting regions that corresponds to things coming from the origin of a scene, named as motion detection. It is the first stage of some important functions like tracking, behavior detection they considered the motion detection as a basic step of them. The main stages of motion

detection are *environment modeling, motion segmentation,* and *object classification*. *Environment modeling* could be categorized into two models: 2-D models in the image plane and 3-D models in the real physical universe. *Motion segmentation* used in series of images to detect region that have moves of object like a person in order to provide a focus point for later processes of tracking and behavior analysis. *Object classification* that classify moving of objects into separated classes such as human, birds, vehicle, etc. [14].

2. Object Tracking
    When the motion detection is completed, the focus point of image direction has been determined. So, typically, surveillance system tracks subject moving at frames based on sequences of detected images. Tracking methods maybe categorized into four categories. The first is *Region-Based tracking* where the algorithms track the object based on its region in the image corresponding to its moving. The second, Active *Counter-Based tracking* which works to extract shapes of subjects and provides effective description. The third and fourth methods are Feature-Based tracking and Model-Based tracking. Feature-Based tracking uses recognition techniques by extracting elements and clustering them into set levels of features for matching them with images [14].

3. Understanding and Description of Behaviors
    Understanding object behavior and interpreting its movement is a critical process that needs to succeed two major tasks, i.e., motion detection and tracking. Depending on the sequences of images, behavior understanding algorithms analyze these images, classify them into data features, and, then, match them with the sequences of represented determine behavior. The major methods used for behavior understanding are listed as follows [14]:

    a) Dynamic time warping (DTW)
    b) Finite-state machine (FSM)
    c) HMMs
    d) Time-delay neural network (TDNN)
    e) Syntactic techniques
    f) Non-deterministic finite automaton (NFA)
    g) Self-organizing neural network.

With respect to behavior description, it is important to define object behaviors in a natural language that is suitable for non-specialist visual surveillance operators. Generally, there are two main categories of behavior description methods: statistical models and formalized reasoning [14].

4. Personal Identification For Visual Surveillance

After motion detection, tracking, and behavior understanding, the question that arises is "Who are currently in the place under surveillance system?". It is an important question to know who are there. For answering such questions, the term of 'personal identification' has to be defined. Generally, surveillance systems can identify a human using some biometric traits such as face, gait, human geometry, etc. At a distance, gait and face are most important for personal identification, where the face detection, face tracking, feature detection of the face, and face recognition are considered as important steps to recognize a person using face trait at visual surveillance systems. In fact, there is no constraints on someone who presented in front of the system, and cooperate property has eliminated. Therefore, it is critical issue to develop an integrated face recognition system with above-mentioned steps, especially for surveillance systems.

Furthermore, the major methods of gait recognition can be classified into [14]:

1. *Model-Based Methods*: it used such parameters as joint trajectories, limb lengths, and angular speeds.
2. *Statistical Methods*: it depends on the motion image description; it used in automatically gait recognition systems.
3. *Physical-Parameter-Based Methods*: to characterize a gait pattern of person, the structural of human body must extracted as a used parameters such as height, stride cadence and length, weight, etc.
4. *Spatio-Temporal Motion-Based Methods*: Based on the spatio-temporal, the motion recognition can be characterized via 3-D image sequence.

However, *Gait Fusion with Other Biometrics* can be adopted so as to provide robust, reliable, and accurate recognition systems with the help of fuse gait characteristics that merged with other biometric traits. Such systems integrate gait recognition and one or more of biometric traits e.g. an integration of gate and face recognition to optimize the performance of systems.

7.3.3   Fusion of Data From Multiple Cameras

For more reliability, multiple cameras-based visual surveillance systems are better than a single camera-based one. For such places or buildings, more than one camera has to be used to cover all sensitive parts of the place and entries. Here, the problem is "how to track the subject in system with multiple cameras?" that needs more processing and leads to an ambiguity because of the occlusion or depth problems. However, multi-cameras-based visual surveillance systems have some critical issues such as installation, calibration, object matching, automated camera switching, and data fusion [14].

7.3.4   Expanding the Use of CCTV

One of Criminology's most common theories is that crime rates dropped in tandem with an effective strategy of regulation and prevention of crime. Nevertheless, applying the monitoring systems as a prevalent method for control of the crime and deviance poses numerous problems in specific aspects of the existence and activities of a person. In this way, privacy remains at risk because communities are more prone to prioritize protection first [16].

In certain countries (CCTV) became a significant tool and traditional tactic in the battle against crime and the enhancement of community safety, and its usage continues to grow. However, the usage of CCTV services is just a single tool among a broad variety of approaches to crime reduction, though it is a rather successful technique [16]. From "crime avoidance" techniques, CCTV services help to make offenders inactive when a target is located elsewhere [16].

To better understand these modern surveillance program approaches, the word 'risk environment' which can explain focus on the safety model of earlier decades. In this sense, the emergence of video monitoring systems in all areas of activities, private as well as public, is a way of deterring crime and in order to collect data about criminals and their behaviors, is becoming a core component of security policies [16].

7.3.5   CCTV Effectiveness

The crucial issue of CCTV discussion is its effectiveness. Yet, by default when CCTV is presented, it is simply that the relevant perpetrators have to know such facts as: they are being monitored, and their data under control. Therefore, it is necessary to be aware while thinking about such crimes or deviant acts. If they do so, there will be detected and strong evidence would be introduced in somewhere else [16].

Despite its future usefulness, what we miss so far is knowing how CCTV technology is developed, applied, and implemented to meet particular safety objectives, and what activities managers operating with CCTV need to perform in order to achieve the goals. Some researches have also focused on the connection between CCTV device architecture and operator execution efforts[16].

A variety of technical deficiencies were found in this context, including inadequate setup equipment, low-quality video capture, and absence of systems integration. Such aspects often reduce the efficacy of CCTV [16].

7.3.6   CCTV Limitations

Some conclusions about efficacy can be learned with caution. Among other things:

1. CCTV performs better in well-defined specific locations (e.g. municipal car parks), but not always broad places (e.g. residential situations);
2. CCTV is more successful in combating property crime, and not strong instruments for reducing violence or chaos;
3. Strong public ties would significantly boost the efficiency of the program, so it needs cooperation from the police side;
4. High-quality CCTV devices will support criminal inquiries (at least in certain cases), so, high-quality CCTV is needed [16].

7.3.7   Privacy and CCTV

The definition of privacy extracted from it describes to us the foundations for a discussion of the shortcomings of privacy which may occur in very different places or circles where a person interacts with her or his social life [16]:

1. The basic close relation circle of social and personal life, where the intimate relationship is sacred in that space known as "the home";
2. The after field starts as a one's passes the line and reaches a "no-one's place" or public square (security and fairness will be handled in the same manner, including an appreciating of privacy such as anonymizing);
3. Eventually, one can try to cross a border or certain boundaries for getting the third type level (where "the possessor" can impose his laws, without limitations, in any way).

7.4   Legality to Surveillance and Biometrics vs. Privacy and Human Rights

As new technologies are being developed, the biometrics is continuously improving. There are of course many fears and controversial issues about biometrics, along with privacy and possible misuse of the new technology, and also issues about accuracy. Yet civil rights activists claim the gains exceed the risks.

Legally, some general guidelines for allowing the installation of CCTV cameras in public places may be defined. Clearly placed, the cameras need to be accurate, proportionate and required. In some opinion, it depends on studying the actual situation, the extent of risks and the hazards in different ecosystems to explain the reasons for the nature and scope of the actions to be taken for regulation [16].

The operation of an installed CCTV would have to clear a three-part examination according to the European Court of Human Rights doctrine:

1. Check the "suitability", that determines the appropriateness measure, likely to satisfy the goals reasonably;
2. Check the "necessity": determining the neediness, if there are certain, less restrictive methods capable of producing the same outcome; and
3. Check the "proportionality" in the specific meaning of the term, consisting of balancing priorities under which the effects on basic rights are measured against the significance of the desired goal.

So, the greater the violation, the more powerful the lawful aim at any situation [16].

The concept of proportionality in data security law is focused on the legality of data handling, as well as on the appropriateness and significance of the methods employed to accomplish these objectives in a democratic culture.

Both sides of the principle of proportionality, the legitimacy of the target and the tools used to this end must be evaluated with regard to video surveillance [16]. The implementation of a biometrics program would serve a valid and lawful intent because of the concept of proportionality, whereas certain approaches as efficient as surveillance are not possible but less invasive. At specific, the risk of the right to self-determination with information has to be sufficient for the intended intent. Consequently, the balance here has one result: the greater the risk of the rights concerned, the greater its interference with the right to self-determination with information. On the opposite, this suggests that the console will not employ invasive measures so long as there is no concrete danger [17].

Individuals don't have an absolute right in their rights since they are communicating necessarily in the society personally. Even when information is based on an individual, it's still a reflection of actual society thus cannot be correlated solely with the person concerned. The intensity among people and their community was determined by fundamental law in favor of community relations and binding over individual being. In principles of proportionality, the biometric system has pursuit of a legal and rightful objective. The purpose pursued must be bigger in order to interfere with the individual right to informational self-determination. Because of its challenges, biometric system is bound to process the data obtained in a legitimate purpose. The principles of "data avoidance" and "data dissolution" states that data processing be made such that it cannot identify individuals hence, processing is small and storage period is short [17].

All collected data are nicknamed and protected against unlawful access to reduce identification of personal data obtained by biometric system, and when pursued purpose is achieved all data be deleted or kept in anonymous state [17].

In order to decrease the ability of identification of the collected personal data, the program must be built in such a way that ensures the security of all data from unauthorized access. Data should not be personal so as to apply the principle of obtaining and processing data only when necessary to pursue the legitimate purpose. That is, those data must be aggregated or non-person related. Getting the pursued purpose achieved, those data is to be deleted or be anonymized [17].

However, while the individual has his right that does not mean absolute mastery of their rights. An individual is only a character in growing connections within the society. Even if it is based on personality, it is a reflection of social reality and cannot be linked exclusively to one individual in particular. According to the Basic Law definition, tensions between an individual and society goes in favor of being connected to society [17].

In brief, the personal interest is less important than the public one. Every person has the right to claim reservation of his own privacy, especially when it can be of any harm to his. The society has the right to be secured and live peacefully. Therefore, an authorized body must exist to guarantee no violation of individual privacy, and to ensure peace for the community.

7.5   Proposed Work (Biometric-Based CCTV System)

A crime is an illegal act which arises from a criminal intention. It is considered a deviation from the standards of society. To prevent crimes, penalty and precautionary measures are imposed.

The crime is presumed to take place when the victim and the perpetrator meet in the absence of a capable guardian. Perception of a potential perpetrator increases that he/she may be monitored as perceived risk of abuse at this specific location, and, then reduces the drive to abuse. Regardless of this deterrent effect, other justifications for using CCTV include the effective deployment of police to areas where criminal activity is or is likely to occur and that photographic evidence is easy to be detected [15].

Project First, is one of INTERPOL's projects to help law enforcement in member countries improve their border security through the use of biometric data—such as fingerprints and facial recognition—on FTFs and other terrorist-related individuals [4].

However, biometrics is here to stay, and for those who work to solve crime, this is a very good thing. Using CCTV systems, the environment considered under unconstrained sense where some biometric traits can be acquired but in low quality sometimes. Therefore, persistent video surveillance is considered a successful crime deterrent and, as a result, surveillance cameras have proliferated rapidly around the world, especially in large metropolitan areas. Figure 7.8 explains how the accuracy recognition affected regarding the cooperating individuals and constrained environment.

However, real-time video processing and recognition is rarely performed either to predict, detect or identify an incident or the offender [11].

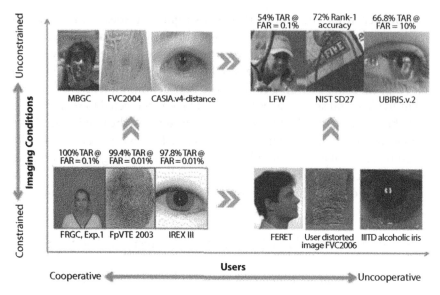

Figure 7.8 Accuracy recognition.

Using face recognition techniques, in a real-time biometric system can detect specific persons and identify them.

Using face image/video, there are several tasks including *face identification* which is intended to determine the identity from database, *face verification* which decide whether the identity of the given face is the same as the claimed by the user or not, and *face per matching* is determine whether two images represent the same subject or not [8]. Moreover, fusion Gait with other biometrics can be certified provide robust, reliable and accurate recognition systems with the help of extract gait features combined with other biometric traits. These systems combine gait recognition and one or more biometric features such as gate integration and facial recognition to improve system performance.

To track a subject/person as he/she passes in the CCTV system, a problem rises as how to re-identify the same person was detected, where face recognition it will a challenging problem because of the poor quality of face images captured using CCTV and the desired subject is uncooperative [11].

7.5.1 Biometric Surveillance System

7.5.1.1 System Component and Flow Diagram

The proposed framework is a multimodal biometric and multi-cameras surveillance system, where the biometric systems identify the offender based on his/her biometric traits and/or based on his/her weapon detected by the surveillance system.

System components can be classified into:

- *Surveillance System*: which monitor the area and fed biometric system with image captured when the moving happened.
- *Multimodal Biometric System*: which manipulate received images and process it to identify any suspects or criminal tools moved at the area under surveillance.
- *Database*: To store biometric data of captured criminals.

As shown in the flow chart of the system (Figure 7.9), the system begins the process of *capturing* any movement sensed, this captured image must be examined by *detecting* process to ensure whether it contains any of the crime tools or people.

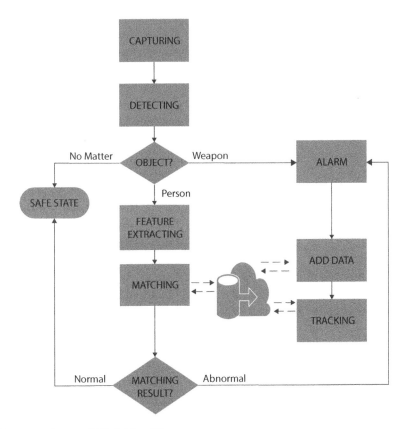

Figure 7.9 Proposed Work Flow Diagram.

In case the image contains any of the crime tools such as the weapon, the system issues a warning alert to the security men, and then tracks this tool according to the cameras map of the area under surveillance, updating its location in the database and drawing the path of the movement that was discovered.

Second case, if one or more people are found in the image, the system works to extract the biometric features of each person in the image which called as *feature extraction* process, and then compare them with all the data in the database which called as *matching* process. If this person is identical to any of the people added to the database, the person is considered a suspect and the area under surveillance is in a near-dangerous condition. Therefore, the system must raise a warning alert, track this person which called as *tracking* process, and add his data to the database, pending confirmation of this suspected case.

The last case, if nothing appears in the captured image, then the area under surveillance is safe.

Moreover, the system is in a state of permanent work and in the form of a continuous loop of taking pictures and processing them to ensure that the place is safe i.e. free of any suspect or any of the crime tools.

7.5.2   Framework

The proposed framework (Figure 7.10) is designed with the consideration that the offenders' data have already been enrolled in the central biometric database system which officially is done by the home office, i.e., police. Furthermore, the technical methods of extracting the features of offenders' biometric are followed in the proposed framework so as to provide perfect results in the matching process. Consequently, the proposed framework includes three stages included in surveillance, processing, and tracking stage, and the stage may involve a set of phases as follows:

- Surveillance Stage: it is the first stage, where the system senses any moving at the served place and captured it when it's happening, it can include two phases as:

  - *Sensing phase*: a process of sensing any moving surrounding, it may use an intelligent cameras.
  - *Capturing phase*: depends on the sensing at the first stage, cameras have to capture the place and send the image to the next stage.

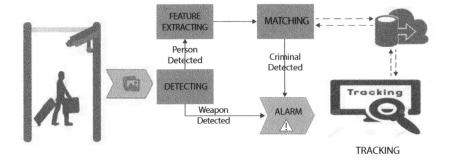

Figure 7.10 Proposed Frame Work.

- Processing Stage: here is the main work of the system, where the system receives an image and then checks whether it matches to any offender or any part of the crime instrument. At this stage, image received previously must be detected to ensure that the movement was safe. So, all objects in an image must be detected to determinate their behaviors. Several phases included at this processing stage as:

  • *Detection phase*: where all objects at the image must be detected as possible. After fetching the component of the image, there are three situations as a result of detecting are nothing detected which lead to nothing will happen; crime instrument which decides that something abnormal moving, system must rise alarm and track it till the security catches it; and the last situation is there are person detected which needs it identify her/hem through the upcoming phases.

  • *Feature extraction phase*: when one or more persons are detected as a result from previous phase, the current phase must extract all features for each person detected in order to fetch these features to the next stage.

  • *Matching phase*: here the main process that looks at offenders' database for matching any similarity with the detected features. There are two cases, once the similarity is low, then the system under normality; and the another is when the similarity is high, then, it is an abnormal case, system have to alarm the security and track the offender.

Figure 7.11 Intelligent Identification System.

    – Tracking stage: Tracking is a complex process, especially if the area under surveillance is large and contains a large number of cameras and routes. Tracking algorithms are also complex and requires significant processing and time. Therefore, dividing the large area into sub-regions and distributing independent surveillance systems leads to speeding up the detection of suspicious cases and thus raising the efficiency and performance of the system.

The idea behind the system is shown in Figure 7.11 where the biometric features of the person marked in red color are identical to a high percentage with the data of one of the criminals stored in the database. So he became a suspect. The rest of the people who were identified through the full personal body or through the face were marked yellow, because no data matching their biometric features has been found in the system database.

7.6   Conclusion

This chapter started with a general introduction in which the crime and its environment were defined, and the possible treatments represented in surveillance systems and the necessity of linking them to biometric systems. The first section dealt with introducing biometric systems, how they work, and available techniques to measure the extent of similarity in identifying people. The second part presented the monitoring systems, their types, objectives, and stages, which are sensitivity to motion detection, object tracking, understanding the behaviors, and personal identification.

The legality of surveillance and capturing the biometric data, human rights and privacy, compared to maintaining safe community, was discussed in Section 7.3.

In the fourth section, theoretically the main topic of this chapter was discussed, biometric surveillance system to secure the interested areas, system components, flow diagram, framework supported by illustrations and figures.

References

1. Jain, A.K., Nandakumar, K., Ross, A., 50 years of biometric research: Accomplishments, challenges, and opportunities. *Pattern Recognit. Lett.*, 79, 80–105, 2016.
2. Park, H.H., Oh, G.S., Paek, S.Y., Measuring the crime displacement and diffusion of benefit effects of open-street CCTV in South Korea. *Int. J. Law, Crime Justice*, 40, 3, 179–191, 2012.
3. Senior, A. *et al.*, Enabling video privacy through computer vision. *IEEE Secur. Priv.*, 3, 3, 50–57, 2005.
4. INTERPOL, Biometric data plays key role in fighting crime and terrorism. *INTERPOL*, 2017. [Online]. Available: https://www.interpol.int/es/Noticias-y-acontecimientos/Noticias/2017/Biometric-data-plays-key-role-in-fighting-crime-and-terrorism
5. Akhtar, Z., Hadid, A., Nixon, M. S., Tistarelli, M., Dugelay, J. L., & Marcel, S. Biometrics: In search of identity and security (Q & A). IEEE MultiMedia, 25, 3, 22–35, 2018.
6. Of, C. and Acm, T.H.E., B Iometric. *Commun. ACM*, 43, 2, 91–98, 2000.
7. Bhattacharyya, D., Ranjan, R., F. A., a, Choi, M., Biometric Authentication: A Review. *Int. J. Serv. Sci. Technol.*, 2, 3, 13–28, 2009.
8. Tistarelli, M., Sun, Y., Poh, N., On the use of discriminative cohort score normalization for unconstrained face recognition. *IEEE Trans. Inf. Forensics Secur.*, 9, 12, 2063–2075, 2014.
9. Jain, A., Klare, B., & Ross, A. (2015, May). Guidelines for best practices in biometrics research. In 2015 International Conference on Biometrics (ICB) (pp. 541–545). IEEE.

10. Trader, J., 5 Ways Biometrics Help Solve Crimes. M2SYS, 2015. [Online]. Available: http://www.m2sys.com/blog/comments-on-recent-biometric-news-stories/5-ways-biometrics-help-solve-crimes/.
11. Jain, A. K., & Ross, A. Bridging the gap: from biometrics to forensics. Philosophical transactions of the Royal Society of London. Series B, Biological sciences, 370 (1674), 20140254, 2015.
12. Dantcheva, A., Elia, P., Ross, A., What else does your biometric data reveal? A survey on soft biometrics. *IEEE Trans. Inf. Forensics Secur.*, 11, 3, 441–467, 2016.
13. Ben Mabrouk, A. and Zagrouba, E., Abnormal behavior recognition for intelligent video surveillance systems: A review. *Expert Syst. Appl.*, 91, 480–491, 2018.
14. Hu, W., Tan, T., Wang, L., Maybank, S., A survey on visual surveillance of object motion and behaviors. *IEEE Trans. Syst. Man Cybern. Part C Appl. Rev.*, 34, 3, 334–352, 2004.
15. Lawson, T., Rogerson, R., Barnacle, M., A comparison between the cost effectiveness of CCTV and improved street lighting as a means of crime reduction. *Comput. Environ. Urban Syst.*, 68, December 2016, 17–25, 2018.
16. Agustina, J.R. and Galdon Clavell, G., The impact of CCTV on fundamental rights and crime prevention strategies: The case of the Control commission of video surveillance devices. *Comput. Law Secur. Rev.*, 27, 2, 168–174, 2011.
17. Desoi, M., Pocs, M., Stach, B., Biometric systems in future crime prevention scenarios—How to reduce identifiability of personal data. *Lect. Notes Informatics (LNI), Proc.—Ser. Gesellschaft fur Inform.*, P-191, 13, 259–266, 2011.

Rule-Based Approach for Botnet Behavior Analysis

Supriya Raheja[1]*, Geetika Munjal[1], Jyoti Jangra[2] and Rakesh Garg[1]

[1]Department of Computer Science & Enginerring, Amity University, Noida, India
[2]IBM India Pvt. Ltd, Gurugram, India

Abstract

Botnets pose as serious threat and huge loss to organizations. The presence of botnet traffic in any network is a matter of serious concern. They are used for many activities of malicious type like distributed denial of service (DDOS) attacks, mass spam, phishing attack, click frauds, stealing the user's confidential information like passwords and other types of cyber-crimes. The detection of botnets in early phases is very crucial for minimizing the damage. With this aim, the proposed approach uses Network forensic analysis flow exporter tools like Wireshark, NetworkMiner and CapLoader for analyzing and extraction of important features. The botnet traffic flows are analyzed based on the features set extracted by these tools. The impacts of these extracted features are studied with respect to the Botnet malicious activities. A botnet detection model is generated using decision tree. The performance of different algorithms namely Decision Tree, Naïve Bayes and ZeroR are analyzed. It has been observed that the decision tree works better with selective features.

Keywords: Bots, botnet behavior, traffic flow exporter tools, malware, machine learning, cross validation, botnet traffic flow

8.1 Introduction

Today's internet world is rapidly growing and there is a need to protect the data from different kinds of cyber security issues and cyber-crimes which

---

*Corresponding author: supriya.raheja@gmail.com

Subhendu Kumar Pani, Sanjay Kumar Singh, Lalit Garg, Ram Bilas Pachori and Xiaobo Zhang (eds.)
Intelligent Data Analytics for Terror Threat Prediction: Architectures, Methodologies, Techniques and Applications, (161–180) © 2021 Scrivener Publishing LLC

are increasing in the cyber world. To protect the users and any organization's confidential information is significant. The rapid advancement in the technological field has resulted in the evolution of malware forms starting from the initial viruses, worms, Trojan, and other kinds of advance malware like botnets.

Botnets are considered as the advanced form of malwares which are capable of evolution with the changing technological environment. The botnet network consists of the infected hosts which are known as bots. The bots are also known as the infected host machines. The attacker exploits and controls the bots by issuing the commands to the single infected bot on the botnet network to gain control over the entire network to carry out various illegal forms of malicious activities. The attacker is known as the 'botmaster' or 'botherder' [3]. The botnet attacks can lead to most serious and devastating effects that result in major financial, personal, organizational crisis. They are considered as the costliest cyber security issues. Since the botnet attacks influence various areas like finance, organizational, health, cyber security, government sectors, and many more, the early detection of the botnets in the network is of significant importance.

The Botnets are used by an attacker for carrying out various forms of illegal cyber-attacks like DDOS (distributed denial of service attack), Click frauds, users identity theft, stealing of users confidential information like passwords, spamming and phishing attacks [1]. Since the botnets are a cause of serious threat to the world of cyber, it is important to deeply acknowledge the problems that are related to botnet detection in the botnet network.

In literature, different technologies exist to detect the botnets in network traffic. Each technology overcomes the limitation of others. The extraction of significant features from the network traffic flows plays an integral part in the detection of the early botnet attack phase. Therefore, in lieu of early and effective analysis of botnets behavior, it is important to analyze the effect of the network flow features including IP of source, IP of destination, source port, payload bytes, destination port, start time, end time, protocol used and many other features.

The main aim of this work is to focus on these network traffic flow features which are extracted by using the network forensics tools like Wireshark, NetworkMiner and CapLoader and later to deeply analyze how these flows contain the features information that contribute in analyzing the inside secret information of any organization. These features are helpful in extracting the relevant information required for the inspection of the abnormal traffic flows.

Since the infected bot is a part of the compromised botnet network which acts as a zombie and can infect the other host on the same network. By deeply analyzing the bot information through the communication of the bot over the network, it is highly useful in categorizing the normal traffic and the malicious traffic traces. The crucial information regarding the infected host like infected client IP, client Port, services used for attacks and the transport protocol used for the attacks can be extracted by using the network Forensic analyzing tools. These tools are capable of analyzing the pre captured network traffic flows and generate the report based on the features extracted. Data preprocessing and data cleaning is performed using different machine learning algorithms. These algorithms are used further to analyze the selected features from the raw input flows.

The rest of the work is organized as follows: Section 8.2 presents the state of art, Section 8.3 discusses the basics of botnets and botnet architecture, Section 8.4 discusses the data set used and proposed methodology. Section 8.5 discusses the results and analysis. Finally, Section 8.6 concludes the proposed work.

8.2   State-of-the-Art

Different types of malware and botnet detection techniques exist in the literature. Since, the first SPAM message which was sent in early 90s, one of the most common and significant threats faced by the organizations are botnet attacks. The present botnet detection and analyzing methods focus mainly on the control (C&C) protocols and botnet command like HTTP, IRC and many others.

Fadullah *et al.* [1] have proposed a new detection method known as DTRAB to predict the DDOS attacks. The application level protocols are examined for the suspicious attacks. DTRAB technique have successfully detected the novel attacks and also tracked the root of threat on the basis of attacker network traces.

Zhang *et al.* [2, 3] have used flow correlation information for improving the efficiency of the classification process by training the small data set instances. The Naïve Bayes and the K-Nearest-Neighbor classifiers are used to analyze and identify the possible signs of the any malicious traffic on network. Shu *et al.* [4] have proposed a technique which shows how rule-based approach can be utilized for the detection of the anomaly attacks. They proposed the qualitative comparisons between the advantages and disadvantages used by the traditional networking and software networking. It defined the security issues regarding the overall architecture of the network used.

Zeidanloo *et al.* [6, 22] have developed a botnet detection model for the detection of botnets where on the basis of the related communication patterns and results showed by the group of infested hosts can be utilized for the botnet detection. The prior known features are not required in this approach. X-means clustering is used by authors in this framework. Gu *et al.* [7] have proposed a model for novel botnet detection of anomaly based which had no dependency of protocol and structure used by the botnets. They provided an in depth analysis of the traffic flow features like destination IP, source IP, time, destination port, source port, number of bytes and the packets transferred during the communication. It revealed that the bots of the same botnet network show similar C&C communication pattern and the information regarding the malicious activity retrieved is same. Authors have applied the C-plan clustering for similar botnet communication patterns.

Arshad *et al.* [8] have presented another botnet detection of anomaly-based approach that does not require the prior knowledge of the bot attack signatures, C&C protocol information. Amini *et al.* [9] have proposed a method which analyzed the traffic flow features like IP addresses, ports used, packets event times, duration and bytes per packet for the detection of the botnets. Rule-based techniques are deployed to increase the efficiency. Strayer *et al.* [10] have proposed the classification technique for the effective botnet traffic analysis. This approach used the extracted traffic flow features like bandwidth, IP addresses, packet timing and burst duration. J48 decision trees, naïve Bayes and Bayesian classifiers are used for finding the correlation with the malicious botnet traffic flows.

Zhao *et al.* [11] have used a decision tree classifier for analyzing the different network flow features that can be helpful in detection the malicious botnet attack which uses the C&C channel. The flow based features are checked during the specific time intervals for the presence of any suspicious activity related to botnets. Both the supervised and unsupervised techniques are used for the detection of botnets In unsupervised approach, the network traffic flows were clustered to find the anomalous behavior based on the extracted features from the traffic flows of the application. This approach was tested on data set derived from IRC community. This approach is capable of attaining high detection rate and very low false positive rate during botnet detection which is got from computer results [22].

Piyush & Manoj [13] gave a comparative analysis of the machine learning based classification of C&C traffic and P2P botnet traffic. The three models were used like Decision Tree (C4.5), Bayesian Network and Linear Vector Support (LVS). The results were compared and the performance was evaluated and compared. The proposed model gave the better results as compared to the decision tree classifier. The botnet detection approach compared the three different approaches used in categorizing botnet traffic. Kalaivani and Vijaya [14] have presented another approach for analysis and identification of the malicious botnet traffic flows. They have applied the different machine learning algorithms such as support vector machine, naive Bayes and decision trees.

Rajesh and Tajinder [15] have proposed a model of automated system that assisted in the packet capturing, processing multiple logs of the attacks, labeling of the network traffic flows based on the low level features. Lu et al. [16] have described the importance of Honeynets in capturing and analyzing of the botnet anomaly traffic flows. Strayer et al. [20] have used the approach for bulk filtering of the flows and later correlating the remaining flows with the similar characteristics and features found among them. This approach increased the effectiveness of the previous work done by Livadas.

Villamarin and Brustoloni [17] have proposed an anomaly detection approach for DNS traffic filtering to identify the botnet C&C server. Due to the evolution of the botnet communication architecture, it becomes a complex process to detect and analyze the botnet behavior by extracting the significant features from the Network traffic flows which plays a key role in the detection of the early botnet attack phase. It is important to understand the botnet behavior depicted by the bots during execution of any malicious activity. In today's fast growing world of interconnectivity and codependency on internet machines, the major concern is to ensure the security of the data at the personal level and at organizational level. With such advancement in technology, the malwares are also evolving themselves. Botnets are also continuously changing and evolving their communication architecture. The primary concern is to deploy tools and techniques which are feasible to analyze the early botnet malicious behavior shown by botnets.

It is important to study the effect of the network flow features like source IP, destination IP, source port, destination port, payload bytes, start time, end time, protocol used and many other features for effective analysis. Since the botnets use a more complex architecture, they are slowly detected. To choose the correct features from the available feature set is very crucial.

8.3   Bots and Botnets

Day by day, many new forms of malwares are evolving which are threats to the cyber security. The Botnets are also an advance form of malware which are learning new ways to avoid detection by updating their control mechanisms by machine learning approaches.

8.3.1   Botnet Life Cycle

To completely understand the deep analysis of the botnet attack, it is important to have full knowledge about the botnet life cycle. It is crucial to understand the different stages involved in the execution of the botnet attack for successful completion. Figure 8.1 shows the six different phases of the botnet life cycle involved in the completion of the any botnet attack.

The 'initial infection' of the attack compromises the vulnerable host machine by using the bot malware. Thus, the infected host becomes a bot over the specific botnet network. This phase includes downloads by infected websites, through infected email file attachments, through wrong clicks on malicious links, infected hardware, and softwares [16].

'Secondary infection' involves the execution of the malware bot binary from the external source destination onto the compromised host machine, where it installs itself and is ready to become a bot. The different protocols can be used for the downloading of the bot malware binaries like HTTP (Hypertext Transfer protocol), FTP (File Transfer Protocol) and P2P (Peer-to-peer) protocols.

'Communication phase' and 'malicious command transfer' involves the interaction and communication between the infected host machines or bots with the command & control server (C&C server) [18]. 'Update' and 'Maintenance' phase is used for carrying out the malicious activities like DDOS attacks, spam attacks, click frauds, stealing other confidential information like passwords, etc. After the successful execution of the attacks on the compromised bot machines, botnet networks are also searched [19].

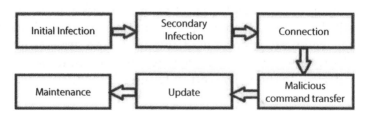

Figure 8.1 Botnet life cycle.

The bots can update themselves and become adaptive to the changing environment by learning the new patterns for further propagation and also to avoid detection over the network. That is why it very difficult to detect botnets easily over any network channel.

8.3.2   Botnet Detection Techniques

Many different researchers have proposed various botnet detection approaches for the effective detection of the botnets as illustrated in Figure 8.2. There are two major types of detection techniques that are proposed to solve the problem for botnets detection. The two main categorized techniques are Host-based detection techniques and network-based detection techniques [18].

The Host Based detection methods are responsible for checking the host machine for any signs of malicious binary file activities onto the machines. These detection methods use Anti-viruses, Anti-spywares, etc; these are installed on the hosts to detect suspicious malware activities. It is an important method as the attack is detected in the initial phase on the infected machine and attack can be stopped.

The Network based detection techniques are much more effective as they are able to scan the entire network for any sign of malicious activity. The Intrusion detection systems (IDS) and Intrusion prevention systems (IPS) are responsible for carrying out the network based detection approach.

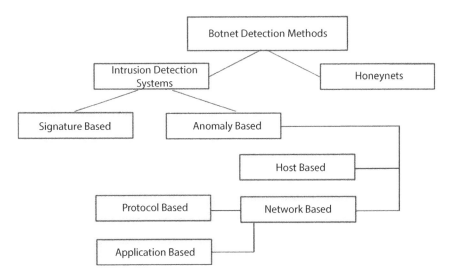

Figure 8.2 Different botnet detection methods.

Within a short duration of time the wide network can be scanned for any malicious attack.

The main aim of this work is to focus on the network based flow features extracted from the captures of network traffic.

8.3.3   Communication Architecture

It is also important to understand the different communication topologies used by the botnets like IRC (Internet Relay Chat) and P2P (Peer to Peer). The botnets use C&C channels for deployment which is used for attack purposes [21].

The command and control channel (C&C) mechanism are the major techniques which are used by the bot-master for issuing the different set of malicious instructions and also gaining the control over the compromised host known as bots. The presence of the C&C channel is the suspected sign for the presence of any botnet network. There are two types of protocols which are mainly used by the bots for the communication over the botnet networks, these are IRC and P2P. On the basis of classification of the protocol topology used by the botnets, they can be broadly categorized as centralized, decentralized and hybrid topology communication architecture used by the botnets. The early botnets used the IRC protocols as a means for communication. The bot-master issues the control command to the bots for performing malicious activities like DDOS attacks, click frauds, spam attacks, etc. The major limitation of IRC protocol type of topology architecture is that it uses a centralized topology for communication which means if the central bot server goes down then no further communication and control can be gained on the remaining bots of the botnet network by the bot-master. In the botnet traffic architecture, once the C&C server is detected and stopped then the whole botnet can be stopped.

With the evolution of the botnet architecture new ways of communication developed which assisted botnets to hide their identity and made it more complex to detect such bots on botnets. To overcome the limitation of the centralized botnet topology architecture, new type of communication topology evolved which is known as the P2P protocol architecture.

The P2P communication architecture uses the decentralized framework as the means for communication. In this type of protocol architecture, the bot-master issues the commands through the C&C channel for the attack to the P2P nodes. These P2P nodes are neutral and independent in their working across the botnet network. Even if the central C&C server is disabled, these P2P nodes can still be used by the bot-master for carrying out malicious activities. However, this P2P communication architecture has its own limitations like it does not guarantee a high degree of reliability, has low latency with respect to C&C communication, which has major impact on the effective working of the botnet attacks.

Nowadays, with the major advancements in the field of technology and internet, the botnets are also evolving their communication architecture. They are learning new patterns to spread and remain anonymous during the attacks. Also, to overcome the limitations of host based detection techniques and network based detection techniques, the new hybrid botnet detection techniques evolved which are a better solution for the detection of the novel attacks. The two types of techniques are majorly used for detection are Signature based approach and Anomaly based approach. The signature based detection approach uses the 'signatures' which are the characteristic patterns of the network traffic. This methodology uses the detection approach where the packets are deeply inspected from the network traffic and recognizes the signatures of the malicious attacks. The major limitation of the signature based approach is that it is only best for detection of known attacks.

However, Anomaly based detection methodology is capable of detection of traffic anomalies that show the possible indication of any malicious attack instance taking place over the network traffic. The major advantage of this approach is that it is possible to detect new attacks high better accuracy.

To analyze the botnet behavior, it's important to focus on the following aspects [23, 25–28]:

- To understand the botnet traffic behavior by deeply analyzing the network traffic flows.
- Understand the feature set extracted by different tools
- Understand the limitations of the botnet data sets
- Commonly used attacks by botnets
- The tools and software's that can be deployed with ease
- Understand the limitations of the previous botnet analysis and detection methods
- Proposed work.

Considering the above mentioned points, we have analyze the botnet behavior by using the three different network forensic analysis flow exporter tools including Wireshark, NetworkMiner and CapLoader. The significant flow features are extracted by using these tools, and later the impact of the network traffic flows that are relevant in the detection are studied and analyzed for the suspicious botnet behavior.

Wireshark is an open source packet analyzer tool. It is a dedicated data collection tool that systematically understands the structure of various network protocols. We can analyze and parse the display fields. Wireshark uses the pcap format to capture packets. It can perform both active and passive analyses of the network traffics but only in the compatible. Features extracted by using the Wireshark tool are as follows are displayed in Table 8.1.

Another tool is NetworkMiner which is a Network Forensic Analysis flow exporter tool. It can be used to passively analyze the .PCAP file for any suspicious botnet attack behavior. It also provides the relevant information regarding operating systems, sessions, hostnames, open ports which are used in research.

NetworkMiner gives an advanced network traffic analysis (NTA) by providing extracted artifacts in an intuitive user interface. The data extracted is simple to understand and simplifies the research analysis.

In case of our botnet analyses, this tool provides the relevant information for performing the high level of analysis of any malware propagating over the network by analyzing the network flows. It also gives information regarding operating system fingerprinting; parse any PCAP file, etc. The features extracted by this tool are Host information, Files, Images, Messages, Credentials, Sessions, DNS, Parameters, Keywords, Anomalies, IP addresses. These features are examined manually for checking the presence of malicious signs shown by the botnets. It's crucial to know the importance of the presence of significant features that influence the botnet activity. This is done by literature survey and doing some research or study work related to botnet communication patterns, etc. [12].

These features contain the information that is used for analyzing and detecting the botnet behavior. The sub categories information of these features include Hosts which includes host information, Other features

Table 8.1 Features extracted from Wireshark.

Features	Meaning
Sequence no.	It depicts the sequence of flow id
Time	Seconds since previous capture packet
Source	Client/Source IP
Destination	Destination IP
Protocol	Protocol used for communication
Length	Packet length (Bytes)
Info	Information contained inside

include files, images, messages, credentials, sessions, DNS, parameters, keywords and anomalies. The file features gives information of file extension, size, host etc. The 'images' feature has all the images which are extracted. The 'messages' include source and destination host, from and to information and subject as well. Timestamp is common attribute for 'file' and 'message' feature. 'Credentials' include Client, Server Protocol, and username, password and other login information. 'Sessions' contains client and server port, protocol Information and start time. 'DNS' include frame number, timestamp, client and server port, IP and DNS TTL, Transaction ID, Type, DNS query and answer. 'Parameters' include its name, value, source and destination host and port and timestamp details. Another feature 'Anomalies' informs about detected anomalies

The third tool used is CapLoader tool is used for handling the large .PCAP files. It is also used for analyzing and extracting the features that used for doing research in case of Botnets and other types of Malware traffic traces. The CapLoader tool extracts different set of features on the bases of Flows, Services and Hosts.

8.4   Methodology

The overall approach adopted to complete the task is shown in Figure 8.3. The dataset used for this research work is taken from the Malware Capture Facility Project [24]. The facility project is an initiative taken by the Czech Technical University ATG Group used for capturing, analyzing and publish genuine long lived malware traffic for the research purpose.

The major objectives of this work are:

- The execution of the real malware traffic for long during of time.
- Analyzing the malicious malware traffic flows both manually and automatically by using different tools and techniques.
- To allocate the ground truth labels to the malicious network traffic flows that include different botnet phases and different attack patterns.
- To provide the acquired dataset to students and researchers so as to assist them in developing effective and better botnet detection techniques.

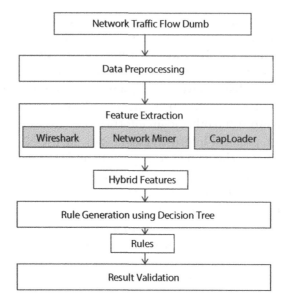

Figure 8.3 Block diagram of proposed methodology.

- The dataset contains the pre-captured malicious botnet traffic files in .PCAP format. The .PCAP file contains the traces of botnet traffic that are used to analyze the behavior of the botnet communication over the botnet.

Using the above mentioned tools, seven features are selected based on their significance related to the botnet analysis and detection which includes ClientIP, ClientPort, ServerPort, Transport, Duration, Payloadbytes, PCR. The details of these features are:

- ClientIP: The client IP Address is used to separately find the client machine for communication. It is most general basic and significant feature present in the net flow traffic field. The client IP address is the unique IP address of the host machine or any web application site that we use for communication. The Client IP address is changed to single last digit format for further processing. Like 147.32.84.165 is denoted as 165. In our case the Client IP of the client machine (Bot) having the IP address as 147.32.84.165 [SARUMAN] (Windows) is the infected Malicious Bot address which is used during the botnet attack.

- Client Port: The client port number, helps to identify and locate the service or web applications to which the data or information needs to be send during communication. The client port number is mostly use to acquire the information during the communication with remote machine that were used for attacking or have been targeted for malicious activities. In our case the client port 138 (UDP domain services) and 137 UPD (name services) are used mostly for malicious Botnet activity of UDP floodattack.
- ServerPort: The server port provides the crucial information to allow us to identify and locate the service or web applications to which the data or information needs to be sending during communication. These server ports are used to acquire information remotely that have been used for malicious activities. The server port 53 is used by Botnet, where the remote attacker sends a large amount of data to port 53 and cause the server to crash.
- Transport: The protocol is the unique set of rules that are used for connection and communication. The Protocols are used to mention communication between the interacting machines. In our case the three major protocols are used. They are TCP, UDP and ICMP. Another attack where attacker overwhelms random ports is "UDP flood". It is a type of on the targeted host with IP packets containing UDP datagram. The presence of excess amount of UDP in this case shows the presence of suspicious botnet traffic behavior.
- Duration: the total time taken to complete the particular flow. The duration rate shows that how much payload bytes are send within the specific duration of time. The presence of large number of the flows on the network with the very minimal time range onto the specific host machine is the sign of botnet attack.
- Payloadbytes: The Total Bytes provides the total number of bytes that the client transmitted for any of the request. The total byte size is used as significant factor for network measurement. The presence of excess number of payload bytes within the very minimum range of time shows the malicious behavior existing in the network flow which is the behavior exhibited by the bots during the communication in the botnet network.

- PCR (Peak CellRate): The PCR is defined as the maximum rate allowed at which the cells can be transported in any asynchronous transfer mode network. The PCR rate is crucial factor in determining how often the cells are sent with respect to time so as to minimize the jitter.

These extracted set of features are studied for the analyzing the botnet behavior. It is checked how these features influence the botnet behavior detection process. In some of the literature surveys, some of these features were used for proposing the model for botnet detection using Machine learning. But in current research work we have tried to refine some of the features that can affect the analyses process used of botnet behavior.

These selected features can further help to analyze the botnet traffic with help of machine learning techniques. The proposed features performance is evaluated by comparing various machine learning approaches and it observed that decision tree can successfully classify botnet data with highest accuracy. Thus these extracted features are fed to C4.5 machine learning approach to identify the rules that may help to classify the botnet traffic in to TCP and UDP. Figure 8.4 shows the decision tree generated using our proposed approach; the tree is formed with the help of WEKA tool [29, 30]. Table 8.2 shows the rules identified using proposed approach for botnet traffic analysis.

The Decision tree Classification method is responsible for generating the output as decision tree which are binary tree like structures, that include branch nodes which represent an alternative between a number of alternatives, and each of the leaf node represent the decision. The Decision

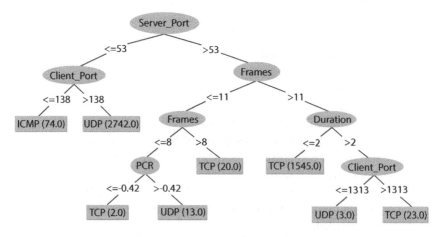

Figure 8.4 Decision tree obtained using proposed approach.

Table 8.2 Rules generated.

S. No.	Rules	Class
1	If Server Port<-53&& client port<=138	ICMP
2	If the Server Port<=53&& client port >138	UDP
3	If Server Port >53 && frames<=8&&PCR<= -0.42	TCP
4	If Server Port >53 && frames<=8&&PCR> -0.42	UDP
5	If Server Port >53 &&(8<frames<=11)	TCP
6	If Server Port >53 && frames>11&&duration<=2	TCP
7	If Server Port >53 && frames>11&&duration>2 && client port <=1313	UDP
8	If Server Port >53 && frames>11&&duration>2 && client port >1313	TCP

Tree approach represents rules to forecast the target variable. This classification technique is efficient, in case there is changing training data and high number of attributes present in the huge dataset.

J48 in WEKA is the simple implementation of the C4.5 decision tree classifier, decision tree for current domain is depicted in Figure 8.4. This machine learning algorithm makes use of the greedy approach to induce decision tree for classification. By analyzing the training data, a decision tree structure is generated and this structure is later used to classify the hidden data. J48 machine learning approach creates the decision trees and the nodes thus generated assess the presence and importance of the single features.

A total of 8 rules are generated, which are depicted in Table 8.2. The above rules are validated using accuracy and error rate.

8.5   Results and Analysis

The result of the different classifiers is assessed and a comparative analysis is done. The accuracy in classification task is used as a key parameter for measuring the performance of classifier. It is defined as the ratio of the total number of the correctly classified instances in the test data set and the total number of test cases. It is calculated as the count of all correct predictions divided by the total number samples in the dataset. The formula for calculating accuracy is as follows

$$accuracy = \frac{TP+TN}{TP+TN+FP+FN} \tag{8.1}$$

Where TP is true positive and TN is true negative. They both sum up to get total sample correctly predicted. FP and FN is false positive and false negative respectively. Both correctly classified and incorrectly classified samples form total sample which is denominator in above equation. Highest possible accuracy can be have 1.0 and worst is 0.0.

Another metrics used for validating our model is Error rate (ERR) expressed as Equation (8.2). It is calculated as the number of all incorrect predictions divided by the total number of samples in the dataset.

$$error \ rate = \frac{FP+FN}{TP+TN+FP+FN} \tag{8.2}$$

The best error rate is 0.0 whereas the worst is 1.0. All the results are validated using cross validation approach. Using the proposed approach we have obtained accuracy of 99.09% where are zeroR which is based on majority classifier gives an accuracy of 0.62 as shown in Figure 8.5. Naïve

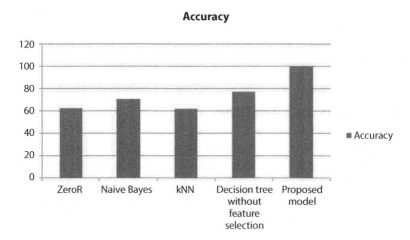

Figure 8.5 Percentage accuracy of various machine learning model and proposed model.

Table 8.3 Error rate.

	ZeroR	Naive Bayes	kNN	Decision tree without feature selection	Proposed model
Error rate	0.37	0.30	0.38	0.22	0.09

Bayes the proposed model classifiers are used for comparison ZeroR, Naive Bayes and kNN is giving any accuracy of 0.75 and 0.60 respectively. We have also observed that decision tree without feature selection gives an accuracy of 0.75 whereas in proposed model i.e. with feature selection decision tree is giving an accuracy of 0.99. Error rate for all these respective algorithms are mentioned in Table 8.3.

8.6   Conclusion and Future Scope

Botnets are becoming the most serious threat on the internet. This research work describes the approach for analyzing botnet behavior by extracting significant features of the botnet traffic flows. The present work generated an effective botnet detection model based on decision tree. It is shown by the experimental results that most of the machine learning models achieved lower classification accuracy, among which the decision tree algorithm gives the best results in terms of accuracy i.e. 78%. Based on this result, we propose to exploit the decision tree algorithm along with relevant features in the suggested botnet detection model. The proposed model has boosted the accuracy to 99.09% for the given dataset. In the future, the proposed model is to be tested on larger dataset. Its effects are also required to be analyzed for domain features identified, on larger and different datasets. Another dimension is to explore more new features to improve the detection accuracy of the proposed model.

References

1. Fadlullah, Z.M., Taleb, T., Vasilakos, A.V., Guizani, M., & Kato, N., DTRAB: Combating against attacks on encrypted protocols through traffic-feature analysis. *IEEE/ACM Trans. Networking*, 18, 4, 1234–1247, 2010.
2. Zhang, J., Chen, C., Xiang, Y., Zhou, W., Xiang, Y., Internet traffic classification by aggregating correlated naive Bayes predictions. *IEEE Trans. Inf. Forensics Secur.*, 8, 1, 5–15, 2012.

3. Zhang, J., Xiang, Y., Wang, Y., Zhou, W., Xiang, Y., Guan, Y., Network traffic classification using correlation information. *IEEE Trans. Parallel Distrib. Syst.*, 24, 1, 104–117, 2012.

4. Zhang, J., Chen, C., Xiang, Y., Zhou, W., Vasilakos, A.V., An effective network traffic classification method with unknown flow detection. *IEEE Trans. Netw. Serv. Manage.*, 10, 2, 133–147, 2013.

5. Shu, Z., Wan, J., Li, D., Lin, J., Vasilakos, A.V., Imran, M., Security in software-defined networking: Threats and countermeasures. *Mobile Networks Appl.*, 21, 5, 764–776, 2016.

6. Zeidanloo, H.R. and Manaf, A.B.A., Botnet detection by monitoring similar communication patterns, 7, 3, 36–45. 2010. arXiv preprint arXiv:1004.1232.

7. Gu, G., Perdisci, R., Zhang, J., Lee, W., Botminer: *Clustering analysis of network traffic for protocol-and structure-independent botnet detection*, 17th USENIX Security Symposium, 139–154, 2008.

8. Arshad, S., Abbaspour, M., Kharrazi, M., Sanatkar, H., An anomaly-based botnet detection approach for identifying stealthy botnets. *2011 IEEE International Conference on Computer Applications and Industrial Electronics (ICCAIE)*, IEEE, pp. 564–569, 2011, December.

9. Amini, P., Azmi, R., Araghizadeh, M., Botnet detection using NetFlow and clustering. *Adv. Comput. Sci.: Int. J.*, 3, 2, 139–149, 2014.

10. Strayer, W.T., Walsh, R., Livadas, C., Lapsley, D., Detecting botnets with tight command and control. *Proceedings. 2006 31st IEEE Conference on Local Computer Networks*, IEEE, pp. 195–202, 2006, November.

11. Zhao, D., Traore, I., Sayed, B., Lu, W., Saad, S., Ghorbani, A., Garant, D., Botnet detection based on traffic behavior analysis and flow intervals. *Comput. Secur.*, 39, 2–16, 2013.

12. Lu, W., Rammidi, G., Ghorbani, A.A., Clustering botnet communication traffic based on n-gram feature selection. *Comput. Commun.*, 34, 3, 502–514, 2011.

13. Barthakur, P., Dahal, M., Ghose, M.K., An efficient machine learning based classification scheme for detecting distributed command & control traffic of P2P botnets. *Int. J. Mod. Educ. Comput. Sci.*, 5, 10, 9, 2013.

14. Kalaivani, P. and Vijaya, M., Mining based detection of botnet traffic in network flow. *Int. J. Comput. Sci. Inf. Technol. Secur.*, 6, 535–540, 2016.

15. Kumar, R. and Kaur, T., Machine Learning based Traffic Classification using Low Level Features and Statistical Analysis. *Int. J. Comput. Appl.*, 108, 12, 6–13, 2014.

16. Lu, W., Rammidi, G., Ghorbani, A.A., Clustering botnet communication traffic based on n-gram feature selection. *Comput. Commun.*, 34, 3, 502–514, 2011.

17. Villamarín-Salomón, R. and Brustoloni, J.C., Bayesian bot detection based on DNS traffic similarity. *Proceedings of the 2009 ACM symposium on Applied Computing*, pp. 2035–2041, 2009, March.

18. Zhao, D., Traore, I., Ghorbani, A., Sayed, B., Saad, S., Lu, W., Peer to peer botnet detection based on flow intervals. *IFIP International Information Security Conference*, Springer, Berlin, Heidelberg, pp. 87–102, 2012, June.

19. Feily, M., Shahrestani, A., Ramadass, S., A survey of botnet and botnet detection. *2009 Third International Conference on Emerging Security Information, Systems and Technologies*, IEEE, pp. 268–273, 2009, June.

20. Strayer, W.T., Lapsely, D., Walsh, R., Livadas, C., Botnet detection based on network behavior, in: *Botnet Detection*, pp. 1–24, Springer, Boston, MA, 2008.

21. Haddadi, F., Morgan, J., Gomes Filho, E., Zincir-Heywood, A.N., Botnet behaviour analysis using ip flows: with http filters using classifiers. *2014 28th International Conference on Advanced Information Networking and Applications Workshops*, IEEE, pp. 7–12, 2014, May.

22. Zeidanloo, H.R., Manaf, A.B., Vahdani, P., Tabatabaei, F., Zamani, M., Botnet detection based on traffic monitoring. *2010 International Conference on Networking and Information Technology*, IEEE, pp. 97–101, 2010, June.

23. Barthakur, P., Dahal, M., Ghose, M.K., An efficient machine learning based classification scheme for detecting distributed command & control traffic of P2P botnets. *Int. J. Mod. Educ. Comput. Sci.*, 5, 10, 9, 2013.

24. Garcia, S., Malware capture facility project, cvut, 2013.

25. Nair, H.S. and Ewards, V.S.E., A study on botnet detection techniques. *Int. J. Sci. Res. Publ.*, 2, 4, 319–321, 2012.

26. Masud, M.M., Al-Khateeb, T., Khan, L., Thuraisingham, B., Hamlen, K.W., Flow-based identification of botnet traffic by mining multiple log files. *2008 First International Conference on Distributed Framework and Applications*, IEEE, pp. 200–206, 2008, October.

27. McKay, R., Pendleton, B., Britt, J., Nakhavanit, B., Machine Learning Algorithms on Botnet Traffic: Ensemble and Simple Algorithms. *Proceedings of the 2019 3rd International Conference on Compute and Data Analysis*, pp. 31–35, 2019, March.

28. Hoang, X.D. and Nguyen, Q.C., Botnet detection based on machine learning techniques using DNS query data. *Future Internet*, 10, 5, 43, 2018.

29. Singhal, S. and Jena, M., A study on WEKA tool for data preprocessing, classification and clustering. *Int. J. Innovative Technol. Exploring Eng. (IJItee)*, 2, 6, 250–253, 2013.

30. Witten, I.H. and Frank, E., *Data Mining: Practical Machine Learning Tools and Techniques with Java Implementations*, Morgan Kaufmann, San Francisco, CA, 2000.

9.1   Introduction

The problem of cybersecurity includes the guarantee of data items (e.g. all kinds of media files whether it is content video or anything else) in this way allowing the approved clients to get to the substance that can be accessed in digital sources [1]. Content writers, for example, are incurring loss of scores of rupees each year in their incomes because of unlawful copying and distribution of online media files [2]. So as to curb this overpowering issue, Digital Rights Management (DRM) frameworks are sent for seeing copying as well as distribution of online facts and figures. Commonly included segment of the DRM framework is user verification which decides if the person accessing the content is the legitimate user to get access to the source under advanced medium [3]. The action plan of cryptographic framework is based upon the proprietorship of the user. This means just by verifying some kind of password the system provides you the access to the specific source. Since the encryption of these keys includes special symbols, signs, etc. [4]. These are of huge length which in turn makes them difficult to remember. That's why, such keys are stored at another place (for instance, in the PC, pen drive) and ejected depending on kind of elective identification structure for an instance passcode [5]. Many times, passcodes are so easy to predict that they can be easily hacked (particularly dependent on social building techniques). It isn't astounding that the most generally utilized secret phrase is "secret phrase." Straight forward passwords can be anything but difficult to supposition and, therefore, composite passwords are strenuous to recollect as well as are costly to retain [6]. Some clients tend to "store" composite passwords in effectively open areas. Besides, the vast majority utilize a similar secret key across various applications; an impostor after deciding a solitary secret key would now be able to get to different applications. At long last, in a multi user account situation, passwords can't give non amendment (i.e. under a situation when a secret phrase is revealed to another user, it becomes difficult to figure out the real client: it may dispose of the practicality of the counter-computations [7], for example, considering scheming real clients responsible in an official courtroom). A considerable lot of these impediments related to the operation of passcodes can be improved with the help of fusion of enhanced techniques required for client confirmation [8]. Such kind of confirmation, alludes to setting up personality dependent on the substantial and social qualities (otherwise called characteristics or identifiers) of an individual, for example, the profile, fingerprint, hand geometry, iris, depression of keys on keyboard, signature, voice, and so forth. Biometric frameworks offer a few points of interest over conventional verification schemas [9].

These are naturally much more dependable than the passcode-established verification because biometric attributes can't be strayed or overlooked while the secret keys can be vanished or overlooked; biometric characteristics are laborious to duplicate, dispense, and disseminate (passwords can be reported in programmer sites). It is strenuous to produce similar biometrics as it requires additional time, credits, understanding to get to beneficiaries) and it is unfeasible for an intruder to renounce having reached the computerized source of information using biometrics [10]. Accordingly, a biometrics-based validation conspire is a ground-breaking option in contrast to customary confirmation plans. On certain occasions, biometrics can be utilized related to passwords (or tokens) to improve the certainty offered by the verification framework.

As the innovation time has risen and innovation has become increasingly the mainstream, seniors have wound up at a considerably more noteworthy gap with the youthful age. They experience issues in staying aware of a field that is ever changing constantly and in which relatively few individuals are hoping to help them in proceeding to adjust to it. In an ongoing report led by a researcher from the research centre of PEW, he concluded that lone around 17–19% of more established grown-ups felt happy with figuring out how to utilize gadgets, for example, cell phones and tablets all alone, while around 75–78% demonstrate older people require somebody to provide them with a helping hand through the procedure. Furthermore, senior citizens are regularly debilitated from figuring out how to utilize recently developed innovations because of the physical ramifications that accompany most advancements. As grown-ups age, they are increasingly disposed to create issues and inabilities in their well-being, which later meddle with their use of innovation. Telephones and tabs, for instance, are a colossally well-known methods for correspondence during this time, nonetheless, in light of the fact that they are likewise generally little and are along these lines hard to peruse from for seniors with visual impedances, they are not as famous with more seasoned grown-ups as they are with the more youthful age.

Most as of late, in any case, Smith has discovered that this pattern in suspicion from more established grown-ups towards innovation is moving as albeit new advancements are hard for them to stay aware of, the advantages they have toward regular day to day existence surpass those negative viewpoints. As per Pew Research Centre, 79% of more established grown-ups who utilize the Internet concur with the explanation that "individuals without web get to are at a genuine hindrance due to all the data they may be missing," while 90–95% concur to the explanation that "the Internet makes it a lot simpler to discover data today than before." One of the best focal points and key reasons about why numerous more seasoned grown-ups are moving in the direction of the Internet and innovation currently is web-based life. In an ongoing report directed by scientists from the Wisconsin University, it was discovered that around 40–45% of grown-ups matured said they intermittently utilize person to person communication as it is easy to use, helpful, and mainstream among their correspondence circles. Seniors regularly don't find a good pace numerous social connection as others do because of either being homebound or incapable to travel as often as possible. Web based life is helpful to them right now it permits them to at present feel drew in with the neighbouring surroundings, while staying in the solace of their personal space. As innovation keeps on coordinating itself into the regular daily existences of individuals and people in the future, elderly people must establish good relationships with the new advancements for a superior method of lifestyle. The majority of elderly people are now starting to venture out doing as such, nonetheless, there still should be a lot more headways made in crossing over any barrier between the more youthful age who is familiar with innovation and more seasoned grown-ups who fear it or disheartened by it. Maybe in particular, more established grown-ups must believe must have a move in worldview so they themselves are progressively disposed to find out about these new advances also.

The remainder of the paper is collocated as follows: Section 9.2 explains the basics of biometric systems. Biometric variance illustrated in Section 9.3. Section 9.4 highlights the Performance of Biometric System. Justification of Biometric System has been elucidated in Section 9.5. Assaults on a Biometric System presented in Section 9.6. Section 9.7 shows Biometric Cryptanalysis: The fuzzy vault scheme followed by the conclusion of this paper in Section 9.8.

9.2   Basics of Biometric Systems

With regards to the DRM System, the use of biometrics is as follows: i) to encourage the whole validation instrument, ii) anchor the Morse alphabets that in turn are responsible for security of a particular site or voice files. Various aspects of biometrics are being used for different operations [11]. Every biometric aspect is of its own kind and has its own traits, and final judgement depends upon the operation to which it is put on use. Only a particular biometric is not relied upon to adequately accommodate the entirety of the prerequisites (example, precision, reasonableness, and price) everything being equal (e.g. DRM, get to control, and welfare dissemination). At the end of the day, no biometric is "ideal" despite the fact most of them are "permissible" [12]. Point to be noted that qualities such as sound uttered also the keys pressed over keyboard are self-sufficient for test reaction instrument which is very important for certain applications (e.g., e-banking). A short depiction of the normally utilized biometrics is depicted in Figure 9.1.

9.2.1   Face

Face acknowledgment may be non-invasive technique, and profile images (as shown in Figure 9.1) are probably the premier biometric attribute employed by individual to form physical acknowledgement [13]. The implementations of facial acknowledgment extend from a stable, restrained "mugshot" verification to a dynamic, uncontrollable face verification during a jumbled foundation. The foremost well-known ways to affect face acknowledgment depend upon either: 1) the world and shape official attributes, like the sense organs of the face like nose, mouth, eyes, and jawline and their structural interconnections, 2) the comprehensive analysis of the profile photo that speaks to a face as a alloyed mixture of discrete sanctioned appearances. Despite the validation of decapitation of the facial realization frameworks that are profitably available, they impose a variety of limitations in the way facial pictures are gotten, frequently needing a variety and basic foundation or exceptional enlightenment [14]. These systems even have issues in comparing facial images taken from different sources definitely various perspectives and under various enlightenment possibilities (i.e., shifting transient settings). Facial features are often considered to be unreliable because it lacks any kind of legitimate facts and figures, may be a sufficient reason for perceiving a private from a huge number of personalities with a really elevated level of confidence. All at

Figure 9.1 Face.

once that a facial acceptance shell functions flawlessly particularly conveying, it need to be naturally: i) Identify whether a face is out there within the captured image; ii) Detect the facial image if the one is present before it; iii) Catch sight of the facial image from a common view [15].

9.2.2   Hand Geometry

Hand geometry comprehension frameworks are essentially founded on a wide assortment of approximations taken from the individual's hand, alongside its structure, dimensions of palm and dimensions of the fingers as shown in Figure 9.2. Hand geometry-based validation frameworks for business purposes have been snared in stacks of spots the world over [16]. A basic procedure, uncommonly simple to utilize as well as cheap. Ecological variables, e.g. barren climate or man or lady irregularities on the body surface, for example, wrinkled skin, do never again visible at have any poor outcomes on the confirmation accuracy of such frameworks [17]. The shape of the hand is never again perceived to be exceptionally uncommon and hand geometry-based awareness software's can't be processed up for structures requiring identification of an individual from a huge populace [18]. Further, hand geometry information may moreover not be invariable sooner or later in the blast period of kids. In addition, the personal studs (e.g., bracelets) or limits in potential (e.g., from any kind of disease or injury), can likewise present notwithstanding problems in removing the left-hand structural data. The substantial element of a hand structure-based machine is enormous, and becomes a very strenuous task to install it in small gadgets, for example, smartphones. There exist affirmation structures available which are fundamentally founded over examinations of few fingers only (normally, index and middle) instead of entire paw. These units are lighter than those utilized for hand geometry [19], be that as it may, they are regardless of bounty enormous than these utilized in some different biometrics (for example fingerprints, face, and sound).

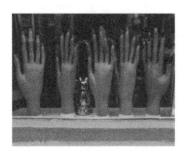

Figure 9.2 Hand geometry.

Figure 9.3 Fingerprint.

9.2.3   Fingerprint

Nowadays most mobile phone companies offer fingerprint sensors in their mobile phones for identification of an individual for an extensive period of time and integrating accuracy utilizing the impression of fingers has been demonstrated to be huge [20]. A fingerprint is the result of crests and troughs on the outlines of a fingertip as shown in Figure 9.3. Even the look alike twins have different fingerprint as compared to each other. As per now, the costs of a fingerprint sensor are about Rs. 800 when demanded in huge amounts including the peripheral expense of implanting a finger-print-based sensor in a system (example smartphones) becomes reasonable in an enormous number of utilizations [21]. The exactness of the presently available fingerprint sensor schemas is gratifying for verification schemas including hundreds of users. Varying fingerprints of a person give an upper hand to permit high scope identification including a large number of characters [22]. In a long run, fingerprints of a small division of the population might be inadmissible for the programmed identification on account of hereditary elements [23] like adulthood, inherent, or arguments associated with work (e.g., human laborers may have countless cuts and wounds on their fingerprints that continue evolving).

9.2.4   Voice Detection

It is a total of physical and conduct biometrics. The major part of the human's voice depends on various vocal parts of the body for example vocal cord, nasal pit, mouth, lips, etc. (as shown in Figure 9.4). All the above-mentioned parts are responsible for various kinds and types of speeches and voices. These physical features of human critique are invariant for an individual, however the social area of the critique of an individual change after some time because old enough, clinical stipulations, (for example, a successive

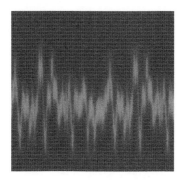

Figure 9.4 Voice detection.

cold), enthusiastic state, and so forth. Voice is also not exceptionally interesting and may now not be stunning for enormous scope identification. A book subordinate voice awareness gadget is essentially founded on the articulation of a fixed foreordained expression [24]. A book free voice mindfulness framework perceives the speaker-autonomous of what the person talks. A book autonomous contraption is more prominent difficult to graph than a book subordinate machine anyway gives additional well-being contrary to extortion. A downside of voice-based authentication is that critique components are delicate to a wide assortment of components, for example, foundation clamour. Speaker insight is generally amazing in telephone-based purposes yet the voice signal over the cell phone is commonly debased in wonderful by the correspondence station.

9.2.5 Iris

It is defined as ring shaped spot of the eye limited with the guide of the understudy and the white of the eye known as sclera on either side as

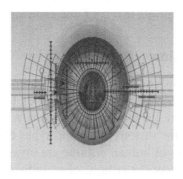

Figure 9.5 Iris.

shown in Figure 9.5. The optical plane of the iris is formed during fatal development and stabilizes out all through the first two years after birth. The mind-boggling iris plane contains exceptionally distinct particulars remuneratively of private cognizance. The precision and speed of by and by sent iris-based insight frameworks is reliable and focuses on the plausibleness of enormous scope identification structures dependent on iris data [25].

9.2.6   Signature

The manner in which a man or lady signs their name is recognized to be a quality of that person as shown in Figure 9.6. In spite of the fact that marks require contact with the composing instrument and an exertion on the period of the client, they have been conventional in government, lawful, and business exchanges an indistinguishable to do verification. Marks are a social biometric that changes over some stretch of time and are influenced by methods for the substantial and enthusiastic stipulations of the signatories. Marks of certain individuals contrast considerably: even progressive impressions of their mark are significantly extraordinary [26]. Further, proficient counterfeiters may also be in a situation to duplicate marks that fool the framework.

9.2.7   Keystrokes

It is conjectured that each man or lady sorts on a console in a characteristic. These social biometrics isn't relied upon to be exceptional to each character anyway it is required to offer sufficient unfair records that let

Figure 9.6 Keystrokes.

in personality verification [27]. Keystroke elements are social biometric; for certain people, one can likewise accept to watch huge forms in typical composing designs. Further, the keystrokes of an individual the utilization of a device could be checked subtly as that character is entering in data. Nonetheless, this biometric supports the relentless verification of a man or lady over a term of time.

The representation schemes along with matching algorithms for Biometric Identifiers are presented in Table 9.1 & Comparisons of Biometric Identifiers on the basis of various factors such as Performance, Acceptability, Collectible, Distinctiveness, Universality etc. are shown in Table 9.2.

Table 9.1 The representation schemes along with matching algorithms for Biometric Identifiers [28, 29].

S. No.	Modality	Matching Algorithm	Representation Scheme
1	Face	Euclidean Distance, Bunch Graph Matching	Principal Component Analysis (PCA), Local Feature Analysis (LFA)
2	Hand Geometry	Euclidean Distance	Length/Width of Finger/ Palm
3	Fingerprint	String Matching	Minutiae Distribution
4	Voice	Hidden Markov Model, Gaussian Mixture Model	Mel-Cepstrum
5	Iris	Hamming Distance	Texture Analysis, Key-Point Extraction

Table 9.2 Comparisons of Biometric Identifiers on the basis of various factors [30–32].

Factors→ Biometric Identifiers ↓	Permanence	Performance	Distinctiveness	Universality	Collectible	Circumvention	Acceptability
Hand	Fair	Fair	Fair	Fair	Good	Fair	Fair
Keystroke	Less	Less	Less	Less	Fair	Fair	Fair
Voice	Less	Less	Less	Fair	Fair	Good	Good
Face	Fair	Less	Good	Good	Good	Good	Good
Iris	Good	Good	Good	Good	Fair	Less	Less
Signature	Less	Less	Less	Less	Good	Good	Good
Fingerprint	Good	Good	Good	Fair	Fair	Fair	Fair

9.3   Biometric Variance

Secret word-based confirmation frameworks never again contain any confounded example center methods (passwords need to coordinate precisely) and, thus, they almost persistently perform precisely as implied through their framework creators. Then again, biometric pointers and their portrayals (e.g. picture of face) of a man or lady change significantly depending on the obtaining strategy, securing condition, client's association with the procurement gadget, and (in some cases) variation in the qualities because of a scope of bearing o-physiological wonders. Underneath, we existing a portion of the incessant thought processes in biometric signal/portrayal varieties [33].

9.3.1   Inconsistent Presentation

The sign caught by methods for the biometric identifier sensor depends upon each genetic biometric identifier trademark as appropriately the biometric identifier is introduced. Along these lines, a gained biometric sign is a non-descriptive piece of a substantial biometric characteristic, the client property management, and the client association encouraged with the guide of the securing link. For an instance, 3-D type fingers get mapped onto the sensor surface of a 2-D surface [34]. As the finger isn't a resolute article and on the grounds that the way of finger surface predictions onto the sensor surface is currently not definitely handled, unmistakable finger impressions are identified with one another with the guide of a number of variations. Further, each impact of a finger may likewise maybe portray an optional segment of its surface. On account of facing security, unique learning may likewise connote exceptional stances of the face. Geometry of hand estimations may likewise be found on explicit hand projections on a planar surface. Distinctive iris/retina (in an eye) acquisitions can likewise relate to uncommon non-frontal iris/retina projections of on to the planes of image.

9.3.2   Unreproducible Presentation

Not at all like the counterfeit identifiers [e.g., radio-recurrence identification (RFID)], biometric identifiers symbolize natural quality management ideas. These identifiers are bent to mileage, unintentional wounds, pathophysiological advancement and breakdowns. Physical work, mishaps, and so many others, inflict mishaps to the finger, in addition to these lines modifying the edge structure of the finger both totally or semi-for all time.

Wearing explicit types of jewellery (e.g. rings) may affect the geometry of hand estimations in an unreproducible manner [35]. Facial hair development (e.g., moustache on face), mishaps (e.g., harmed nose), connections, cosmetics, lump, sore development, and particular hairdos may likewise all compare to irreproducible face portrayals.

9.3.3   Fault Signal/Representational Accession

The sign procurement stipulations in down to earth circumstances are not perfect and thought process superfluous forms in the obtained biometric signal. Be that because it may, the dryness of the skin, shallow/destroyed edges (since of maturing/hereditary qualities), skin disease, sweat, soil, and stickiness discernible all around all befuddle the circumstance taking after in a nonideal contact circumstance. On account of inked fingerprints, off-base inking of the finger as regularly as conceivable results in "disorderly" moo separation (moo quality) pictures, which lead to either deluding or missing fingerprint points of view (i.e., points of interest). Different enlightenments reason unmistakable assortments in facial appearance. Enlightened brightening may moreover render picture acquirement genuinely unsuccessful in various applications [36]. Unexpected on ergonomic conditions, the stamp may besides move significantly. The channel information exchange capacity qualities influence the voice flag. Further, the capacity extraction calculation is flawed and presents size blunders. Different picture handling activities would conceivably acquaint conflicting predispositions with annoy work confinement. A remarkable biometric identifier of two exceptional individuals can be entirely practically identical in view of the inalienable absence of select realities in it or because of the reality of the lacking delineation utilized for the identifier.

9.4   Performance of Biometric System

A biometric framework might be seen as a sign discovery framework with an example acknowledgment engineering that detects a crude biometric signal, forms this sign to extricate a remarkable arrangement of highlights, looks at these highlights against the capabilities dwelling in the database, and either approves an asserted character or decides the personality related with the sign. Biometric frameworks endeavour to inspire repeatable and unmistakable human introductions, and comprise (in principle, if not in real act) of easy to understand, instinctive interfaces for controlling the client in exhibiting the important characteristics. The element extraction organizes disposes of the superfluous and unessential data from the detected estimations and gathers valuable data important for coordinating [37].

The most broadly utilized nearby highlights depend on minute subtleties (particulars) of the fingerprint edges. The example of the particulars of a fingerprint structures a legitimate portrayal of the fingerprint. This portrayal is smaller and catches a significant segment of data in fingerprints; contrasted with different portrayals, details extraction is moderately increasingly hearty to different wellsprings of fingerprint corruption. Most kinds of particulars in fingerprint pictures are not steady and can't be dependably identified via programmed picture handling techniques. The most broadly utilized highlights depend on: 1) edge closure; and 2) edge bifurcation, which are spoken to as far as triplets $[p,q,\phi]$, where $[p, q]$ speaks to the spatial organizes in a fixed picture driven facilitate framework and speaks to direction of the edge at that minutia. Typically, in a real time examination of fingerprint picture of nice grade, around 50–60 particulars are present.

Coordinate estimation of two biometrics. Commonly, a biometric matcher fixes a portion of the intraclass varieties in the biometric estimations to be coordinated by adjusting them to regard one another. When the two portrayals are adjusted, an appraisal of their closeness is estimated. The closeness between the two portrayals is regularly quantified regarding a coordinating score; the higher the coordinating score, the more comparable are the portrayals. For instance, given two (inquiry and format) fingerprint highlight portrayals, the coordinating module decides if the prints are impressions of the equivalent finger by an examination of the question and layout highlights. Just in exceptionally compelled fingerprint frameworks would one be able to accept that the inquiry and format fingerprints delineate a similar part of the finger and are adjusted (regarding removal from the starting point of the imaging coordinate framework and of their directions) with one another. In the wake of adjusting the fingerprints, the quantity of coordinating (or relating) highlights is resolved and a fingerprint comparability is defined as far as the quantity of comparing details. Indeed, even in the best handy circumstances, all particulars in inquiry and format prints are once in a while coordinated because of false details presented by earth/extra smears, varieties in the region of finger being imaged, and removal of the minutia attributable to mutilation of the print from squeezing the finger whose surface is deformable against the flat surface of the procurement gadget; the matcher utilizes a framework parameter—the limit esteem—to choose whether a given pair of prints has a place with the equivalent finger (mated pair) or not [38]. The examples of apps using biometric recognizance represented in Table 9.3.

Table 9.3 Examples of apps using biometric recognizance [39, 40].

Applications	Description
Recovery from loss/theft	Loss of wallet is never again a major issue. Substitution of lost or taken Visas and so on has become simple at this point of time.
E-wallets system	Biometrics takes into consideration advantageous record access with adequate extortion opposition.
Quick medical and emergency services	With the biometrics coming in use process of Mediclaim's and such services has become much easier for the public.
Disaster relief	Quick ID of the dead/hurt disastrous setback and re-unmistakable verification of evacuated suffering people
Security check-in	The verification of the people during check ins has become convenient and cost effective.

9.5 Justification of Biometric System

Biometrics isn't just an entrancing example acknowledgment inquire about the issue be that as it may, if painstakingly utilized, could likewise be an empowering innovation with the possibility to make our general public more secure, lessening cheating hence ensures user convenience (user-friendly man-machine interface) by comprehensively giving the accompanying following functionalities [41].

9.5.1 Authentication ("Is this individual really the authenticate user or not?")

Biometrics can confirm with high conviction the credibility of an asserted enlistment dependent on the info biometric test. Business applications, for example, PC arrange logon, electronic information security, ATMs, Visa buys, physical access control, mobile phones, individual advanced aides

(PDAs), medicinal records the executives, and separation learning are test verification applications. Validation applications are commonly cost-touchy with a solid impetus for being easy to understand.

9.5.2   Recognition ("Is this individual in the database?")

Given an info biometric test, a verification decides whether the information biometric test is related to any of an enormous number (e.g., a great many) enlisted personalities. Average verification operations incorporate progressive payment, Aadhaar cards, fringe supervision, voter ID cards, driving license, a culprit examination, carcass identification, parenthood assurance, missing kids' identification, and so on. These identification applications require an enormous feasible throughput with a meagre human administration could be allowed [42].

9.5.3   Concealing ("Is this a needed person?")

Concealing applications decide if an individual has a place with a watch-list of characters. Instances of concealing applications could incorporate at air terminal surveillance, surveillance in the open occasions also the other observation operations. A concealing watchlist comprises of a reasonable (example—two or three thousand) quantities of characters. Such applications: i) don't have explicit "client" enlistment stage; ii) may anticipate just insignificant power over their affairs and illustrative circumstances; iii) needed to a great extent supportable throughput with a meagre human administration as would be prudent. Concealing can't be cultivated without biometrics (e.g., by utilizing token or information-based verification).

Biometric frameworks are by and large progressively conveyed in regular citizen applications that have a few thousand enlisted clients. Along these lines, biometric frameworks can be utilized to upgrade client comfort while improving security [43].

9.6   Assaults on a Biometric System

A biometric system is more susceptible to attacks which can affect the security of the system and the result of this causes a system failure [44]. All attacks are classified into two basic categories. The attributes of biometric of a cosmopolitan may be similar enough to a legally listed person, resulting in the severance of the security of a system [45]. Zero-effort attacks are linked with the prospect of monitoring the grade of analogy among patterns produced in distinction to types of sources. Adversary Attack refers to the persistent imposter who could be able to pretend as an enrolled user by using a digital artefact of the legally listed person. A person may also rearrange his or her biometric attributes in order to keep away from observations by an automated biometric system.

9.6.1   Zero Effort Attacks

There are different changes that biometric information starting from two people will be very comparative which may lead to the issue of independence in biometrics. The distinction of a few biometric properties may be characterized as the work of interclass similitude and intraclass inconstancy together with its properties or characteristics [46]. For the determination of this issue, one can make the source that gives the biometric signal or demonstrate the parameters for making the format [47]. Within the case of unique mark illustration, the distinction issue can be defined in different diverse ways depending upon which one of the taking after angles of the problem is taking beneath examination:

- Discover out the likelihood of the number of people which will have the same unique mark in a given set of population.
- For a given test unique finger impression, discover out the likelihood of the same unique finger impression in a given set of populaces.
- For a given set of two fingerprints from two distinctive fingers, discover the likelihood that they are very comparable. For a unique finger impression comparison, an upper bound can be built up on the execution of unique finger impression systems.

For deciding the singularity of fingerprints, there are two approaches for a given representation plot and a closeness measure. (i) Empirical Approach: In this approach, different agent tests of fingerprints are collected and with the assistance of a normal unique mark matcher, the precision of the matches on the given tests gives a sign of the uniqueness of the unique mark of a person with regard to matcher. In spite of the fact that, there are known issues in conjunction with the collection of the tests of agents. (ii) Theoretical Approach: In this approach, for distinction estimation, all the practical wonder influencing interclasses and intraclass unique mark design varieties are modeled [48]. For a given similitude metric, one may hypothetically appraise the likelihood of an untrue correspondence. For the most part, hypothetical approaches are restricted by the degree to which the virtual or accepted show acclimates to reality. In a design space, a add up to no of degrees of opportunity (e.g., particulars setup space) does not relate straightforwardly to the discriminability of different designs [49]. With the assistance of intraclass varieties, the compelling estimation of oppressive data can be accomplished [50]. There are various sources of changeability within the numerous impressions of a finger such as irreproducible contact, inconsistent contact, non-uniform contact and imaging artefacts. Within the numerous impressions of the finger, this inconstancy shows itself as: (i) Minutiae Types Transformation, (ii) Detection of Missing Authentic Minutiae, (iii) Deformation or Displacement.

9.6.2   Adversary Attacks

Biometric isn't the same as privileged insights. Physical characteristics like face and fingerprints may well be tricky gotten from the person for making advanced artefacts which can be utilized to parody the character of the lawfully enlisted individual [51]. Separated from this, there are a few assaults that are propelled against an application whose assets are ensured with the assistance of biometrics.

9.6.2.1   Circumvention

To pick up get to the system, agate crasher may balk the biometric matcher and scrutinize delicate information such as restorative records related to the lawfully selected client [52]. Separated from breaching the security of enlisted users, the interloper can adjust the touchy information in which biometric data may be included.

9.6.2.2   Coercion

For allowing the get to of system, a faker may be constrained to the lawfully selected user (e.g., at gunpoint) [53].

9.6.2.3   Repudiation

For the offices advertised by application, a legitimately client may be gotten to it and after getting to he/she claim that a few gate crashers had circumventing the framework. For illustration, a bank receptionist may do changes within the records of a client and after that deny duty by claiming that a few gate crashers have gotten to the record and spoofed her biometric trait [54].

9.6.2.4   DoB (Denial of Benefit)

A trespasser may overcome the assets of the framework to the point where lawfully clients craving get to will be denied service [55]. For illustration, amid handling a server get to ask may be assaulted with a false request, by that over-burdening its computational assets and avoiding the ask from being processed.

9.6.2.5   Collusion

A person with super client prerequisite may intentioned alter the biometric framework qualities to allow invasions by a collaborating intruder [56].

9.7   Biometric Cryptanalysis: The Fuzzy Vault Scheme

Biometric framework (like some other security framework) is powerless against various foe assaults, it is critical to solve the problem of defending plan of the biometric framework. Specifically, one might want to know whether there is a protected strategy for consolidating biometric verification and cryptographic strategies. In a short-sighted biometrics-based key discharge technique [57], a fruitful biometric layout coordinate discharges a cryptographic key. Table 9.4 shows the advantages and disadvantages of biometric system. Figure 9.7 shows the linking format of the biometrics in case of cryptanalysis.

Table 9.4 Advantages & disadvantages of biometric system on the basis of various parameters [58].

Advantages	Disadvantages
Precision: Conventional systems of reliability regularly cost us wealth, resources as well as time. The most familiar collateral frameworks are PIN numbers, security passwords and cards like debit and smart cards which may or may not always be accurate. Though biometric works with physical attributes like fingerprints, palm vein and many more.	**Error rate:** In case of perfection, devices of biometric are not so accurate due to the chances of mistakes. Mainly, there are two types of error in biometric devices. 1. False Acceptance Rate (FAR) 2. False Rejection Rate (FAR) In the case of FRR, the device rejects an authorized person and in FAR, the device accepts an unauthorized person.

(Continued)

Table 9.4 Advantages & disadvantages of biometric system on the basis of various parameters [58]. (*Continued*)

Advantages	Disadvantages
Useful (convenient): In the case of passwords, remembering every single word of password is very hard and due to these there are chances of forgetting it in some situations. There are many portable devices for us to do the job but the convenience of biometric solutions cannot be beaten by none of the above tools because biometric is the best convenient solution ever. So, it is not required that you memorize or note down anything because your credentials are with you forever.	**Delay:** As biometric machines take so much time than time of acceptance and a large line of workers is waiting to join the companies. During scanning the biometric devices in these cases, people must have a hard time. So, to go through a biometric verification is very hard for a person before entering into various places every day such as school, companies, colleges, etc.
ROI (return on our investment): In case of comparison to provide ROI, biometric solutions are the best as compared to other security system. A device and software can be used to keep track of thousands of workers of a company, and on the other hand, you will need to manage a large amount of resources for doing a single job that costs more time than the biometric solution.	**Unhygienic:** There are mainly two types of biometric models. 1. Contact based. 2. Contactless-based Palm vein scanners and fingerprints are included in contact-based models while iris and face recognition are the contactless based models of biometric systems.
Reliable: According to reports, the younger generation can trust biometric solutions more than the other solutions. Security system of a biometrics is also used by a bank to enhance its reliability and security.	**Physical disabilities:** Due to physical damage in the body such as lost or damaged eyes and fingers, some people are not able to participate in the enrolment process. So, in this case these fingerprint and recognition devices are not able to perform.

(*Continued*)

Table 9.4 Advantages & disadvantages of biometric system on the basis of various parameters [58]. (*Continued*)

Advantages	Disadvantages
Cost effective: For the persons to provide the more accurate government services with less amount of cost, governments are putting their money to establish a national biometric database. For the accurate information with saving money and time corporation adopting biometric system. With a little money, any company can reduce the cost which they are paying for years and track their clients.	**Integration in addition hardware:** There are some biometric models which need some additional features which are very complex and also have a very high cost. So, it is also very hard to manage these types of biometric models.
Safety or Security: Mostly we use passwords with numbers, characters and some symbols which are becoming very easy to hack day by day due to increasing technologies. Due to which there are many incidents in which millions of passwords is hacked and we all lose our money continuously.so for the security purpose biometric technology bring various types of arrangements which are about difficult to hack and this is very helpful in business for security purposes for a long time.	**Physical Attributes are not changeable:** Biometric models work with physical traits such as fingerprints, iris, palm vein etc. In case of passwords, we can change our passwords if it is stolen but in case of fingerprints and recognition it is impossible because we have just a couple of eyes, certain quantities of fingerprints, and other organs that are not mutable.
Accountability: There are different confirmation techniques in which anyone can utilize your secret phrase and hack your own data which is dangerous and we are experiencing this continually. So, to permit 100% responsibility for every one of your exercises, biometric security needs your immediate communication to get access to the security framework.	**Cost:** Biometric devices are more costly as compared to the other traditional devices. Due to the biometric software, programmers, devices servers and other relative equipment, the cost of these combined in a large amount of money.

(*Continued*)

Table 9.4 Advantages & disadvantages of biometric system on the basis of various parameters [58]. (*Continued*)

Advantages	Disadvantages
Scalability: For all types of projects, biometrics are highly scalable solutions. In various fields like government projects, workforce management, banking security systems etc., biometric technologies are used. Due to scalability of its solutions it is possible.	**Complexity:** Exceptionally specialized and complex framework that makes up the entire procedure is the greatest burden of biometrics. More abilities are required in an individual to comprehend this framework. Organizations procure profoundly experienced and talented developers just because of the complexities of biometric models.
Time reliable: In case of time, biometric solutions are highly time-conserving. To pass the system you just need to look at a retina device or put your finger on a device. Also, on the opposite side, regular strategies have layers of issues and cross examination which become upsetting and inadmissible.	**Difficulties in scanning:** There are some difficulties that occur during implementation of biometric models like face recognition can go through scanning difficulties. Eyelids, eyelashes, lens and reflection from the cornea are the main reasons behind this.
Flexibility: There is no need to memorize numbers, alphabets and various types of symbols for creating a complex password because you have your own security credentials due to the flexibility security solution of the biometric system.	**Environment and usage matters:** It can affect overall measurement taken. Mainly, in high cold regions, there are more chances of error which create unnecessary mistakes over the whole system.

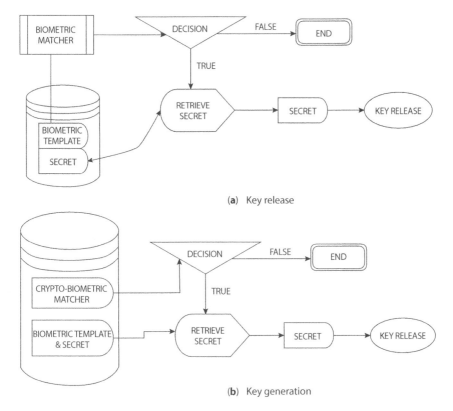

(a) Key release

(b) Key generation

Figure 9.7 (a), (b) Forms of linking biometric framework with cryptanalysis.

9.8   Conclusion & Future Work

Biometrics presents significant specialized, arrangement, and framework challenges that must be comprehended in light of the fact that there's not a viable replacement for this innovation for tending to numerous basic data security issues. Considering the ongoing government commands for national and global utilization of biometrics in conveying significant cultural capacities, there's earnestness to additionally create fundamental biometric abilities, and to incorporate them into functional applications. Since biometrics can't be effectively shared, lost, or fashioned, the resultant security is more solid than current secret key frameworks and doesn't burden the top client with recalling long cryptographically solid passwords. Biometric-based director access to delicate client data bears successful responsibility.

While biometric innovation has all the earmarks of being appropriate to give a client helpful segment of secure individual character linkage, there might be social, cultural, and strict obstruction toward acknowledgment of this innovation. For instance, one of the crucial wellsprings of data fraud issue is the basic dependence on the linkages to and data in heritage personality the executive's frameworks. While biometric innovation can alleviate a portion of the enlistment issues (e.g., different characters), it can't tackle the issue of depending on blemished inheritance personality the executive's frameworks. One may need to depend on process designing (e.g., guaranteeing enlistment during childbirth as is right now done in neighbourhood birth registers) for a few ages before we could guarantee flawless enlistment. In the meantime, we may need to depend on a fragile parity of discouragement and location of character extortion guided by sound open approach. An ineffectively executed biometric framework can be the reason for lack of concern, fiasco, and a further reason for opposition. Then again, a well-executed biometrics framework with sufficient protection shields might be an unmistakable prerequisite in the speedy reaction to regular or man-made disasters. Much stays to be cultivated as far as general training of the end clients, framework executives, integrators, and generally significant, open approach creators.

The constraints of the present condition of the biometric innovation ought not be understood to infer that it isn't as of now valuable in numerous applications. Actually, there are an enormous number of biometric arrangements that have been effectively sent to give helpful incentive in common sense applications. For instance, the hand geometry framework has filled in as a decent access control arrangement in numerous organizations, for example, college dormitories, building passageway, and time and participation applications. AFIS frameworks have been giving terrific incentive to society, incorporating programmed and manual procedures. Further iterative patterns of innovation advancement, application to new spaces, reasonable execution assessment, and institutionalization endeavours will encourage the pattern of construct test-share for changing the innovation into business arrangements. The multifaceted nature of structuring a biometric framework dependent on three primary components (size, scale or accuracy of the information, and ease of use). Numerous application areas require a biometric framework to work on the extraordinary of just one of the three tomahawks and such frameworks have been effectively sent. The stupendous test is to structure a framework that would work on the boundaries of these three tomahawks at the same time. This will involve conquering the basic obstructions that have been astutely kept away from in planning the at present effective specialty biometric arrangements. Tending to these center research issues in the assessment of the creators will essentially propel the best in class and make biometric frameworks increasingly secure, hearty, and financially savvy. This, we accept, will advance appropriation of biometric frameworks, bringing about conceivably expansive monetary and social effect.

References

1. Yan, Z. and Zhao, S., A usable authentication system based on personal voice challenge. *Proc. Int. Conf. Adv. Cloud Big Data (CBD)*, pp. 194–199, Aug. 2016, J. Clinton, commencement address at Morgan State University, Baltimore, MD, May 18, 1997.

2. Proov, A.B., Facing the future: The impact of Apple Face ID. *Biometric Technol. Today*, 2018, 1, 5–7, Jan. 2018.

3. Blasco, J., Chen, T.M., Tapiador, J., Peris-Lopez, P., A survey of wearable biometric recognition systems. *ACM Comput. Surv.*, 49, 3, 43, Dec. 2016. F. James, "Body scans could make ID process truly personal," Chicago Tribune, June 4, 1997.

4. Padma, P. and Srinivasan, S., A survey on biometric based authentication in cloud computing. *Proc. Int. Conf. Inventive Comput. Technol. (ICICT)*, vol. 1, pp. 1–5, Aug. 2016.

5. Bhushan, B. and Sahoo, G., Recent Advances in Attacks, Technical Challenges, Vulnerabilities and Their Countermeasures in Wireless Sensor Networks. *Wireless Pers. Commun.*, 98, 2, 2037–2077, 2017.

6. Shen, C., Zhang, Y., Guan, X., Maxion, R.A., Performance analysis of touch-interaction behavior for active smartphone authentication. *IEEE Trans. Inf. Forensics Security*, 11, 3, 498–513, Mar. 2016.

7. Matsumoto, T., Matsumoto, H., Yamada, K., Hoshino, S., Impact of artificial 'gummy' fingers on fingerprint systems. *Proc. SPIE*, 4677, 275–285, Apr. 2002.

8. Alegre, F., Vipperla, R., Evans, N., Fauve, B., On the vulnerability of automatic speaker recognition to spoofing attacks with artificial signals. *Proc. 20th Eur. Signal Process. Conf. (EUSIPCO)*, pp. 36–40, Aug. 2012.

9. Ross, A., Nandakumar, K., Jain, A.K., *Handbook of Multibiometrics (Biometrics)*, Springer-Verlag, New York, NY, USA, 2006.

10. Goel, A.K., Rose, A., Gaur, J., Bhushan, B., Attacks, Countermeasures and Security Paradigms in IoT. *2019 2nd International Conference on Intelligent Computing, Instrumentation and Control Technologies (ICICICT)*, 2019.

11. Ross, K., Nandakumar, Jain, A.K., Introduction to multibiometrics, in: *Handbook of Biometrics*, Springer-Verlag, Berlin, Germany, 2008.

12. Yu, J., Zhang, B., Kuang, Z., Lin, D., Fan, J., iPrivacy: Image privacy protection by identifying sensitive objects via deep multi-task learning. *IEEE Trans. Inf. Forensics Security*, 12, 5, 1005–1016, May 2017.

13. Braun, M. and Van Swol, L., Obstacles to Social Networking Website Use among Older Adults, in: *Obstacles to Social Networking Website Use among Older Adults*, University of Wisconsin, n.d. Web., 5 Jan.2017.

14. Schuckers, S., Liveness detection: Fingerprint, in: *Encyclopedia of Biometrics*, pp. 924–931, Springer-Verlag, Berlin, Germany, 2009.

15. Marasco, E., Johnson, P., Sansone, C., Schuckers, S., Increase the security of multi-biometric systems by incorporating a spoofing detection algorithm in the fusion mechanism. *Proc. 10th Int. Conf. Multiple Classifier Syst.*, pp. 309–318, 2011.

16. Marasco, E., Ding, Y., Ross, A., Combining match scores with liveness values in a fingerprint verification system. *Proc. 5th IEEE Int. Conf. Biometrics, Theory, Appl. Syst.*, pp. 418–425, Sep. 2012.

17. Sharma, A., Singh, A., Sharma, N., Kaushik, I., Bhushan, B., Security Countermeasures in Web Based Application. *2019 2nd International Conference on Intelligent Computing, Instrumentation and Control Technologies (ICICICT)*, 2019.

18. Chingovska, Anjos, A. and Marcel, S., Anti-spoofing in action: Joint operation with a verification system. *Proc. IEEE Conf. Comput. Vis. Pattern Recognit.*, pp. 98–104, Jun. 2013.

19. Zhu, L., Zhang, Z., Qin, Z., Weng, J., Ren, K., Privacy protection using a rechargeable battery for energy consumption in smart grids. *IEEE Netw.*, 31, 1, 59–63, Jan./Feb. 2017.

20. Bhushan, B. and Sahoo, G., A comprehensive survey of secure and energy efficient routing protocols and data collection approaches in wireless sensor networks. *2017 International Conference on Signal Processing and Communication (ICSPC)*, 2017.

21. Ionescu, T.B. and Engelbrecht, G., The privacy case: Matching privacy-protection goals to human and organizational privacy concerns. *2016 Joint Workshop Cyber-Phys. Secur. Resilience Smart Grids (CPSR-SG)*, 1–6, 2016.

22. Jadhav, A. and Shahane, P.N. Privacy Preserving Biometric Verification. *Int. J. Eng. Res.*, 3, 1, 6–8, 2014.

23. Gomez-Barrero, M., Maiorana, E., Galbally, J., Campisi, P., Fierrez, J., Multi-biometric template protection based on Homomorphic Encryption. *Pattern Recognit.*, 67, 149–163, 2017.

24. Poh, N. and Bengio, S., Database, protocols and tools for evaluat- ing score-level fusion algorithms in biometric authentication. *Pattern Recognit. J.*, 39, 2, 223–233, Feb. 2006.

25. Hastie, T., Tibshirani, R., Friedman, J.H., *The Elements of Statistical Learning*, Springer-Verlag, New York, NY, USA, 2001.

26. Lui, Y.M., Bolme, D., Phillips, P.J., Beveridge, J.R., Draper, B.A., Preliminary studies on the Good, the Bad, and the Ugly face recognition challenge problem. *Proc. IEEE Comput. Vis. Pattern Recognit. Workshops (CVPRW)*, 9–16, Jun. 2012. https://ieeexplore.ieee.org/document/6239209

27. Varshney, T., Sharma, N., Kaushik, I., Bhushan, B., Architectural Model of Security Threats & their Countermeasures in IoT. *2019 International Conference on Computing, Communication, and Intelligent Systems (ICCCIS)*, 2019.

28. Bailly-Baillire, E. *et al.*, The BANCA database and evaluation protocol. *Proc. Int. Conf. Audio- Video-Based Biometric Person Authentication (AVBPA)*, pp. 625–638, 2003.

29. Martin, F. and Przybocki, M.A., The NIST 1999 speaker recognition evaluation—An overview. *Digital Signal Process.*, 10, 1–3, 1–18, 2000.

30. Przybocki, M., Martin, A., and Le, A. NIST Speaker Recognition Evaluation Chronicles - Part 2. *2006 IEEE Odyssey - The Speaker and Language Recognition Workshop*, 2006.

31. Martin, F. *et al.*, The DET curve in assessment of detection task performance. *Proc. Eurospeech, 1997*, Scholar Publishing, Cambridge, UK, pp. 1895–1898, 2015.

32. Schuckers, S.A., Spoofing and anti-spoofing measures. *Inf. Secur. Tech. Rep.*, 7, 56–62, 2002.

33. Yang, W., Hu, J., Fernandes, C., Sivaraman, V., Wu, Q., Vulnerability analysis of iPhone 6. *Proceedings of the 14th Annual Conference on Privacy, Security and Trust (PST)*, Auckland, New Zealand, pp. 457–463, 12–14 December 2016.

34. Arora, A., Kaur, A., Bhushan, B., Saini, H., Security Concerns and Future Trends of Internet of Things. *2019 2nd International Conference on Intelligent Computing, Instrumentation and Control Technologies (ICICICT)*, 2019.

35. Tan, B. and Schuckers, S., Liveness detection for fingerprint scanners based on the statistics of wavelet signalprocessing. *Proceedings of the Conference on Computer Vision and Pattern Recognition Workshop(CVPRW'06)*, New York, NY, USA, p. 26, 17–22 June 2006.

36. Coli, P., Marcialis, G.L., Roli, F., Fingerprint silicon replicas: Static and dynamic features for vitality detectionusing an optical capture device. *Int. J. Image Graphics*, 8, 495–512, 2008.

37. Tiwari, A., Sharma, N., Kaushik, I., Tiwari, R., Privacy Issues & Security Techniques in Big Data. *2019 International Conference on Computing, Communication, and Intelligent Systems (ICCCIS)*, 2019.

38. Galbally, J., Alonso-Fernandez, F., Fierrez, J., Ortega-Garcia, J., A high-performance fingerprint liveness detection method based on quality related features. *Future Gener. Comput. Syst.*, 28, 311–321, 2012.

39. Kim, W., Fingerprint liveness detection using local coherence patterns. *IEEE Signal Process. Lett.*, 24, 51–55, 2017.

40. Jung, H. and Heo, Y., Fingerprint liveness map construction using convolutional neural network. *Electron. Lett.*, 54, 564–566, 2018.

41. Jaidka, H., Sharma, N., Singh, R., Evolution of IoT to IIoT: Applications & Challenges. (May 18, 2020). *Proceedings of the International Conference on Innovative Computing & Communications (ICICC) 2020*, 2020. Available at SSRN: https://ssrn.com/abstract=3603739 or http://dx.doi.org/10.2139/ssrn.3603739

42. Kundargi, J. and Karandikar, R., Fingerprint liveness detection using wavelet-based completed LBP descriptor. *Proceedings of the 2nd International Conference on Computer Vision and Image Processing, Roorkee, India, 9–12 September 2017*, Springer, Berlin, Germany, pp. 187–202, 2018.

43. Sharma, M., Tandon, A., Narayan, S., Bhushan, B., Classification and analysis of security attacks in WSNs and IEEE 802.15.4 standards: A survey. *2017 3rd International Conference on Advances in Computing, Communication & Automation (ICACCA) (Fall)*, 2017.

44. Xia, Z., Lv, R., Sun, X. Rotation-invariant Weber pattern and Gabor feature for fingerprint liveness detection. *Multimed. Tools Appl.*, 77, 14, 18187–18200, 2017.

45. Zuev, Y.A. and Ivanon, S., The voting as a way to increase the decision reliability. foundations of information/decision fusion with applications to engineering problems. *Proc. Foundations of Information/Decision Fusion with Applications to Engineering Problems, Washington D.C.*, pp. 206–210, Aug. 1996.

46. Jaitly, S., Malhotra, H., Bhushan, B., Security vulnerabilities and countermeasures against jamming attacks in Wireless Sensor Networks: A survey. *2017 International Conference on Computer, Communications and Electronics (Comptelix)*, 2017.

47. Kaushik, I. and Sharma, N., Black Hole Attack and Its Security Measure in Wireless Sensors Networks, in: *Advances in Intelligent Systems and Computing Handbook of Wireless Sensor Networks: Issues and Challenges in Current Scenarios*, pp. 401–416, 2020.

48. Brunelli, R. and Falavigna, D., Person identification using multiple cues. *IEEE Trans. Pattern Anal. Mach. Intell.*, 12, 10, 955–966, Oct. 1995.

49. Bigun, E.S., Bigun, J., Duc, B., Fischer, S., Expert conciliation for multi modal person authentication system using bayesian statistics. *Proc. Int. Conf. Audio and Video-Based Biometric Person Authentication, Crans-Montana, Switzerland*, pp. 291–300, Mar. 1997.

50. Sinha, P., Jha, V.K., Rai, A.K., Bhushan, B., Security vulnerabilities, attacks and countermeasures in wireless sensor networks at various layers of OSI reference model: A survey. *2017 International Conference on Signal Processing and Communication (ICSPC)*, 2017.

51. Jadon, S., Choudhary, A., Saini, H., Dua, U., Sharma, N., Kaushik, I., Comfy Smart Home using IoT. (April 1, 2020). *Proceedings of the International Conference on Innovative Computing & Communications (ICICC) 2020*, 2020. Available at SSRN: https://ssrn.com/abstract=3565908 or http://dx.doi.org/10.2139/ssrn.3565908

52. Frischholz, R.W. and Dieckmann, U., Bioid: a multimodal biometric identification system. *IEEE Comput.*, 33, 2, 64–68, Feb. 2000.

53. Jain, A.K. and Ross, A., Learning user-specific parameters in a multibiometric system. *Proc. IEEE Int. Conf. Image Processing, Rochester, NY*, pp. 57–60, Sep. 2002.

54. Singh, A., Sharma, A., Sharma, N., Kaushik, I., Bhushan, B., Taxonomy of Attacks on Web Based Applications. *2019 2nd International Conference on Intelligent Computing, Instrumentation and Control Technologies (ICICICT)*, 2019.

55. Ross, A. and Govindarajan, R., Feature level fusion using hand and face biometrics. *Proc. SPIE Conf. Biometric Technology for Human Identification II*, pp. 196–204, Mar. 2005.

56. Tiwari, R., Sharma, N., Kaushik, I., Tiwari, A., Bhushan, B., Evolution of IoT & Data Analytics using Deep Learning. *2019 International Conference on Computing, Communication, and Intelligent Systems (ICCCIS)*, 2019.

57. Ho, T.K., Hull, J.J., Srihari, S.N., Decision combination in multiple classifier systems. *IEEE Trans. Pattern Anal. Mach. Intell.*, 16, 1, 66–75, Jan. 1994.

58. Prabhakar, S. and Jain, A.K., Decision-level fusion in fingerprint verification. *Pattern Recognit.*, 35, 4, 861–874, 2002.

10

The Role of Big Data Analysis in Increasing the Crime Prediction and Prevention Rates

Galal A. AL-Rummana[1], Abdulrazzaq H. A. Al-Ahdal[1] and G.N. Shinde[2*]

[1]*School of Computational Sciences, S.R.T.M. University, Nanded, India*
[2]*Yeshwant College, Nanded, India*

Abstract

Nowadays, cyber-crime is growing in the world exploiting the personal informa-tion of internet users. The emergence of the field of big data and the conventional analysis techniques to handle a huge amount of data leads to unsatisfactory results; viz, the generated data isn't handled effectively. Consequently, the rate of crime prediction and prevention would be low. Therefore, there is a need to use big data analysis techniques to increase the prediction and prevention of the crime-rate.

In this chapter, an overview of BigData and cyber-crime are presented along with the need of big data analysis in cybercrime. Moreover, different BigData anal-ysis techniques like methodology of Van der Hulst, The Process Cross Industry for Data Mining (CRISP-DM) methodology, and the methodologyof AMPA are discussed to present their roles in crime prediction and prevention. Also, the most important big data security techniques.

This chapter is organized in five sections as follow: first section provides the aims of the present chapter. Second section provides a brief overview of big data and cyber-crime. Third section discusses different big data analysis techniques. In the fourth section, the important big data security techniques are explored. Finally, the last section will be devoted for the conclusion.

Keywords: Big data analysis, big data security techniques, cyber-crime, crime prediction, criminal network, Van der Hulst, CRISP-DM, AMPA

Corresponding author: shindegn@yahoo.co.in

Subhendu Kumar Pani, Sanjay Kumar Singh, Lalit Garg, Ram Bilas Pachori and Xiaobo Zhang (eds.) *Intelligent Data Analytics for Terror Threat Prediction: Architectures, Methodologies, Techniques and Applications*, (209–220) © 2021 Scrivener Publishing LLC

10.1 Introduction: An Overview of Big Data and Cyber Crime

In the past, the crime data were in hard copy forms and manually entered at police offices which can be represented in the complaints. Meanwhile, its analysis is very tedious and time consuming. Due to technological development, the crime data became available on the electronic level. In comparison with the analysis of the traditional data with big data in respect to time consumption, the analysis of big data shows amazing results. Before talking about data analysis methods, a brief description of big data is given. It describes massively of structured, semi-structured as well as unstructured data that are analyzed to find behavior trends and patterns. We note that, the more data increased, the more crimes occurred, and this is the main issue facing human society which leads to the need cyber security [1]. In the same path we need to know about characteristics of big data such as value, variety, volume, velocity, variability, and veracity, and note that these characteristics affect the security in big data. It is no secret that the huge amount of the generated data through different sources nowadays makes the crime prediction so challenging. Therefore, there is a dire need to develop some techniques to deal with the huge amount of data, i.e., BigData.

The motive of doing a cybercrime is to earn money and there is a type of an organized crime whose motive is a result of ideological, philosophical, political, racial, religious or ethnic background. Criminal network systematic analysis is seen as a viable means of gaining a more thorough understanding of criminal behavior.

At the present, data generated cannot efficiently be handled using traditional analysis techniques. So, it's better to adopt big data analysis techniques. These techniques can help to predict the class and intensity of cyber security threats. In addition, it allows using current and historical data used to collect statistical understanding of which trends are acceptable or which are not from cyber security stand point. Big data has shown new possibilities for security solutions to protect data and stop future cyber-attacks. Intelligent big data analytics enable specialists to create a predictive model which is capable of issuing an alert once it sees an entry point for a cyber-security attack.

Over the past three decades, the applications of different data analysis techniques to security and criminal enforcement have demonstrated the development, progression, and maturation of criminal analysis.

Machine learning and artificial intelligence has a significant role in the development of such mechanisms, which is where such solutions, backed up by machine learning and artificial intelligence, give businesses hope and cyber security breach and hacking processes can be kept secure. You can enhance your data management strategies and cyber threat detection mechanisms with the power of big data, and allow you to predict and plan for future events in the process.

10.2   Techniques for the Analysis of BigData

The analysis of BigData is a complex process that needs such tools as Van der Hulst's, CRISP-DM and AMPA [2]. A big data project's success depends on the proper mix of expert analysts and good tools. Additionally, it requires an effective project management and sound methodology.

A BigData analysis' life cycle is broken down into six phases; data understanding, understanding of business, preparation of data, modeling, measurement, deployment. Note that phase sequence isn't strict. The criminal intelligence application can be used for investigating individual crimes in many different ways; and criminal networks [3]. McCue [4] states that steps of criminal investigation are similar to criminal data mining steps, too. She also points out that forensic police theory utilizes case-based reasoning techniques. From that kind of point of view, the crime data mining can also use the same sources of all data used by the police. Therefore, the police investigation process can be divided into five steps: Collecting details of the offence, processing and storing data & documents on crime, scanning & recovering, obtaining relevant details & examining information to locate leads and using the information for criminal proceedings.

Identifying available data sources is important for determining the best method of information discovery and effective investigation. During an investigation the police usually use the following data sources:

I.   Information on Demographics of Offender:
Surname, name, birth date, birth's place, number of the social security and so on. Such documents are usually kept in electronic databases however the police may not access them quickly.

II.   Information Regarding Criminal Backgrounds:
When a person is wanted against the background of previous crimes or even the possibility of another person participating in the crime.

III. Previous Files to Investigate:
After discovering a suspect previously convicted, police are looking for reports of suspected suspects from past

investigations. Examples include text, image, video, CCTV, bank & credit card statements, telephone calls, e-mail sending records, flight and travel itineraries, Intelligence Reports, forensic reports, Police Reports, witness and victim statements, lawyer, and statements and confessions on criminal matters.

IV. Police Arrest Records:

Police officers apprehend suspects immediately and hold them in police custody after general searches and routine requests, or calling for service investigation. There are different methods of data mining that are used to uncover information of counter-terrorism. Skillicorn [5] divides them into four major groups namely: understanding relations, clustering, prediction, and understanding the internal world of others which can be described as follows:

a) Prediction:
By collecting and finding its properties it is as determining the results or meaning of a given situation [6].

b) Clustering:
It means putting objects or situations into groups whose members look like one another and who are like members of other groups. If category or group membership has not been previously identified, techniques of clustering can be used to uncover natural relationships or patterns in the data. For example, it can detect and group related crimes in which perpetuators resemble a known profile.

c) Understanding connections:
The meaning of understanding connections is the understanding of how people are connected to objects and processes. In the crime context, it requires information of who is a friend of whom, knowing the criminal connection. To identify such links, analysts use data visualization tools.

d) Understanding other's inner world:
Understanding someone else's inner life helps us to infer what other people may think or feel. In the crime domain, through sharing information, expertise, and tools, it involves sentiment analysis or assessment of which criminal groups are linked to cooperative groups.

Table 10.1 Four forms of knowledge discovery in crime cases.

Cases	Prediction	Clustering	Understanding connections	Understanding the internal world of others
Crime	Prediction of unsolved crimes	Finding similar and dissimilar crimes	Detecting interrelated series of crimes	Detecting common attributes of crimes
Criminal	Prediction of next attack of a serial criminal	Detecting similarly behaving criminals	Detecting friendship link of criminals	Detecting relationship of criminals
Criminal network	Prediction of a missing member in a criminal network	Detecting cliques and subgroups in a criminal network	Positional analysis of criminal network members	Detecting similarity of groups and finding emerging networks

In Table 10.1, there are four knowledge forms of discovery that can be applied to three types of cases: crime, criminal, and criminal network are shown.

Regarding the recent data mining methodologies for crime, there are a number of methods used to analyze the data in big data. Some of those techniques are discussed here.

A. Van der Hulst's Methodology

It known as Social network analysis (S.N.A.) which is designed especially forcriminal network analysis. It is one of the techniques used in big data analysis and one of the tools which can help to reveal clandestine and adversary networks systematically. S.N.A. is seen as the certain equivalent of the analysis of the links. It consists of three principal steps [7]:

1. Preparing Data:
   This phase includes defining the network boundaries and accessing data from the network.

2. Processing Data:
   In this phase, information is collected on the social ties of actors. Then, the activities, attributes, and database of individual attributes and affiliations associated with the actors get identified.

3. Data analysis and reporting:
   This step involves collecting data and information, as well as analyzing it and making sure that all the required data is completed through some specific procedures and required measures and stored correctly in a database. Finally, outcomes are reported in an interpretative way.

B. Methodology of CRISP-DM
   It is a comprehensive process model for carrying out data mining projects. The (CRISP-DM) is one of standard framework which based on both the used technology and industry sector. The aims of this model are to make large data mining projects which are more reliable, less costly, faster, and more manageable. A hierarchical process of the (CRISP-DM) methodology is consisting of four levels of abstraction:

   At the beginning, the process of data mining is to be organized into a small number of phases. Every phase includes several generic tasks of second-level. Second level is called generic; this level is meant to be general enough to cover all possible situations of data mining. The third level is known as specialized task level that describes how to carry out actions in the generic tasks in specific situations. The level number four is the process instance level which refers to the record of actions, decisions, and results of an actual data mining engagement [8, 9].

C. AMPA Methodology
   The Actionable Mining and Predictive Analysis (A.M.P.A.) model includes variable selection, operationally relevant recoding, security specific evaluation, public safety, and a focus on operationally feasible output [4].

   The (AMPA) model for actionable mining is for Public Safety and Protection. Actionable mining includes the following phases:

   1. Problem or Challenge: Present protocols and records are reviewed in this process to better clarify the complexity of the issue.

2. Data Collection and Fusion: these are useful when designing models for specific questions using different data sources at this level. Depending on the nature of the query the required data is placed in the same format.
3. Operationally Appropriate processing includes variable selection and recoding of this process.
4. Recoding: the consumer gets acquainted with the data at his stage and develops a rough understanding of their sequence. In addition, data transformation and cleaning can be done.
5. Variable Selection: This stage involves the utility of variables as well as significant experience in current crime domains.
6. Definition, characterization, and modeling: the definition, characterization and modeling of the data is applied at this stage to characterize the available data.
7. Specific Evaluation of Public Safety: At this point, the models are checked to see if they answered the question during the initial phase or not.

Table 10.2 Comparison of methodology.

Available methodologies		
Van der Hulst's Methodology	CR1SP-DM Methodology	AMPA Methodology
Data preparation	Business Understanding	Question or Challenge
Data preparation	Data Understanding	Data Collection and Fusion
Data preparation	Data Preparation	Operationally Relevant Processing and recoding
Data preparation	Data Preparation	Variable Selection
Data processing	Modelling	Identification, Characterization, Modelling
Data analysis and reporting	Evaluation	Public Safety Specific Evaluation
Data analysis and reporting	Deployment	Operationally Actionable Output

8. Operationally Actionable Performance: planning the performance for end users to meet their operational production expectations at this level.

The limitation of (AMPA) requires different analytical approaches, especially in such a technically diverse area as security analysis and applied public safety, numerous issues, methods, techniques, and sources. The (AMPA) model may therefore be considered to be in similarity of a building code, that specifies the particular item that needs to be addressed and provides a suggested sequence of measures that should be covered in the larger phase.

Table 10.2 demonstrates crime data mining methodologies focused on the above concepts and explanations.

10.3 Important Big Data Security Techniques

We know about the importance of security data as well as big data, so there are different techniques used such as safeguard distributed programming frameworks, security of non-relational data, homomorphic encryption, secure multiparty computation and attribute-based encryption. They are briefly introduced as follows:

a. Safeguard distributed programming frameworks
Distributed programming framework allows the processing of a lot of data in a distributed environment. Hadoop is one of the popular frameworks and it is a distributed open source project. It effectively uses MapReduce programming to deal with big data, as it can exploit parallel processing. Hadoop's architecture is demonstrated in Figure 10.1. The Cloud Security Alliance (CSA) suggests that companies use methods such as Kerberos Authentication, while maintaining compliance with predefined security policies. After that, "de-identify" the data by decoupling all Personally Identifiable Information (PII) from the data so as not to violate personal privacy. This helps you to permit access to files with predefined security policies, ensuring that untrusted code will not leak information across device resources. Eventually, the complex task is over what remains of securing data with regular maintenance against data leakage.

b. Security of Non-relational data
A Non-relational database is the database that does not adopt the conventional relational database management

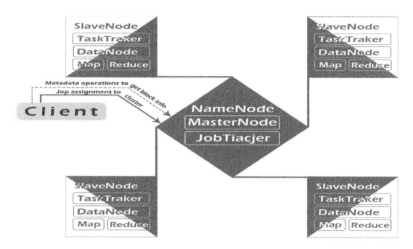

Figure 10.1 Architecture of Hadoop.

system based model. This category of databases, also called NoSQL databases, was developed with the growth of big data applications in recent years. It has become very popular because essentially they were built to solve the limitations of relational databases in addressing big data demands. Big data refers to data that develops and travels too quickly, and is too structurally complex to manage traditional technologies. Although these NoSQL technologies differ considerably, these databases are more scalable and flexiblethan their equivalents in comparison to them [10].

c. Homomorphic encryption (HE)

It is a particular cryptographic method, it is an encryption scheme that enables a third party as a (cloud, service provider) to perform some computable functions on the encrypted data while maintaining the purpose and format features of the encrypted data to suit the results of the operations performed on the plaintexts after decryption [11].

The three types of HE scheme are (Partially Homomorphic Encryption P.H.E.), (Somewhat Homomorphic Encryption S.W.H.E.), and (Fully Homomorphic Encryption F.H.E.) as shown in Figure 10.2.

In recent years, P.H.E. and S.W.H.E. schemes are being progressively replaced by F.H.E. schemes. Big data used F.H.E. for security and privacy Purposes.

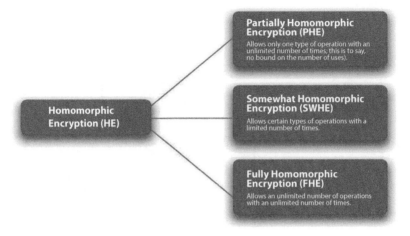

Figure 10.2 Types of Homomorphic Encryption.

d. Secure Multiparty Computation

It was suggested by seminal researches of Yao [12]. It lets multiple parties calculate a function f with their private inputs in a distributed cloud environment. After computation, the proper calculation results are given to all honest parties [13].

e. Attribute-based encryption

It is the most effective and known technique of core encryption in order to secure access to data suggested by Sahai *et al.* [14] called Attribute-based encryption. Data owners mark all keys and ciphertexts with the set of attributes in Attribute-based encryption, and then the users are expected to show legal user authority for these attributes. Subsequently data is downloaded and decrypted by matching the key and ciphertext attributes. Traditional encryption based on attributes is classified into two groups, namely ciphertext-policy attribute-based encryption (CP-ABE) and key-policy attribute-based encryption (KP-ABE). The major difference between the two types is the technique that embeds access protocols.

The access protocols are implemented in CP-ABE scheme with homologous cipher texts. In contrast, the access protocols in KP-ABE scheme are related to users' private keys [15].

10.4   Conclusion

Technological development leads to creating a huge amount of data which results in the emergence of a new area called big data. Simultaneously, cyber-crime has also grown rapidly hand in hand with the development of technology. So there should be appropriate techniques that can deal with these huge amounts of data effectively and efficiently. In this study, we discussed some of these techniques that can be used to analyze these data as well as the ability to predict the crimes before they happened. These techniques play a vital role in the prevention of crimes through the prediction of crimes before their occurrence. The study also made a comparison among different cases of crimes: crime, criminal and criminal network. The comparison was conducted in terms of the prediction level, clustering level, understanding level as well as understanding the internal world with others. Then the study presented the important big data security techniques which are safeguard distributed programming frameworks, security of non-relational data, homomorphic encryption and Attribute-based encryption

As a matter of fact, the BigData area is evolving rapidly and tremendously in the past few years. Therefore, great efforts have to be done on the field of BigData analysis in order to computing the big data growth and also to get effective and appropriate results.

References

1. Abdullah, F.M., Using big data analytics to predict and reduce cyber crimes. *Int. J. Mech. Eng. Technol.*, 10, 1, 1540–1546, 2019.
2. Pramanik, M.I., Lau, R.Y.K., Yue, W.T., Ye, Y., Li, C., Big data analytics for security and criminal investigations. *Wiley Interdiscip. Rev. Data Min. Knowl. Discov.*, 7, 4, 1–19, 2017.
3. Morselli, C., *Inside Criminal Networks*, (Springer Science+Business Media, New York, NY, USA) vol. 8, 2009.
4. McCue, C., *Data mining and predictive analysis: Intelligence gathering and crime analysis*, Second. UK, Butterworth-Heinemann, 2014.
5. Skillicorn, D., *Knowledge discovery for counterterrorism and law enforcement*, CRC Press, Taylor & Francis Group, Boca Raton, FL, 2008.
6. Chen, M., Chung, H., Xu, W., Wang, J.J., Qin, G., Chau, Y., Crime Data Mining: A General Framework and Some Examples. *Computer (Long. Beach. Calif.).*, 37, 50–56, 2004.
7. van der Hulst, R.C., Introduction to Social Network Analysis (SNA) as an investigative tool. *Trends Organ. Crime*, 12, 2, 101–121, 2009.

8. Pete, C. *et al.*, Crisp-Dm 1.0. *Cris. Consort.*, 76, 2000.
9. Wirth, R., CRISP-DM : Towards a Standard Process Model for Data Mining. *Proc. Fourth Int. Conf. Pract. Appl. Knowl. Discov. Data Min.*, pp. 29–39, 2000.
10. Sowmya, Y., A Review on Big Data Mining, Distributed Programming Frameworks and Privacy Preserving Data Mining Techniques. *Int. J. Adv. Res. Comput. Sci.*, 6, 1, 121–126, 2015.
11. AL-Rummana, G.A. and Shende, G.N., Homomorphic Encryption for Big Data Security A Survey. *Int. J. Comput. Sci. Eng.*, 6, 10, 503–511, 2018.
12. Yao, A.C., Protocols for Secure Computations. In 23rd annual symposium on foundations of computer science (sfcs 1982), IEEE, 160–164, 1982.
13. Bogetoft, P., Christensen, D.L., Damgård, I., Geisler, M., Jakobsen, T., Krøigaard, M., Secure multiparty computation goes live. In International Conference on Financial Cryptography and Data Security (pp. 325-343). Springer, Berlin, Heidelberg, 23–26, 2009.
14. Sahai, A. and Waters, B., Fuzzy Identity-Based Encryption. In *Annual International Conference on the Theory and Applications of Cryptographic Techniques*, pp. 457–473, 2005.
15. Bao, R., Chen, Z., Obaidat, M.S., Challenges and techniques in Big data security and privacy: A review. *Secur. Priv.*, 1, 4, e13, 2018.

11

Crime Pattern Detection Using Data Mining

Dipalika Das[1]* and Maya Nayak[2]

[1]Dept. of MCA, Trident Academy of Creative Technology, BBSR, India
[2]Dept. of CSE, Orissa Engineering College, BBSR, India

Abstract

In the current scenario as crime is increasing day by day it is becoming a challenge for the investigating agencies to have control on this. Again criminals are adopting new techniques and formulae to perform crime so that it would be difficult for law enforcement department to catch them. Hence crime analysis, detection and prediction becomes essential now-a-days. For this we need to go through previous crime records, analyze them, then classification/regression algorithms can be applied basing on requirement in order to predict the next occurrence of crime. So that next crime can be checked before being committed. As a procedure learned rules from training set are applied on test set in order to obtain predicted output. Several other data mining techniques can be a great help towards solving the problem. By going through this literature one can have a brief idea regarding what has been done in this regard and can acquire knowledge in facing the problem in a different way. This paper also puts light on several criminal analysis methods in use till date.

Keywords: Data mining, crime analysis, crime prediction, algorithm

11.1 Introduction

Crime can be defined as any deed done by any person which is against the law and causes harm to another and the person who does this is known

---

*Corresponding author: dipalika.das@gmail.com

Subhendu Kumar Pani, Sanjay Kumar Singh, Lalit Garg, Ram Bilas Pachori and Xiaobo Zhang (eds.) *Intelligent Data Analytics for Terror Threat Prediction: Architectures, Methodologies, Techniques and Applications*, (221–236) © 2021 Scrivener Publishing LLC

as a criminal. The deviation from normal behavior may be due to social, economic and environmental conditions. Every government in the entire world is giving emphasis on safety and security. The main aim of each government is to minimise the existence of crime. It is seen each criminal activity is associated with some sort of new practice and innovative idea. Statistical data related to crime are monitored and analysed by various investigating bodies so that various strategies can be planned to prevent crimes from further happening. Now the work of data mining and machine learning starts on huge volumes of data that are being properly stored and maintained. Data mining uses a variety of techniques (association, correlation, clustering, and decision tree) to analyse previously stored data and make predictions about future. Here main aim is to identify patterns of crime and find relation between them digitally. As the criminal offence increases day by day, it becomes difficult to find out which ones have been committed by whom or by the same human being. There are several software tools available in order to better understand patterns of crime and identification of suspects.

11.2   Related Work

Sharma *et al.* [15] did a survey and found that previous crime records would be helpful in predicting the future crime occurrence. They realized that out of several data mining techniques the most commonly used were classification and clustering. They concluded that an advancement in clustering could enhance the evaluation of classifier.

Rohith *et al.* [1] provided the perception about crime trends and suspect prediction. In order to predict suspects, depending on the type of crimes, there were many kinds of constraints. For example during chain snatching, the constraints could be like location, time, criminal height, appearance, type of vehicle, weapon used, color, etc. Thus, the paper provided insight about the techniques used for crime trends and suspect prediction.

Vijayalakshmi *et al.* [2] clustered the different attributes present in the dataset. Then they used SVM to do prediction regarding forthcoming crime. They found the output in the form of clusters and prediction in the form of graph. They mapped both of them on a box plot. They showed that the results would support the police in planning their strategies and implementing the same to prevent crimes from further happening.

Murthy *et al.* [3] showed the study of various frequently occurring patterns and calculations related to rules which could be implemented in finding crime patterns. They explained different frequent pattern calculations:

1. candidate generation, 2. without candidate generation, and 3. vertical layout approach. They focused on how it could be connected to various zones especially in wrong doing design identification. This paper helped the research scholars in implementing the algorithms related to frequently occurring patterns found in various datasets.

David *et al.* [4] performed survey on several supervised and un-supervised learning techniques generally used for identifying criminals. From the survey they could find out several data mining techniques meant for analyzing and predicting crime to happen next.

Pande *et al.* [5] tried to find out patterns related to crime and represented them on a graph. They applied several algorithms related to regression, classification, decision tree, forecasting models, artificial neural networks in order to measure crime patterns and compared the results to find out the best algorithm giving correct prediction. They used the WEKA tool for their analysis.

Jaglan [6] grouped similar crimes taking place against women in India using clustering algorithm. He did classification of crime dataset based on several predefined conditions. He tried to help governing bodies to reduce crime through mapping of crime. He tried to provide better explanation of crime patterns through various prediction and visualization methods.

Wang *et al.* [11] proposed a mechanism called subspace clustering. They first constructed a similarity graph by linking similar crimes. Secondly they used an integer linear programming approach to find crimes in cores and at the end the full crime series was constructed by merging all together. They proposed methods which could be used to detect general patterns as well as crime series patterns.

Sonawanev *et al.* [9] analyzed and correlated the available crime datasets, then did predictions about the next crime. They did correlation between crime and location. They found that correlation could be done on the basis of age, location and type of crime. They did prediction using several pictorial representations like pie chart, heat map, spike, graph, etc.

Marchal *et al.* [13] introduced a system that was based on automation. It could check, identify and analyse phishing sites. This system could interact with any server or proxy server. The experimental evidence shown in this paper could be able to find out phishing sites. They worked upon the query data from various commonly used search engine sites and did feature extraction from the words that formed an URL. They used these features to classify the URLs that are phishing sites from the original datasets. Their proposed system achieved high confidence rate. Further they started implementing on big data and advanced data.

Wang *et al.* [18] developed a new algorithm 'Series Finder' meant for pattern detection. It was helpful in identifying crime patterns committed by the same criminal. It was capable enough to match correctly crimes to patterns that might be missed by analysts. As per the working mechanism the algorithm searched for similarities between crimes in a growing pattern and tried to identify the modus operandi of a particular offender. As the number of crimes increased, the modus operandi could be more defined.

Zhuang *et al.* [19] developed a system which could automatically categorize phishing and malware sites by applying clustering algorithms. They proposed a framework which was based on clustering mechanism in order to group malware as well as phishing sites separately.

Zhang *et al.* [21] worked upon Bayesian network approach to find a completely new framework to detect phishing websites. Their framework was capable enough to differentiate between original web site and the web site under suspicion. They applied classifiers like text, image or combination of both to distinguish between original and false web page. They were capable of estimating matching threshold.

Rajan *et al.* [22] found a crime information system which was completely automated and new. They did this by implementing a clustering approach based on k-means to detect, locate and identify the crime and group the same.

11.3   Methods and Procedures

The diagram below reveals the steps to be followed:

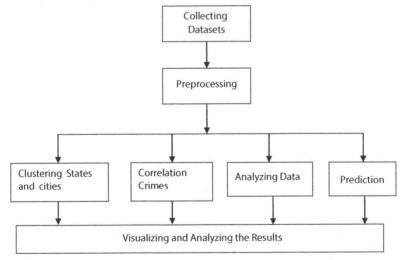

1. Collection of Data

Huge collections of crime records are gathered annually in several investigating departments. All sorts of crime records are available in National Crime

Bureau. It provides a statistical report of different cases occurred throughout the country in the entire year. Generally raw data is available, quite possible that it may contain erroneous and absence of values. So pre-processing is essential in view of getting data in appropriate and pure form. Pre-processing and cleaning are both requisite for pre-processing phase.

2. Classification of Data

Classification of records into several groups is possible by considering features of data objects. Grouping of crimes are done basing on regions and localities. Crimes are classified by taking into account the already occurred crimes. Data with similar features are clustered by implementing K-Means clustering technique.

- K-Means Algorithm

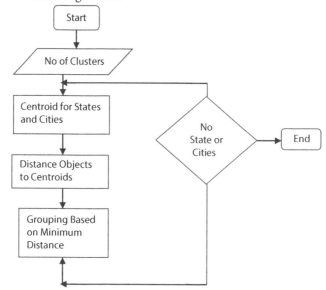

Here mean is the main criteria to distinguish the clusters from each other. The algorithm begins with assumption of having K clusters. Computation of mean value refers to mean distance between corresponding objects. It implements the iterative technique to move objects from one cluster to other till repetition occurs. Following are the steps of K-means algorithm:

Input: Assume number of groups

1. Randomly pick 'K' objects as centroid points from a dataset named 'D' containing 'N' objects.

2. Objects are placed in a cluster which are at less distance or similar to centroid points
3. Compute mean value for each cluster

Output: Final set of 'K' clusters

K-means algorithm is a base for all other clustering algorithms.

4. Correlating Crimes

Generally crimes are interrelated. It may be related to another crime or criminal. Identifying the correct correlation helps in computing values that are omitted due to some reason. Predictions are based on correlation. Identifying the correlation between two variables in past assumed that it would pursue to correlate in future. The value of a known variable can be used to predict the other variable in future. Generally Pearson's Correlation Coefficient can be evaluated by the ratio of the Covariance of the two variables to the product of their individual standard deviations.

$$\rho(X, Y) = \frac{cov(X, Y)}{\sigma_X \sigma_Y}$$

Here cov = covariance, σ_X refers to the standard deviation of X and refers to the standard deviation of Y. This equation gives a result that lies between +1 and −1, where +1 stands for positive correlation, 0 represents no correlation and −1 stands for negative correlation.

5. Predicting Crime

Predicting crime can be a great help to the investigating departments in reducing events related to crime. Possibility of occurrence of an event in future is called prediction. Linear regression can be an approach to predict crime. This helps in predicting different crimes and their places of occurrence without mistake. This approach relates a dependent variable with one or more independent variable. Simple linear regression is based on one independent variable. The value of one variable is derived from the value of other by the process of prediction in this simple linear regression method. The predicted variable is known as criterion variable and is represented by Y. X is known as the predictor variable as this is the variable on which prediction is based upon. When Y is plotted against X a straight line is generated in simple linear regression. Obtaining the best fitting straight line through the given points is the main objective of linear regression. The line that minimizes the sum of the squared errors of prediction line that minimizes the sum of the squared errors of prediction is the best fitting line. The regression equation of a straight line is as below:

$$Y = bX + a$$

Here
Y = predicted score, b = slope of the line, a = Y intercept
Slope 'b' can be expressed as

$$b = \gamma \frac{S_X}{S_Y}$$

And the intercept 'a' can be computed as

$$a = M_Y - bM_X$$

Where,

M_X = mean of X
M_Y = mean of Y
S_X = Standard Deviation of X
S_Y = Standard Deviation of X and Y
γ = Correlation between X and Y

11.4   System Analysis

There are two approaches of system analysis:

i. Functional Requirements

a) Datasets Generation
National Bureau of Crime Records can provide the crime data. Basing on what parameter we want to detect or predict several datasets can be generated.

b) Cleaning of Dataset
This refers to pre-processing stage where collection of data is organized so that we can easily perform analysis and obtain stable outcome. Then data filtration is done.

c) Cleaning of Dataset
Several techniques are to be implemented for the data analysis task at the end. The results obtained from this step need to be stored and used as per requirement. Mainly investigating authorities use the result of this step in order to check crime in their own localities. For better understanding purpose this data can be visualized.

ii. Non Functional Requirements

1. *Performance*
How quickly the system will be able to run analysis task measures the performance of the system. The system is quick enough to produce crime patterns basing on type and volume of data to be extracted. Performance is to be maintained in order to get accurate result.

2. *Safety and Security*
The system should be protected in such a way that it should be less prone to 3rd party intervention. Third party not only changes the integrity of the data but also the system as a whole resulting in loss of confidentiality or data loss.

3. *Data Integrity*
Data integrity should be enforced so that the system uses this data efficiently resulting in correct output. The output of data mining or machine learning algorithm is never 100% accurate but it always ensures that the input data is uniform, without error and not corrupted. Like input data the output must also maintain integrity as a little change in input can lead to drastic change in final output resulting in reduced accuracy of algorithm.

4. *Availability*
Availability ensures that system should be readily available to use, up to date and implemented whenever needed. During emergency investigating departments may use system to prepare reports and analyze statistics.

5. *Portability*
Portability of a system refers to:
> a) The system should perform normal function on any device with different hardware configuration with same frequency, efficiency and accuracy as that of original one.
> b) It should be operational on every platform, operating system and software.

This feature is given more importance because of its use in multiple places and multiple situations. Another criteria for portability is its versatile nature.

6. *Maintainability*

Since every device needs to be maintained and repaired on regular basis, every system needs to be monitored and repaired regularly in order to attain full operability, capability and longevity. Errors and bugs are checked on regular basis. Software is given utmost importance failing which we may not obtain full functioning of the system leading to incorrect results.

7. *Software Quality Assurance*

   a. Reliable:

   A system is said to be reliable if:
   - it behaves properly in every event.
   - it functions properly in difficult conditions where decisions are to be taken.

Hence system can be relied upon on any situation.

   b. Robust:

   This is a property of the system to perform in unfavourable conditions. Circumstances in which complex datasets are to be handled with different parameters, the system works effectively.

   c. Efficient:

A system is said to be efficient if:
- Its processes are simple and user-friendly.
- Its processing requires less amount of time to search for required information and data.
- It does not halt and can run with the original hardware.
- It is capable of removing errors and bugs.

   d. Compatible:

A system is said to be compatible if:
- The software has a tendency to work with different configurations.
- As the system strictly follows rules and regulations of industry standard, the software can run on any platform and can be implemented easily.
- If the system is portable, it is automatically compatible.

   e. Modular:

A system is said to be modular if:
- It divides the system into modules for better functionality.
- It refers to the software consisting of separate, interchangeable components.
- It increases cohesion and reduces coupling.

- It is capable of extending functionalities and maintaining the code.
- It is capable of reducing system overhead.

iii. Use_Case Diagram

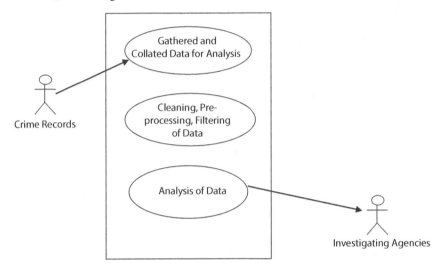

In the above diagram the user is the investigating agency. Crime records are the input datasets on which analysis is being done to present it to the investigating agency.

At the first step, collection and organization of data are done in such a way that the steps followed to find the target variables from the predictor variables become easier. At the next step, data is pre-processed in order to remove any redundant attributes so that predicting the target variable becomes faster. During pre-processing phase, empty fields if any, are omitted, any data mentioned by-mistake is rectified, hence data is cleaned and filtered thoroughly. At the end, after the pre-processing phase is over, analyzed by any of the data mining algorithms to determine the value of the target variables.

11.5 Analysis Model and Architectural Design

I. Modeling of Data

Level 0:
Crime data are made input from investigating organisations at this level. Here the raw data is fed into the system, then predefined values of specified attributes are displayed as results.

Level 1:

This level depicts the general work flow of the proposed system. Initially crime records are fed into the system as data. Then these records are analysed using some data mining techniques for finding useful patterns. The predicted values of the specified target variables are displayed next.

Level 2:

This level depicts the in-depth representation. Here the data which is collected from several sources are the crime records. Now these records are pre-processed by filtering and cleaning. Once pre-processing is over data mining techniques are implemented on the dataset so that predictions of specified target variables are possible in a presentable format to the user.

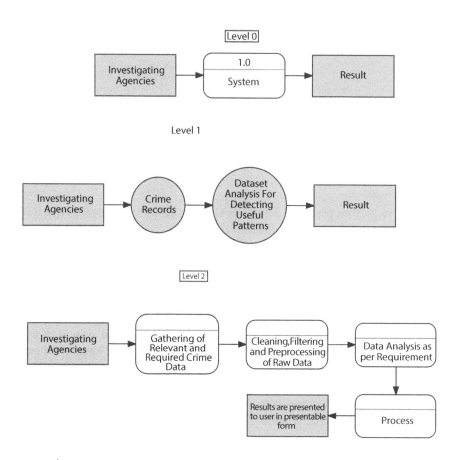

II. Activity Diagram

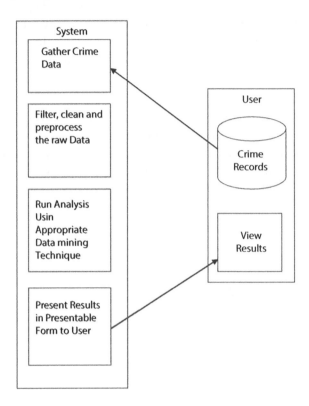

The above picture provides detail working of the software used in the system. It depicts the functionalities of the system. Gathering and aggregating the raw crime data, then pre-processing it using tools like WEKA and finally presenting it to the user, are several functionalities of this system architecture. The system also extracts meaningful patterns from the dataset and shows the result at user end.

Briefly we can say as is depicted in above picture that data from various investigating sources are made input into the proposed system in the form of crime records. Then first step is the gathering and aggregation of all crime data. The second step includes pre-processing of raw data and analyzing using various data mining algorithms. It finds several patterns, derives learning rules and forecasts future values of specified attributes. Finally it represents the result in presentable format.

11.6   Several Criminal Analysis Methods in Use

A. Text, Content and Nlp-based Methods
Hamdy *et al.* [10] worked upon people's interaction with social network sites and cell phone usage based on Location Markers and Call Logs. Their work was based on finding out several suspicious activities going on social network sites. They tried to develop a new system which would help in making faster crime analysis and precise decision making. They used a sequence of inference rules to determine the criminal activities. Their model was capable enough to predict and categorise human behavior from real data.

Sharma [14] worked for achieving no crime in the society. He made use of data mining algorithms for detecting suspicious criminal activities and designed a useful application for the purpose. He delivered a tool which was based on enhanced decision tree algorithm to detect suspicious emails meant for destructive purpose. In order to produce a better and faster decision tree based on information entropy, he tried ID3 algorithm with an enhanced feature selection method and attribute importance factor.

B. Crime Patterns and Evidence-Based Methods
Agarwal *et al.* [16] tried to support investigating personnel in identifying and analyzing patterns related to crime responsible for reducing recurrence of events that were similar and providing steps to reduce crime by using K-means clustering of data mining. They had implemented clustering technique by using open source tools of data mining like WEKA, R, Rapid Miner, etc. They did clustering with the help of Rapid Miner tool. They analyzed homicide, a crime committed by a human being by killing another human being.

Kiani *et al.* [12] developed a new framework for clustering and predicted crime based on real data. They used GA (Genetic Algorithm) in that framework. They preferred this algorithm to improve outlier detection in the pre-processing phase and fitness function based on accuracy and classification error parameters. The importance of framework used here were: removal of low value attributes, optimization of outliers, generation of training and testing data.

C. Spatial and Geo-Location-Based Methods
Rizwan *et al.* [17] did classification of crime dataset to predict crime category for different states of United States of America. They worked on a real dataset. They presented a comparison between two classification

algorithms namely: Naïve Bayesian and Decision Tree for predicting crime category or different states in USA. Experimental outcomes revealed that Decision Tree performed better than Naïve Bayesian. They used WEKA tool for their experiment. They had planned for applying other classification algorithms as well as other feature selection techniques on crime data to evaluate their prediction performance.

Chen *et al.* [23] developed a general framework for crime data mining. They shared the experience gained by the researchers of Coplink project at Arizona. Their work put focus on the relationship between crime types and link between criminal organisations. In order to locate criminals they also used a space approach.

D. Prisoner-Based Methods

Sheehy *et al.* [7] proposed an idea which would be beneficial for the treatment of prisoners who were mentally ill. In order to identify properly mentally ill criminals they had linked criminal personal records and crime career records with social security number. Their research work categorized the criminals into high, medium, low levels of recidivism risk potential. Recidivism means the act of a person to repeat crime even after he is punished. Their main objective was to elaborate and segregate the criminals. Their activities were observed and continuously recorded. Hence criminals could be differentiated from other criminals who were harmful and could cause damage to other inmates. They classified criminals basing on mental health into 2 categories: referred and non-referred. With this guards would be able find out, the prisoners who were referred for mental health check-up and who were not.

E. Communication-Based Methods

Taha *et al.* [8] developed a forensic investigation tool. It helped in identifying and locating the criminal leaders. It helped to identify the immediate leaders. They knew that by removing those members who were beneficial to criminal organization would weaken the criminal activity. They devised a new model known as SIIMCO. It was based on graphical representation of criminal groups as a network based on crime records. In the graph the vertex represented a single criminal and the link represented the communication link between those criminals. They derived a formulae keeping in mind importance of each vertex in the network relative to other vertices in the graph. Their model could identify the immediate leaders with weighted graph that connected other criminals.

11.7   Conclusion and Future Work

As crimes are increasing day by day at various levels it is becoming difficult to store crime details year after year manually and retrieving the crime and suspect information as and when required. Hence automation is the need of the hour. This can be better simplified and apprehended with the help of several mining and machine learning techniques. Various data mining techniques are helpful in analyzing crime and provide a meaningful way towards solving and minimizing criminal activity.

In future basing on requirements of various investigating bodies throughout the world the appropriate mining technique would minimize the difficulty faced till date. The information received from various approaches could be essential in adopting several methods to control forthcoming criminal activity. Hence future scope could be based on real time data analysis of crime data, cyber-crimes, comparison of various forecasting, predicting and classification models so that user could select any of them basing on result obtained.

References

1. Rohith, V. and Sneha Deborah, V., An Improved Optimized Association Rule Technique for Crime Pattern Detection and Suspect Prediction. *JARDCS*, 05-Special Issue, 10, 1886–1891, 2018.
2. Vijayalakshmi, M., Bhatt, S., Goyal, H., Crime Pattern Recognition And Prediction Using Optimised K-Means And Svm. *Int. J. Appl. Math.*, 118, 22, 581–586, 2018.
3. Murthy, K.S.N., Pavan Kumar, A.V.S., Dharmaraju, G., Analysis of Crime data using data mining. *J. Eng. Sci. Math.*, 6, 8, 1059–1071, December 2017.
4. Benjamin Fredrick David, H. and Suruliandi, A., Survey On Crime Analysis And Prediction Using Data Mining Techniques. *IJSC*, 07, 03, 1459–1466, April 2017.
5. Pande, V., Samant, V., Nair, S., Crime Detection using Data Mining. *IJERT*, 5, 891–896, 01, January-2016.
6. Jaglan, V., Review of modelling technologies used for Predicting Crime. *IJRRA*, 3, 4, 71–76, December 2016.
7. Sheehy, K., Rehberger, T., O' Shea, A., Hammond, W., Evidence-based Analysis of Mentally Ill Individuals in the Criminal Justice System. *Proceedings of IEEE Systems and Information Engineering Design Symposium*, pp. 250–254, 2016.

8. Taha, K. and Yoo, P.D., SIIMCO: A Forensic Investigation Tool for Identifying the Influential Members of a Criminal Organization. *IEEE Trans. Inf. Forensics Secur.*, 11, 4, 811–822, 2016.

9. Sonawanev, T., Shaikh, S., Shaikh, S., Shinde, R., Sayyad, A., Crime Pattern Analysis, Visualization And Prediction Using Data Mining. *IJARIIE*, 1, 4, 681–686, 2015.

10. Hamdy, E., Adl, A., Hassanien, A.E., Hegazy, O., Kim, T.-H., Criminal Act Detection and Identification Model. *Proceedings of 7th International Conference on Advanced Communication and Networking*, pp. 79–83, 2015.

11. Wang, T., Rudin, C., Wagner, D., Sevieri, R., Finding Patterns with a Rotten Core: Data Mining for Crime Series with Cores, in: *Big Data*, vol. 3, no.1, Original Articles, Mary Ann Liebert, Inc. Publishers New Rochelle, NY, USA, Mar 2015.3-21.

12. Kiani, R., Mahdavi, S., Keshavarzi, A., Analysis and Prediction of Crimes by Clustering and Classification. *Int. J. Adv. Res. Artif. Intell.*, 4, 8, 11–17, 2015.

13. Marchal, S., François, J., State, R., Engel, T., PhishStorm: Detecting Phishing With Streaming Analytics. *IEEE Trans. Netw. Serv. Manage.*, 11, 4, 458–471 Dec. 2014.

14. Sharma, M., Z-Crime: A Data Mining Tool for the Detection of Suspicious Criminal Activities based on the Decision Tree. *International Conference on Data Mining and Intelligent Computing*, pp. 1–6, 2014.

15. Sharma, A. and Kumar, R., The obligatory of an Algorithm for Matching and Predicting Crime—Using Data Mining Techniques. *IJCST*, 4, 2, 289–292, April–June 2013.

16. Agarwal, J., Nagpal, R., Sehgal, R., Crime Analysis using K-Means Clustering. *Int. J. Comput. Appl.*, 83, 4, 1–4, 2013.

17. Iqbal, R., Murad, M.A.A., Mustapha, A., Panahy, P.H.S., Khanahmadliravi, N., An Experimental Study of Classification Algorithms for Crime Prediction. *Indian J. Sci. Technol.*, 6, 3, 4219–4225, 2013.

18. Wang, T., Rudin, C., Wagner, D., Sevieri, R., Learning to Detect Patterns of Crime. *ECML PKDD 2013, Part III, LNAI 8190*, pp. 515–530, 2013.

19. Zhuang, W., Ye, Y., Chen, Y., Li, Ensemble Clustering for Internet Security Applications. *IEEE Trans. Syst. Man Cybern.*, 42, 6, 1784–1796, Nov. 2012.

20. Shekhar, S., Mohan, P., Oliver, D., Zhou, X., *Crime pattern analysis: A spatial frequent pattern mining approach*, TR 12–015, (CS&E), University of Minnesota, USA May 10, 2012.

21. Zhang, H., Liu, G., Chow, T.W.S., Liu, W., Textual and Visual Content-Based Anti-Phishing: A Bayesian Approach. *IEEE Trans. Neural Networks*, 22, 10, 1532-1546, Oct. 2011.

22. Babu Renga Rajan, S., Srinivasagan, K.G., Ramar, K., Meenachi Sunderasan, S., An automated crime pattern detection using k-means clustering. *Int. J. Adv. Oper. Manage.*, 3, 3/4, 220–229, 2011.

23. Chen, H., Chung, W., Xu, J.J., Wang, G., Qin, Y., Chau, M., Crime Data Mining: a General Framework and Some Examples. *Computer*, 37, 4, 50–56, 2004.

12

Attacks and Security Measures in Wireless Sensor Network

Nikhil Sharma[1], Ila Kaushik[2*], Vikash Kumar Agarwal[3], Bharat Bhushan[4] and Aditya Khamparia[5]

[1]*HMR Institute of Technology & Management, Delhi, India*
[2]*Krishna Institute of Engineering & Technology, Ghaziabad, India*
[3]*RTC Institute of Technology, Ranchi, India*
[4]*School of Engineering and Technology, Sharda University, Greater Noida, India*
[5]*Lovely Professional University, Phagwara, India*

Abstract

Wireless Sensor Network comprises of nodes that are randomly distributed over the network. This type of network operates over radio wave frequency band. The nodes are free to move in any direction as they do not require any fixed infrastructure. The characteristic features of the network are dynamic topology, no infrastructure, fast in operation, etc. But due to its increase in the network, these types of network are prone to many attacks. As security is considered as one of the main constraints in any type of network, it becomes very important to take into consideration the key elements of security which are availability, integrity and confidentiality. Confidentiality means that the data transfer in the network must be kept secret in any transmission process. Integrity implies that the sent data must be preserved during transmission process. Availability means the data must be made available in the network for transmission. Wireless network follows layered approach where different layers perform different functionalities. In this paper we present different layer attacks along with security mechanisms to avoid the effect of attack in the network.

Keywords: Wireless Sensor Network, attacks, authentication, security, threat detection, security schemes, intrusion detection system, cryptography

Corresponding author: ila.kaushik.8.10@gmail.com

Subhendu Kumar Pani, Sanjay Kumar Singh, Lalit Garg, Ram Bilas Pachori and Xiaobo Zhang (eds.) *Intelligent Data Analytics for Terror Threat Prediction: Architectures, Methodologies, Techniques and Applications*, (237–268) © 2021 Scrivener Publishing LLC

12.1   Introduction

Wireless Sensor Network (WSN) is at a mercy of many attacks due to its distinctive attribute that are effectual topology, self-planning, restrained resources and many more. The data collected from a network can be affected by an attack that may cause a network peculiarity. The network attack can be detected by the collected data and that data is inestimable. However, the data can help us to detect security threats, attacks and intrusions. In different kinds of WSN applications, security data is generated. Some security data are sensory data and some are special data, depending on various detection methods. Security defense for obstruct intrusions and security menacing in WSN is supported by attack detection, thus it plays a vital role in maintaining the security of a wireless sensor networks. Stepping forward for working measures of WSN security and understanding the relative state of arts in field of attack detection, the related security data and attack detection methodology is very indispensable [1]. Internet of things (IoT) has a pivotal role in realizing positioning, intelligent identification, monitoring, environmental management, tracking and many more. The things in cyber world and physical (real) can be connected together using IoT, thus making the anthropoid (human) life very easy and comfortable. A wireless sensor network supports many of the functions used in IoT [2]. IoT carries WSN as a requisite part of it, which can be used by many IoT applications to record the situation such as smart home, intelligent healthcare and disaster caution [3].

WSN is basically a resource hindrance network. Regarding communication range, restricted energy, memory space and computation capacity, each node of WSN has the disadvantages.

- Memory constraints: In each sensor node the memory is generally being composed of random-access memory and the flash memory [4]. RAM has its own functionality which is usually used to store sensed data, application programs, and intermediate computations. Now, flash memory administers to accumulate downloaded applications [5]. The node has limited memory space and do not have adequate space to process huge data and execute intricate algorithms.
- Restricted Energy: Energy is one of the most significant resources in the WSN. A sensor's energy is mainly used for sensor transducer, communication and computation [6]. But, consumption of energy for communication in WSN is more [7]. Hence, we have to minimize communication for saving the energy in attack detection.

- Transmission Constraints: Transmission Latency, Transmission Stretch and Unreliable Transmission, all these aspects can be considered as a transmission constraint. Packet collision and channel fault [8] can cause loss of packet and damage in an unreliable wireless channel. Also, multi-hop routing and network clogging may cause high latency [9]. Energy of a node and other environmental elements are the main reason for actual transmission range. Hence, there is a requirement to consider data quality, retransmission mechanism and synchronization issues for a better communication [10].

The rest of the paper is designed as follows: Section 12.2 discussed Layered Architecture of WSN. Security threats on different layers are explained in Section 12.3. The threat detection on different layers has been described in Section 12.4. Section 12.5 illustrated Various parameters for security data collection in WSN. In Section 12.6, different security schemes in WSN have been elucidated followed by the Conclusion of this paper in Section 12.7.

12.2   Layered Architecture of WSN

WSN follows layered architecture in which each layer performs different functionalities. The layered approach can also be considered as stack protocol structure in which header is added in each layer and removed at other end. There are five layers in WSN as shown in Figure 12.1.

12.2.1   Physical Layer

For providing a path to send binary bit stream data by means of signal detection, modulation, data encryption, frequency selection and carrier frequency generation, this layer is responsible for all these. Eavesdropping attack, compromised node attack, replication node attack and basic jamming attack [11] are considered to be in this layer.

12.2.2   Data Link Layer

A devoted communication channel to neighboring nodes is provided by data link layer. In a protocol namely, Media Access Protocol, the entity takes care of communication channel using the carrier sense which are impuissant to different attacks that are Denial of Sleep (DoS) Attack [12], Collision Attack, Unfairness Attacks and Intelligent Jamming. The conviction behind

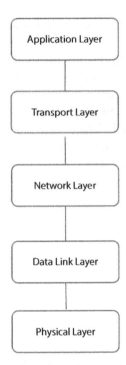

Figure 12.1 Architecture of WSN.

attacks in data link layer is to overtire the power resources of the nodes and secondly, demeaning service promptness. There are many similarities between jamming attacks in the physical layer and collision attacks in physical layer. The intruder tries to degrade the efficiency of the protocol and hence forcing the network to disburse more energy [13].

12.2.3   Network Layer

In WSN, the network layer gives the vanquish service to nodes. Also, at this layer, numerous attacks may buckle the availability of network. Hackers mainly launch attacks on vanquish such as Sybil Attack, Sinkhole Attack, Spoofing Attack, Wormhole Attack and many more [14]. The reliability at scuttle layer mostly depends upon confirmation.

12.2.4   Transport Layer

The point-to-point connections and designate trustworthy transport of packets are the main function of transport layer. The attacks which are particular to this layer only, in other words a main attack at transport layer consists of flooding and desynchronization. Authentication is the only and typical solution to fight against an attack.

12.2.5 Application Layer

For demanding and furnish data for each sensor node and interactivity with the end user is being done on this layer that is the application layer of WSN. One more function of the application layer is to take note of the physical topology. This layer provides numerous feasible entreaties. This particular layer of WSN is prone to attacks on authenticity and spiteful code that may create pernicious effect on application nodes.

12.3 Security Threats on Different Layers in WSN

Security in WSN for each of the particular node becomes very crucial. An intruder might attack with the help of the malicious code to any of the network node. Since WSN contains numerous nodes if we do not take care of this, our data might be at a risk of loss [15]. Transmission and reception of information on the network can be only by the authorized user, any other person except the authorized user considered being an intruder. Users can also perform the different tasks like online banking, shopping, billing and other useful tasks over the network. Nowadays, networks not only carrying the business or financial data but also carrying the personal data as useful information [16]. Thus, to protect the network is not only important but a must thing. So, that our communication becomes effective and useful. The security threats on different layers in WSN are as follows:

12.3.1 Threats on Physical Layer

The different types of threats on Physical Layer are explained as follows:

12.3.1.1 Eavesdropping Attack

Eavesdropping attack involves an eavesdropper or intruder who keeps the track of the activity taking place in between the transmission nodes. It is a kind of passive attack. Eavesdropper surveillances the transmission takes in between the source and recipient node but does not alter the data packets [17]. It is the requisite of many other attacks. A spiteful node tracks the message transmission and stops it. If the data packets are transmitted without the encoding then it is easy for an eavesdropper to attack on it. To shield our network against the attack like this we can use the appropriate encoding and safety protocols.

12.3.1.2   Jamming Attack

Jamming attack is some sort of an act to exploit the energy to obstruct transmission among the nodes. Jamming attack is further divided in two categories that are basic jamming attack and the intelligent jamming attack [18]. Basic jammer release radio signals to shatter the transmission of data packets. Basic Jamming attack gets split into the four categories according Xu *et al.* [19] i.e. Deceptive jamming, Reactive jamming, Random Jamming and constant jamming. Deceptive Jamming perpetually radiates consistent packets without an intervening time to mislead legitimate nodes into a recipient state. In Reactive Jamming the jammer stays shut till the information comes in the channel as faster the information or data packets come in the channel the jammer assaults the transmission nodes. To preserve energy the random jammer, transform into jamming and sleeping. Constant Jammer perpetually radiates signal to detain transmission channels and sensor nodes are prevented using the sending messages. Jamming stops a recipient from receiving the data packets and so make it more complex to figure out.

12.3.1.3   Imperil or Compromised Node Attack

Original legitimate node that is maintained by adversary can be considered as a imperil node attack. The intruder can effortlessly apprehend a sensor node in delicate security applications in WSN such as intelligence troops to spy and collect the data packets.

12.3.1.4   Replication Node Attack

Many a time the WSN is disclosed to on unsecure environment, in that it is very comfortable for an adversary to redevelop the programming the grabbed node and create duplicate of it. The duplicate node can enter and acts as a normal node in the network because it has legal id and key as it is inherited from the true node.

12.3.2   Threats on Data Link Layer

The different types of threats on Data Link Layer are explained as follows.

12.3.2.1   Collision Attack

An eavesdropper manages to give attenuation to the byte values of each data packets. As a consequence, the terminus node will relinquish this data packet reason for this is the checksum mismatch. Further, purposeful packet retransmission will demolish a lot of resources.

12.3.2.2   Denial of Service (DoS) Attack

The most valuable concern in WSN is the energy also the sensor nodes have restricted resources for communication. Many a times, it becomes critical to shield the sensor nodes with the appropriate mechanism. The adversary neglects the service which is being requested by the authentic user. In this way the denial of service affects the WSN system.

12.3.2.3   Intelligent Jamming Attack

Intelligent jamming attack is when the emission of data packets that directly disobeys the certain protocols. Furthermore, they create interference in the transmission of data packets and also power consumption of a node is increased. When the transmission of data packets is on the regular basis to a sensor node, jamming attack may take place easily.

12.3.3   Threats on Network Layer

The different types of threats on Network Layer are explained as follows.

12.3.3.1   Sybil Attack

Newsome et al. [20] describe that the malicious node acquires multiple peculiarities or identities concurrently and deceives original nodes to have faith that they have the original or main neighbors. It has the preparedness to distort the network integrity functions. An entrusted center to conform identities of transmission entities to cure from the Sybil attack.

12.3.3.2   Gray Hole Attack

Gray hole attack [21] also known as the selective forwarding attack. Gray hole attack is a certain or special type of the black hole attack as in this some part of the data packets is being dropped and pass on the data packets after it creates an illusion that it has the shortest path to reach the recipient node [22].

12.3.3.3 Sink Hole Attack

A malicious node tries to attract as much congestions as possible throughout a sink from fetching right packet. An intruder is appealing to neighboring nodes with an unreliable routing. Adjacent nodes send the data packets or message to sink via malicious node, an adversary also influenced the adjacent nodes.

12.3.3.4 Hello Flooding Attack

Various routing technique in WSN uses the Hello message to determine adjacent nodes and create network transmission. A node that collects Hello message from other node is set to have in the radio span of Hello message initiator and hence adjacent of the sender [23]. An eavesdropper may use high-energy transmitter to cover huge area of entities to make them amnesia.

12.3.3.5 Spoofing Attack

To initiate the attack by adversary in the network layer whether to get the data or to manipulate it, a malicious code is used to imitate the other device. An adversary can conceal the network congestion and provoke flaw information by method of distort, replay and attracting routing message in this particular attack.

12.3.3.6 Replay Attack

Data packets sent in WSN is being received by the malicious node and then it replays them again and again to the authenticated node in a particular sequence to manipulate its bounded power and hegemonies the transmission channel. The functioning of the entire WSN will be influenced by this kind of attack if the designing of the network system is below par.

12.3.3.7 Black Hole Attack

This attack is also same as the denial of service attack in the data link layer as it may consequence in a zero-packet transportation ratio and also the propagation delay is high. Many at times it occurs close to a cluster head or a sink to attract a greater number of data packets [24]. A malicious node invalidly replies request to reply message to delude a real node, similar to a black hole.

12.3.3.8   Worm Hole Attack

The straight transmission between two malicious nodes with the connection with less potency and effectiveness is high, like an efficient wireless connection [25]. It snares the packets first and then in second part it disseminates via its reserved connection to contort a primary routing protocol. It affects a lot of authentic nodes of surrounding to transmit the packet as it proclaims the shortest path to their terminal node.

12.3.4   Threats on Transport Layer

The different types of threats on Transport Layer are explained as follows.

12.3.4.1   De-Synchronization Attack

A transmission responsible attack is also known as the desynchronization attack. A trustworthy transport protocol makes sure that the detection can be done for every loss of data packet and also the lost data packet can be resent till they find their final or end node. An adversary models the data packets either with sequence number or with control flags in this attack.

12.3.4.2   Flooding Attack

An intruder tries to transmit the huge number of unproductive data packets authentic node in order to obstruct the normal transmission, also debase the network. An adversary through a lot of link establishment request to a node. Once the node collects them, it sends the acknowledgement packet to it and holds for a link. It also appraises the storage space for communication control. This attack engages the network resources and also obviates the normal working of network.

12.3.5   Threats on Application Layer

The different types of threats on Application Layer are explained as follows.

12.3.5.1   Malicious Code Attack

The attacker infuses the virus in a node to own the control over the node or breaks it down. Which may degrade the efficiency of the network and can play his predetermined programs.

12.3.5.2 *Attack on Reliability*

The intruder tries to inject the malicious node betwixt the transmission nodes to originate wrong data packets. Reliability attack can also cause the collision in the network and abruptly escalate the energy consumption.

12.3.6 Threats on Multiple Layer

Above mentioned attacks can be used as a combination which results in new type of attack. The attacks can operate on different layers at a same time which results in destruction in the functioning of the layer.

12.3.6.1 *Man-in-the-Middle Attack*

An eavesdropper recites in between the transmitting nodes and sometimes can manipulate the data packets; this will be done without giving any information to the user. The intruder surveillance the communication and fetch the information from that is beneficial for the intruder.

12.3.6.2 *Jamming Attack*

It is a kind of attack in which the attacker resists the intended nodes from using the channel bandwidth to communicate. In jamming attack, the interference is done by the attacker to gain the knowledge of the transmission taking place in between the nodes.

12.3.6.3 *Dos Attack*

Denial of service (DoS) attack is an attack in which the limited resources of the network are consumed and also the authentic user is being resisted from accessing the network and services. Network congestion can be done in this attack. Adversary directly infracts the certain protocol and sends information without any delay to raise the collision effect and cause energy loss.

12.4 Threats Detection at Various Layers in WSN

In this particular section, we discuss the various kinds of attack in different layers of WSN system. This includes the Flooding Attack, Sinkhole Attack, Gray Hole Attack, Black Hole Attack, Worm Hole Attack, Sybil Attack, Replication Attack, Denial of Service Attack, Jeopardize Node Attack, Jamming Attack, Hello Flooding Attack.

12.4.1   Threat Detection on Physical Layer

The different types of threats detection on Physical Layer are explained as follows:

12.4.1.1   Compromised Node Attack

This attack can be detected by two techniques [26]. The first technique can be named as the performance-based technique that may only consider different attributes like the advent rate of the data packet, advent time of data packet, locales of the node and energy consumption of a particular node, but will not retract the jeopardize node. Another method is software testimony-based technique, this technique has higher overheads besides that it can retract the jeopardize or compromised node.

12.4.1.2   Replication Node Attack

A protocol to sense the replication node attack in the static WSN is needed. Named RED (randomized effective distributed), the protocol has been proposed by Conti *et al.* [27]. Each and every node knows its locale and also stores its unique id-based set keys. Every node transmits its id and locale [28].

12.4.2   Threat Detection on Data Link Layer

The threats detection on Data Link Layer which is explained as follows:

12.4.2.1   Denial of Service Attack

To preserve the node energy and perpetuate the lifespan of the sensor node numerous Media Access Control (MAC) protocol is suggested by the researchers [29]. Let's take an example, consider a sensor node activates between the sleep mode and the active mode in operation cycle-based media access control protocols like X-MAC and B-MAC in this the recipient node is prepared by the initiator node by conveying the particular prelude data packet. A hierarchical work is being proposed by the Bhattasali *et al.* [30] specifically conjoint technique to find the denial of service attack. A cluster is being carve up into various sectors. A control node is allocated in each of the sector named as the in-charge node and that main node is responsible for cumulating the data from various node. Control node has all the right to judge that whether the data is genuine or not. If the number of information packets for a particular node surpasses the threshold value then that node is named as the distrust node and that node is being marked by the control node.

12.4.3 Threat Detection on Network Layer

The different types of threats detection on Network Layer are explained as follows:

12.4.3.1 Black Hole Attack

To cumulate and evaluate the packet delivery ratio (PDR) from the adjacent node to perceive the black hole attack. The expected node may be an adversary node if and when the packet delivery ratio is zero or null. But sometimes this technique may not be in picture as when it experiences the congestion attack, the PDR approaches to zero there arises an ambiguity. Prachi *et al.* [31] create the use of time respite and PDR to reveal the black hole attack in the wireless sensor network. That node is considered to be a black hole node in which the PDR approaches to zero for a distinct time. Authors designed the shielding techniques which makes the usage of two cluster heads. Each actuate cluster head hoard the member id and detach adversary member id in cluster. The sink detaches the black hole node form the cluster and another cluster head is triggered. Whole scenario is being used for the static network.

12.4.3.2 Worm Hole Attack

Zaw *et al.* [32] proposed a technique resides on the presumption that the number of malicious adjacent node exceeds the original normal node. Initiator node sends the route request in Round trip time and the commensurate route reply is transmitted by the terminator node in the ad-hoc on-demand vector routing protocol, also if there exists an intruder node then it is being raised. Let us consider two nodes namely X and Y then they may be the worm hole node if and when the root request of adjacent nodes of X and Y exceeds the threshold value. This technique can detect the adversary node and also can applied to the static network. Transmission overhead and any kind of auxiliary peripherals are not being demanded by this method to trace the worm hole attack. Now, if the two worm hole nodes are below five gateways apart then the efficacy for this technique to detect the attacker node decreased drastically. Passive and actual span worm hole detection technique known as the "Pworm" is being proposed by Luo *et al.* [33], which will trace and find the locale of the adversary node, also this technique finds an application in the static network. As this technique originate very small amount of transmission overhead so the consideration for efficacy and proficiency is crucial.

12.4.3.3   Hello Flooding Attack

In Ref. [34], every node in the network establishes a threshold for Received Signal Strength Indication (RSSI). A number of cryptographic centric approaches are discussed to shield the hello flooding attack. If the accrued received signal strength indication for a particular node matched the specified gesture potency then node handles the initiator as companion. And if the accrued RSSI exceeds the specified gesture potency then the node acts like an unaccustomed [35]. Node sends an explore message to the initiator when the received signal strength investigation is approximately equals the threshold but not same as the threshold value and waits for a specified, if it collects an acknowledged message within that specified time then the node acts like a companion otherwise it behaves like an outsider. The preliminary technique is being ameliorated by Magotra *et al.* [36]. In the above method test message and the response message is being used, but in this case those messages are being replaced by the coordinate data of the initiator node and the result arises in a positive manner. Now in this case, nodes having the distance and RSSI values both inside the range of threshold value are acknowledged as the friend. The methods can locate adversary node efficiently and also meet the efficacy and proficiency goals.

12.4.3.4   Sybil Attack

Various techniques are being proposed by Newsome *et al.* [20] to trace the sybil attack specifically the wireless source testing technique. In this technique, to initiate and collect information with more than one channel concurrently is presumed to be deactivated. The tracer initiates the information with the adjacent nodes using various wireless channels and holds for a while. Sybil nodes can be traced in the absence of the acknowledgement signal as well, since the sybil nodes contains the same core widget and does not collects the information with more than one channels concurrently. The transmission expenses are substantial reason to execute numerous rounds of duplication reach better authenticity. If a node is in the sleep mode then it may be recognized as the sybil node. A lightweight technique is being proposed by the Murat *et al.* [37] for successfully detection of the sybil node. Concept behind this technique is that the node can reveal the locale if not less than four nodes track the proportion signal at the same time [38].

12.4.3.5   Gray Hole Attack

Detection of Gray Hole Attack is comparatively complex as the operation performed by the adversary mainly coincides with the original packet drop. A detection technique is proposed by the Park *et al.* [39], this comes out to be an energy proficient technique. Mean transmission time of each node is being recorded in the sink. The sink triggers the detection technique and sends a resending signal to the main node if the value of genuine transmission delay of a node transcends the threshold. Various checkpoint node transmits the acknowledgment signal to sink afterwards the retransmission request signal is collected, also transmits the acknowledgement signal to the initiator node succeeded by the reception of the retransmission signal. Li *et al.* [40] suggest a mechanism, after the reception of a packet drop signal from a node the cluster head executes the consecutive mesh test. This mechanism can also be utilized to trace the black hole attack. In Ref. [41], Ren *et al.* presented a mechanism established on the reliability evaluation method. Node keep observing the forward congestion of its adjacent node and calculates the reliability levels focused on the variation between confirmed packet dropping ratio and the mean packet dropping ratio. Various threshold is being set to attenuate the effects of the surroundings and contemplate quality of data by having the reliability reports form the surrounding nodes.

12.4.3.6   Sink Hole Attack

In Ref. [42], Guerroumi *et al.* presented a detection mechanism to effortlessly trace the sink hole attack, network is configured in a manner that acts as a virtual grid of having multiple cells. Greater dissemination rate is used to reduce the throughput, delay and energy usage in a static network sink displaces itself in an erratic manner to a cell. The detection rate of this mechanism is better as in this technique the number of stable nodes is elevated. Salehi *et al.* [43] proposed a mechanism in static network. Sink inspects the uniformity of information to detect the troop of adversary node and then trace a particular adversary by investigating the network congestion. This mechanism can be applied to the static network to find out the adversary node. In Ref. [44], Chen *et al.* present a mechanism to take the note of the reliability of the memory usage by every individual node. Memory usage will expand throughout the stretch of processing numerous data packets as the adversary sensor node consumes a lot of information designated to the sink.

12.4.4   Threat Detection on the Transport Layer

The different types of threats detection on Transport Layer are explained as follows.

12.4.4.1   Flooding Attack

Rolla *et al.* [45] come up with the time established window mechanism that is dynamic in nature. Prevention against the flooding attack by the successful detection of this attack in the static network can be done by this mechanism. Initiator node will convey the RREQ (route request) signal to the earlier part of the sensor node, also it enlightens the next part of sensor node about the adjacent sensor nodes and in order to evaluate the forwarding window or dynamic time, schedule at which the route request signal was generated is also given. The network is being flooded with route request signal. If the affected node or adversary node is being detected. If time span for a node is greater than the forwarding window or dynamic time than that node will an adversary node. The method is most suitable for the sensor node in the static network.

12.4.5   Threat Detection on Multiple Layers

The threat detection on Transport Layer is explained as follows.

12.4.5.1   Jamming Attack

Since, many of the detection mechanism traces both the jamming attacks that are basic and intelligent jamming, to differentiate between these two becomes complex. In Ref. [19], Xu *et al.* describes three properties which are very basic and that are packet distribution ratio, carrier sensing time and the third is received signal strength indication to judge whether the jamming attack occurs or not. Packet delivery ratio, packet dropping ratio, energy exhaustion and various other performance standards are being remarkably influenced by jamming attack [46]. They discern the normal congestion with other jamming attacks excluding the reactive jamming throughout the huge number of simulation demonstration based on the RSSI. Deceptive jammer and constant jammer using carrier sense time can be used to trace effectively, also it can distinguish traffic from jamming [47].

Eventually, differentiating the jammer prototype with the normal congestion PDR can be used as an effective tool.

12.5   Various Parameters for Security Data Collection in WSN

Various parameters required in security against various attacks operating
at different layers of layered architecture and different standards for security measures are explained in this section.

12.5.1   Parameters for Security of Information Collection

The parameters for security of Information collection as depicted in
Figure 12.2 are explained as follows:

12.5.1.1   Information Grade

In security information collection, Information Garde has a pivotal role.
Wireless message is liable to its surroundings and also the data transmitted
via wireless medium is pregnable. Wireless transmission is liable to various
circumstances like power consumption, communication energy and ability
of the recipient to receive it. A real entity is able to retrieve sunken quality
information, due to many reasons to make sure information standards is
up to the mark.

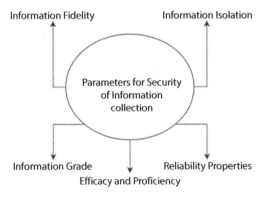

Figure 12.2 Different parameters for security of information collection.

12.5.1.2   Efficacy and Proficiency

Higher level of efficacy and proficiency is advisable for better information transmission, also to shield our data effectively. In order to reduce the energy consumption and restrained the resources better efficacy is important. In WSN, the nodes consume the power or the main focus in WSN is on the power consumption by each node during transmission, we generally give concern to the transmission overhead. If there is any issue to security of information handling then it may be considered with reference to the computational intricacy. Transmission overhead is generally associated with the expanse of the transmitted information congestion.

12.5.1.3   Reliability Properties

With reference to security information collection for assault identification numerous prerequisites are to be needed and they are.

> ➤ *Authentication*: A recipient node of WSN is able to authenticate the originality of the intended sender node. Also, if the originality or authentication for an intended sender is not proved then the recipient will not receive the data packets.
> ➤ *Integrity*: Integrity can be acknowledged by cross checking the data, during communication the wholeness of the message is not to be lost or tempered by an adversary. So that the property is appeased.
> ➤ *Confidentiality*: This property may satisfy by making sure that the information is being passed between the intended nodes and also the authentic nodes that are initiator and terminator are being able to get the information. In this particular way we preserve the main soul of the information.

12.5.1.4   Information Fidelity

To improve the standards of the collected information secretly this particular feature has a major impact to do this task. Adversary nodes may indulge in the system to produce an impact on the authentic nodes so that they don't work properly and also can create a question mark on the secrecy of the information being transmitted through the nodes, sometimes may defame the original nodes. Sometimes, the network basics like the power depletion can produce an effect to information fidelity or can render the fidelity. To shield the normal nodes, slander by the adversary node and pass the true information checkpoints like cluster heads are being used.

12.5.1.5   *Information Isolation*

The isolation of the information would not be pregnable in the operation of collecting the sensed information, if this is not done then we loss the data packets. Once a node is attacked by the intruder and gains the data, they may betray the information of the intended node. Location isolation and data isolation are the part of information isolation. Location isolation means that the location of the information will not be revealed during the communication that includes the initiator node, mediator node and the terminator node.

12.5.2   Attack Detection Standards in WSN

The various Attack Detection standards as depicted in Figure 12.3 are explained as follows:

12.5.2.1   *Precision*

Precision for the detection of attack is most supreme measure to give emphasis on. Precision can also be defined as the capability of attack detection technique to discern between the authorized node and adversary

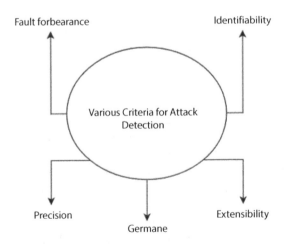

Figure 12.3 Various standards for attack detection.

node. We can utilize the various parameters to calculate the precision of the attack detection.

12.5.2.2   Germane

A method to detect the attack on nodes in WSN is relevant with the special constraints. Germane in reference to WSN can be understood as the particular attack detection method is relevant or not. Generally, it refers to two different kinds of WSN that are static or immobile network and mobile network. This criterion is also very important to take the concern as various detection techniques can be applicable in WSN.

12.5.2.3   Extensibility

In WSN, thousands of sensor nodes are being deployed to transmit the data packets for a large area. Attack detection is being contemplated through extensibility to attain all the probability. Some detection techniques can fulfil their duties in a low number of sensor nodes, the efficacy of the techniques become disgraceful as the system enhances. We can preconize the attack detection technique pleases the extensibility as if the efficacy, proficiency and precision increases as the system extends.

12.5.2.4   Identifiability

Identifiability is one of the criteria which majorly plays a role to define an attack detection technique. If an attack detection technique is able to identify the adversary node with precision and efficacy, then the technique may refer to have better identifiability. To allow the upcoming shielding of the WSN system, identifiability not only point out the attack but also clearly able to detect the location of the attack to give better resistance.

12.5.2.5   Fault Forbearance

An attack detection mechanism would have high ratio of magnanimity to resist against the adversary node. Fault forbearance is utilized to explain the adjustability of an attack detection mechanism to very raucous surroundings. Faulty forbearance ratio can be elucidating as the ratio of the adversary node with the sensor nodes. We can postulate that a detection mechanism has better fault forbearance if and when the method steers conventionally as the faulty ratio increases.

12.6   Different Security Schemes in WSN

There are various security schemes which are as follows [48].

12.6.1   Clustering-Based Scheme

Whole network consisting of nodes is being carve-up into the clusters and the clusters also has one cluster head which is used to detect the black hole attack and also it enlightens to the network about the attack. Main functioning of the cluster head is to accumulate the information from the nodes and then accord it to the base station or the server. For a proficient transmission protocol this clustering technique is used. The main focus to employ this clustering technique is to curtail the total communication energy of the sensor node. In wireless sensor networks, clustering focused routing algorithm transforms it into an indispensable routing protocol. As this has many of the utilities particularly low load, less amount of power consumption, more robustness and high scalability.

12.6.2   Cryptography-Based Scheme

Technologies like digital signature used for encryption, symmetric key cryptography, verification and integration purpose, all these are included in the solutions of cryptography so that they are able to defend the network from any kind of the feasible attack. A new protocol which enhances the security of a wireless network is named as the Ad Hoc On-demand Distance Vector protocol, in this the nodes of the network works only when we need them to transmit the data i.e., when we are required to transmit the data on various nodes then only they create a network or the network is created on-demand network. AODV also enables the use of pre distribution scheme for computing.

12.6.3   Cross-Checking-Based Scheme

This particular scheme is known for having a cross-checking option, the source node or the main node used to do a cross-check operation with the other node which is being involved in doing the transmission with it, so that the nature can be identified. In this technique, Blackhole node has been detected which means that while transmitting data packet in the network intruder drops the packet in between transmission and creates vacant space in the network which act as black holes. The solution to above problem is to use cryptography-based hashing technique which uses concept of public and private key.

12.6.4   Overhearing-Based Scheme

To check the loyalty of the neighbor's transmission, this scheme consists of a solution to overhear it. The node of the network declared as the malicious node if its neighbor node is spotted as doing some uncommon event and also the information is transmitted in the network. Due to the multicast nature of wireless transmission all the reconcilable recipient in the communication range of the initiator aerial will be collecting the data within a communication for the same thing. So, the radio devices will consider transmission by their bordering nodes even when they are not straightly involved. The data packet is being produced when a stimulating event is found by the sensor node that incorporates the data observed, id of the sensor node and succession number. Transmission of data packet to sink via multiple-hop wireless transmission.

12.6.5   Acknowledgement-Based Scheme

After every successful transmission of data packet using the different nodes of network, the recipient node sends the acknowledgement signal. This action confirms the good communication between the nodes. For getting greater proficiency the protocol uses the probability. Initiator node evaluates the probability for an information that will transported effectively to the valid number of intended recipients. The possibility or likelihood is contemplated to be a probabilistic acceptance. Successful possibility can be evaluated on the basis of the properties like the received data packet ratio also the past retransmission. The possibility for error free transmission of the data packet depends upon the retransmission. Retransmission threshold is a value that will be achieved by transmission of information to achieve the better possibility.

12.6.6   Trust-Based Scheme

On the basis of neighboring transmission, the trust value of the node is calculated which plays an important role in defining whether the node is normal or not for transmission. Now, the solution comes out by having a trust value and if the trust value is more than the predefined threshold value then node is declared as normal, if less than the threshold value than considered as a malicious node.

12.6.7   Sequence Number Threshold-Based Scheme

The initiator node is used to calculate the threshold value by making the use of terminator sequence number parameter of the response packet if it has the greater sequence number as compare to threshold value. This technique captures blackhole and gray hole attack of network layer which drops the packet in between network topology and a false request for data packet is being send by the malicious node. A peak value is calculated based on the number of requests a packet sends, number of reply a packet receives and sequence number in the routing table. The peak value is calculated by adding above three parameters in the previous value. Before establishment of node, sequence number is checked by peak value, if the value is greater than peak value packet is not taken into consideration.

12.6.8   Intrusion Detection System-Based Scheme

Special nodes known as intrusion detection system nodes which are having the ability to recognize the malicious activities by a process called as overhearing its near transmitting node and when abnormality is noticed, the node broadcast the signal to the server and also sometime to the user. Intrusion detection system in WSN mainly contains the two phases and those are recognition and respond, the preceding communication of the data procuring fulfilled on the network irregularity identification. IDS trace the doubtful activities and also provoke the alarm when any kind of attack or intrusion exists in the system. Since, the sensor node in the WSN mainly fabricated for small and cheap purpose also they do not contain the adequate hardware asset, creates a bit complex to implement the IDS technique in the wireless sensor networks. So, to implement the IDS method in WSN, the method should be of high proficiency in tracing the adversary that contains the unknown attacks.

12.6.9   Cross-Layer Collaboration-Based Scheme

Two or more layer collaborate or connect internally with each other to find the malicious attack on the network to save the network nodes from attacks. In this technique an approach related to distance vector routing is used in which on demand of data transfer network is being set up and the routing table containing network id, send and received packet information is being updated when data packet id transferred from source to neighboring nodes. This reduces the network size as on demand of particular node transfer of data network is built. Table 12.1 presents the benefits & snag of Security Schemes in WSN.

Table 12.1 Benefits & Snag of security schemes in WSN.

S. no.	Schemes	Benefits of schemes	Snag of schemes	Justifiable or description
1	Clustering Based Scheme	Better resistance to single black-hole, collusive black-hole.	Feasible opportunity for a malicious node turning into cluster head as gray hole node act as a real node. Cluster generation and improvement overhead in a high portability scenario.	This particular scheme is best suited for low portability scenario as cluster head is appointed among the nodes and in case of high portability scenario computational overhead is more, it creates the complexity.
2	Cryptography Based Scheme	Remarkably good in shielding against the external attacks	Transmission and computational overhead are the main concerns in this scheme	Generally, in many of the fixed or static networks this scheme is used and has better packet drop ratio that means loss of packets is less and turnout as a key is to be shared by nodes to other nodes is done clandestinely. Also, in dynamic environment the transmission and routing overhead will be high due difficulty faced in sharing a key.

(Continued)

Table 12.1 Benefits & snag of security schemes in WSN. (*Continued*)

S. no.	Schemes	Benefits of schemes	Snag of schemes	Justifiable or description
3	Cross Checking-Based Scheme	Remarkable against the communal black hole attacks in instance of cross-checking with the data routing information table	Delay and routing overhead are increased drastically in this particular scheme. Energy squandering is more.	The scheme is more suitable for low mobility scenario due to less movement, the initiator node has the ability to cross check the transitional nodes resulting in better packet drop ratio, routing overhead is more in high portability scenario, reason for this is persistent disconnections and more control packets. Delay of intermediate nodes increases in dynamic portability scenario.
4	Overhearing Based Scheme	Recognize the individual and multiple black hole nodes, this is very crucial.	Demerits include the high false positive. Dissipation of energy in this scheme is also a concern.	Throughput and packet drop ratio for moderate and high mobility scenario, for simulation this scheme outstands the better among all. So, overhearing based scheme can be used for high mobility scenario.

(*Continued*)

Table 12.1 Benefits & snag of security schemes in WSN. (*Continued*)

S. no.	Schemes	Benefits of schemes	Snag of schemes	Justifiable or description
5	Acknowledgement Based Scheme	At low mobility speed of the network the detection rate is very good.	Due to additional control acknowledgement packets in this scheme the routing overhead is huge. In high mobility, false positive increases drastically.	Acknowledgement based scheme is mainly suitable for the static or stable mobility plot as the acknowledgement signal is sent after every successful reception of the transmitted data packet, which may not be receive by the intended sender node. Routing overhead is very high in case of high mobility.
6	Trust Based Scheme	Black hole nodes that are individual and multiple both can be detected in trust-based scheme.	Periodic exchange of the trust values routing overhead increases. Maintaining the track record for the congestion in the neighboring nodes and computing the threshold values creates a reason for more energy consumption.	Based on the activity in network, determination of trust values for a node is being done in this scheme. Rather in dynamic network the performance is better in static environment. As the mobility speed increases the routing overhead and delay creates drawback for this scheme.

(*Continued*)

Table 12.1 Benefits & snag of security schemes in WSN. (*Continued*)

S. no.	Schemes	Benefits of schemes	Snag of schemes	Justifiable or description
7	Sequence Number Threshold-Based Scheme	Detection of single black hole node as well as multiple black hole nodes.	Not able to notice and prevent the attack, within the threshold value. Routing overheads and delay increases in case where waiting for multiple respond packet by the initiator node.	This is one of the rare schemes which are suitable for both the dynamic and static environment. If we compare the static threshold value with the dynamic one, dynamic threshold value gives the good result, as MANET is dynamic in nature. Terminus sequence number escalates after recurrent disconnection, creates a reason for static based threshold approach not to be efficient.

(*Continued*)

Table 12.1 Benefits & snag of security schemes in WSN. (*Continued*)

S. no.	Schemes	Benefits of schemes	Snag of schemes	Justifiable or description
8	Intrusion Detection System-Based Scheme	IDS nodes are often used to detect the individual and multiple black hole attacks.	Fortuitous positioning of the IDS nodes will steer to less detection of the malicious nodes. Full coverage of the network area is needed.	This particular scheme is suitable for dynamic and static both, since, special kind of nodes is being utilized in a network which notices the functionality of the nodes in the network and has less routing overhead. Detection rate is directly dependent on the ids nodes, more the ids nodes are high is the detection rate
9	Cross Layer Collaboration-Based Scheme	Less false positive or false alarm is low. High detection accuracy is being ensured	Major demerit is that the layer dependency is more. Modifications are required in more than one layer.	For static network this scheme is generally suited, also this scheme is built on the multiple layer synergy.

12.7   Conclusion

As wireless network possesses a number of characteristic properties, but they lack certain features too such as routing, security aspects which mainly focus on attacks operating at various layers of layered architecture model of the network, energy constraints, etc. In this paper, we focused on attacks at different layers along with their security measures such as Clustering-based scheme, Cross checking-based scheme, overhearing-based scheme, Acknowledgement-based scheme, Sequence number threshold-based scheme, Intrusion detection system-based scheme, Cross layer collaboration-based scheme, etc. A comparison table of all security measures listing the key features of the techniques are formulated. Further the work can be extended by implementing any of the technique in the network to draw an analysis of the effect of the attack with and without security measure.

References

1. Cui, K., Kumar, A., Xavier, N., Panda, S.K., An intelligent home appliance control-based on WSN for smart buildings. *IEEE International Conference on Sustainable Energy Technologies, Hanoi, Vietnam*, pp. 282–287, 2016.
2. Amarlingam, M., Mishra, P.K., Prasad, K.V.V.D., Rajalakshmi, P., Compressed sensing for different sensors: A real scenario for WSN and IoT. *IEEE World Forum on Internet of Things, Reston, VA, USA*, pp. 289–294, 2016.
3. Bysani, L.K. and Turuk, A.K., A Survey on Selective Forwarding Attack in Wireless Sensor Networks. *International Conference on Devices and Communications, Mesra, India*, pp. 1–5, 2011.
4. Venkatraman, K., Daniel, J.V., Murugaboopathi, G., Various Attacks in Wireless Sensor Network: Survey. *Int. J. Soft Comput. Eng.*, pp. 208–211. http://www.ijsce.org/wp-content/uploads/papers/v3i1/A1352033113.pdf 3, 1, Mar. 2013.
5. Sharma, M., Tandon, A., Narayan, S., Bhushan, B., Classification and analysis of security attacks in WSNs and IEEE 802.15.4 standards: A survey. *2017 3rd International Conference on Advances in Computing, Communication & Automation (ICACCA)*, 2017.
6. Bhushan, B. and Sahoo, G., A comprehensive survey of secure and energy efficient routing protocols and data collection approaches in wireless sensor networks. *2017 International Conference on Signal Processing and Communication (ICSPC)*, 2017.
7. Kaushik, I. and Sharma, N., Black Hole Attack and Its Security Measure in Wireless Sensors Networks, in: *Advances in Intelligent Systems and Computing Handbook of Wireless Sensor Networks: Issues and Challenges in Current Scenarios*, pp. 401–416, 2020.

8. Bhushan, B. and Sahoo, G., Recent Advances in Attacks, Technical Challenges, Vulnerabilities and Their Countermeasures in Wireless Sensor Networks. *Wireless Pers. Commun.*, 98, 2, 2037–2077, 2017.

9. Sharma, N., Kaushik, I., Singh, N., Kumar, R., Performance Measurement Using Different Shortest Path Techniques in Wireless Sensor Network. *2019 2nd International Conference on Signal Processing and Communication (ICSPC)*, 2019.

10. Liu, Y., Dong, M., Ota, K., Liu, A., ActiveTrust: Secure and Trustable Routing in Wireless Sensor Networks. *IEEE Trans. Inf. Forensics Secur.*, 11, 9, 2013–2027, Sept. 2016.

11. Ponniah, J., Hu, Y.C., Kumar, P.R., A System-Theoretic Clean Slate Approach to Provably Secure Ad-Hoc Wireless Networking. *IEEE Trans. Control Network Syst.*, 3, 2, 206–217, June 2016.

12. Nadeem, A. and Alghamdi, T., *Detection Algorithm for Sinkhole Attack in Body Area Sensor Networks using local information*, International Journal of Network Security, vol. 21, no. 4, pp. 670–679, 2019. URL: http://ijns.jalaxy.com.tw/contents/ijns-v21-n4/ijns-2019-v21-n4-p670-679.pdf no. September 2018, 2019.

13. Nithiyanandam, N., Parthiban, P.L., Rajalingam, B., Scholar, R., *Effectively Suppress the Attack of Sinkhole in Wireless Sensor Network using Enhanced Particle Swarm Optimization Technique*, International Journal of Pure and Applied Mathematics, vol. 118, no. 9, pp. 313–329, 2018.

14. Iwendi, C., Zhang, Z., Du, X., ACO based key management routing mechanism for WSN security and data collection. *Proc. IEEE Int. Conf. Ind. Technol.*, vol. 2018-Febru, pp. 1935–1939, 2018.

15. Sinha, P., Jha, V.K., Rai, A.K., Bhushan, B., Security vulnerabilities, attacks and countermeasures in wireless sensor networks at various layers of OSI reference model: A survey. *2017 International Conference on Signal Processing and Communication (ICSPC)*, 2017.

16. Pruthi, V., Mittal, K., Sharma, N., Kaushik, I., Network Layers Threats & its Countermeasures in WSNs. *2019 International Conference on Computing, Communication, and Intelligent Systems (ICCCIS)*, 2019.

17. Kaushik, I., Sharma, N., Singh, N., Intrusion Detection and Security System for Blackhole Attack. *2019 2nd International Conference on Signal Processing and Communication (ICSPC)*, 2019.

18. Zhang, R. and Xiao, X., Intrusion Detection in Wireless Sensor Networks with an Improved NSA Based on Space Division. *J. Sens.*, 2019, 20, 2019.

19. Xu, W., Trappe, W., Zhang, Y., Wood, T., The feasibility of launching and detecting jamming attacks in wireless networks. *International Symposium on Mobile Ad Hoc Networking and Computing, Urbana-Champaign, IL, USA*, pp. 46–57, 2005.

20. Newsome, J., Shi, E., Song, D., Perrig, A., The Sybil attack in sensor networks: analysis & defenses. *International Symposium on Information Processing in Sensor Networks, Berkeley, CA, USA*, pp. 259–268, 2004.

21. Stehlík, M., Matyáš, V., Stetsko, A., Towards better selective forwarding and delay attacks detection in wireless sensor networks. *2016 IEEE International Conference on Networking, Sensing, Control,* Mexico City, Mexico, pp. 1–6, 2016.

22. Alajmi, N.M. and Elleithy, K., A new approach for detecting and monitoring of selective forwarding attack in wireless sensor networks. *IEEE Long Island Systems, Applications and Technology Conference,* Farmingdale, NY, USA, pp. 1–6, 2016.

23. Chong, C.Y. and Kumar, S.P., Sensor networks: evolution, opportunities, and challenges. *Proc. IEEE,* 91, 8, 1247–1256, 2003.

24. Bansal, V. and Saluja, K.K., Anomaly based detection of Black Hole Attack on leach protocol in WSN. *2016 International Conference on Wireless Communications, Signal Processing and Networking (WiSPNET),* Chennai, India, pp. 1924–1928, 2016.

25. Zhao, Z., Wei, B., Dong, X., Yao, L., Gao, F., Detecting Wormhole Attacks in Wireless Sensor Networks with Statistical Analysis. *Wase International Conference on Information Engineering,* London, UK, pp. 251–254, 2010.

26. Thaile, M. and Ramanaiah, O.B.V., Node Compromise Detection based on NodeTrust in Wireless Sensor Networks. *International Conference on Computer Communication and Informatics,* Coimbatore, India, pp. 1–5, 2016.

27. Conti, M., Pietro, R. D., Mancini, L. V., & Mei, A. A randomized, efficient, and distributed protocol for the detection of node replication attacks in wireless sensor networks. *Proceedings of the 8th ACM International Symposium on Mobile Ad Hoc Networking and Computing - MobiHoc '07,* 2007.

28. Newsome, J. and Song, D., GEM: Graph EMbedding for routing and data-centric storage in sensor networks without geographic information. *International Conference on Embedded Networked Sensor Systems,* Los Angeles, CA, USA, pp. 76–88, 2003.

29. Mohiuddin, M.M., Adithyan, I., Rajalakshmi, P., EEDF-MAC: An Energy Efficient MAC Protocol for Wireless Sensor Networks. *International Conference on Advances in Computing,* Mysore, India, pp. 1323–1329, 2013.

30. Bhattashli, T., Chaki, R., Sanyal, S., Sleep Deprivation Attack Detection in Wireless Sensor Network. *Int. J. Comput. Appl.,* 40, 15, 19–25, Feb. 2012.

31. Prachi, D., Gafandeep, S.N., Vishal, J., Detection and Prevention of Black Hole Attacks in Cluster Based Wireless Sensor Network. *International Conference on Computing for Sustainable Global Development,* New Delhi, India, pp. 3399–3403, 2016.

32. Zaw, T. and Aung, H.M., Wormhole Attack Detection in Wireless Sensor Networks. *Int. J. Electr. Comput. Energetic Commun. Eng.,* 2, 10, 545–550, 2008.

33. Luo, G., Han, Z., Lu, L., Hussain, M.J., Real-time and passive wormhole detection for wireless sensor networks. *IEEE International Conference on Parallel and Distributed Systems,* Hsinchu, Taiwan, pp. 592–599, 2015.

34. Wu, D., Hu, G., Ni, G., Research and Improve on Secure Routing Protocols in Wireless Sensor Networks. *IEEE International Conference on Circuits and Systems for Communications,* Shanghai, China, pp. 853–856, 2008.

35. Oliveira, L.B., Wong, H.C., Bern, M., Dahab, R., Loureiro, A.A.F., SecLEACH—A Random Key Distribution Solution for Securing Clustered Sensor Networks. *IEEE International Symposium on Network Computing and Applications,* Cambridge, MA, USA, pp. 145–154, 2006.

36. Magotra, S. and Kumar, K., Detection of HELLO flood attack on LEACH protocol. *IEEE International Advance Computing Conference (IACC),* Gurgaon, India, pp. 193–198, 2014.

37. Murat, D. and Youngwhan, S., An RSSI-based scheme for sybil attack detection in wireless sensor networks. *2006 International Symposium on a World of Wireless, Mobile and Multimedia Networks,* Buffalo-Niagara Falls, NY, USA, pp. 566–570, 2006.

38. Zhong, S., Liu, Y.G., Yang, Y.R., Privacy-Preserving Location based Services for Mobile Users in Wireless Networks. *Yale Comput. Sci.,* 1–13, 2004. http://cs.yale.edu/publications/techreports/tr1297.pdf

39. Park, J., Seong, D.O., Yeo, M., Lee, B.Y., Yoo, J., An Energy Efficient Selective Forwarding Attack Detection Scheme Using Lazy Detection in Wireless Sensor Networks. *Lect. Notes Electr. Eng.,* 214, 1, 157–164, Nov. 2012.

40. Li, G., Liu, X., Wang, C., A sequential mesh test based selective forwarding attack detection scheme in wireless sensor networks. *International Conference on Networking, Sensing and Control,* Chicago, IL, USA, pp. 554–558, 2010.

41. Ren, J., Member, S., Zhang, Y., Zhang, K., Member, S., Adaptive and Channel-Aware Detection of Selective Forwarding Attacks in Wireless Sensor Networks. *IEEE Trans. Wireless Commun.,* 15, 5, 3718–3731, May, 2016.

42. Guerroumi, M., Derhab, A., Saleem, K., Intrusion Detection System against Sink Hole Attack in Wireless Sensor Networks with Mobile Sink. *International Conference on Information Technology—New Generations,* Las Vegas, NV, USA, pp. 307–313, 2015.

43. Salehi, S.A., Razzaque, M.A., Naraei, P., Farrokhtala, A., Detection of sinkhole attack in wireless sensor networks. *IEEE International Conference on Space Science and Communication, Melaka, Malaysia,* pp. 361–365, 2013.

44. Chen, C., Song, M., Hsieh, G., Intrusion detection of sinkhole attacks in large-scale wireless sensor networks. *IEEE International Conference on Wireless Communications, Networking and Information Security,* Beijing, China, pp. 711–716, 2010.

45. Rolla, P. and Kaur, M., Dynamic Forwarding Window Technique against DoS Attack in WSN. *2016 International Conference on Micro-Electronics and Telecommunication Engineering (ICMETE),* Ghaziabad, India, pp. 212–216, 2016.

46. Jaitly, S., Malhotra, H., Bhushan, B., Security vulnerabilities and countermeasures against jamming attacks in Wireless Sensor Networks: A survey.

2017 International Conference on Computer, Communications and Electronics (Comptelix), 2017.

47. Tripathi, M., Gaur, M.S., Laxmi, V., Comparing the Impact of Black Hole and Gray Hole Attack on LEACH in WSN. *Procedia Comput. Sci.*, 19, 1101–1107, 2013.

48. Gurung, S., & Chauhan, S. A survey of black-hole attack mitigation techniques in MANET: Merits, drawbacks, and suitability. *Wireless Networks*, 26, 3, 1981–2011, 2019.

13

Large Sensing Data Flows Using Cryptic Techniques

Hemanta Kumar Bhuyan

Department of Information Technology, Vignan University (VFSTRU), Guntur, Andhra Pradesh, India

Abstract

The sensor devices have been used widely to assemble independent sensor networks for a various appliances like smart cities; tidy physical condition, caring cultivation and manufacturing manage systems. Such mechanisms generate diversity information and dispatch those into the corresponding server for more data flows. A Data Stream Manager (DSM) at the server assembles the data flows as a large data to carry out genuine data analysis on significant uses. Most of the time malicious adversaries try to access the data in transit. It is a difficult job to execute the actual data with the help of safety properties such as confidentiality and integrity. The sensitive information is considered as confidentiality of collected data veracity for large sensing data flows. It needs encryption method to protect large sensing data flows that assures the needed numerous levels of privacy and data reliability. The perceptive information is most important to identify several crimes.

The replicated crimes create smart offences using cyberspace by criminals. Cyber communications are highly susceptible to imposition hazards. It needs additional complicated replicated security systems to identify the criminal activities. Frequent bio-inspired work out methods of Artificial Intelligence can be used in pretend offence finding and deterrence. It can demonstrate the detection and prevention of cyber attacks by pertaining AI techniques for contesting pretend crimes.

Keywords: Big sensing data, wireless sensor network, selective encryption, crimes attack

Email: hmb.bhuyan@gmail.com

Subhendu Kumar Pani, Sanjay Kumar Singh, Lalit Garg, Ram Bilas Pachori and Xiaobo Zhang (eds.) *Intelligent Data Analytics for Terror Threat Prediction: Architectures, Methodologies, Techniques and Applications,* (269–290) © 2021 Scrivener Publishing LLC

13.1   Introduction

A large amount of tidy sensor appliances in a heterogeneous surrounding have been issued in critical systems such as calamity managing system, pretend material transportation systems and data control system. These are sensitive factors which are solved by the Internet of Things (IoT) applications. Data Stream Managers (DSM) produce data for practicing and choice making of this sensitive information. The various applications with data sources need for data processing where only truthful reliable information is judged for decision making processes. Data security such as data integrity and confidentiality is an effectual process to guarantee data reliability/dependability. Thus data dependability is promised throughout the lifecycle of large sensing data flows processing.

The large data flows are exceptionally small due to incessant in environment [1, 2]. Such data flows in significant uses have huge volume and velocity, but the data flow practicing need to complete at right time. It cannot go after the conventional store and progression group work out model [3]. Data flow engines adopt the followings:

(i)   It does not require to store huge amount of data and
(ii) It able to maintain real time working out wanted by emerging uses.

The decision making is created significant by using data flows analysis at right time without accessing wicked adversaries. This carry out broad research problems in large data flows. The full security makes sure for data flow practicing with safety data properties (i.e. integrity, confidentiality, authenticity and freshness) [1, 4–6].

Various securities are needed for diverse emerging significant uses. The applications comprise of global monitoring and disaster management based on data integrity for several scrutiny of data. Thus the system requires high self-assurance for perceived events from data flow practicing. But confidentiality is not always significant in such uses [7–9]. Moreover, several applications like martial applications, healthcare, and SCADA are needed both in data confidentiality and integrity. The data confidentiality is defined over both uses and data types. Numerous uses contain martial monitoring for several levels of data confidentiality [4, 7]. Generally sensitive data is compared to more important than confidentiality data. Thus, in this case, sensitive data is highly needed to detect the adversary activities in border area of country.

Generally, data security applied in cryptographic model and encryption keys is a cryptic model which will be identified for security of broadcast data. The cryptographic encryption strategies contain two basic sorts: (a) asymmetric and (b) symmetric. Normally, symmetric key is much faster than asymmetric key cryptography [10, 11]. Thus, it plans to make a fresh safety system for large data flows to maintain data privacy and data reliability.

With the above cryptic analysis, it challenges to design and develop a selective encryption method (SEEN) to protect and preserve secrecy for large data flows. This method is used as a distinctive allocated key for exclusive of needed retransmission.

13.2 Data Flow Management

13.2.1 Data Flow Processing

Stanford stream data Manager (STREAM) [12] generates the data flow Management System to compact with the high volume data and huge number of nonstop queries through resource allotment. The hypothetical and wide-ranging models are concerned with STREAM address. The implementing comprehensive models compact with high velocity data flows and in instantaneous response.

Several data flow management systems such as STREAM [13], Aurora [14], and Borealis [15], have concerned with the queries by the identical client. From this period, it distributes Seq-window supervisors by above management systems as follows.

(a) As per STREAM, it supervisors are reprocessed by processing on identical flows.

(b) Excluding the developments of distributed parts between understandings, Aurora research emphasizes on improved effecting process. Aurora obtains this process using group supervisor as per essential presentation.

(c) Input data assist to execute query for distributed and updated data by fresh queries.

For huge extendable data flows, StreamCloud is considered as a reliable data flowing system to manage huge extendable data flows on clouds [16]. StreamCloud uses a fresh strategy to break up input quarries into sub-queries that assigned to open planning of hubs to decrease the flow transparency. The performance of query processing is emphasized without much more security concerns in data flow. Nehme *et al.* [17] emphasized the safety concern of data flow. The little explanation on security concerns are as follows.

13.2.2   Stream Security

The securing data streams are focused on data safety concerns. It always tries to keep away from unlawful data flows or data safety as per practical secure framework. Security concern of managing data flow access is suggested in Ref. [18]. The access control approach is used at each time for more operate security concern before transforming of actual data. The security concerns have practiced by data flow protect (a unique filtration) as per query strategies. Practical secure query in distributed manner is suggested in Ref. [19]. For the data flow protect concept, the authors used several phase systems to impose right of entry manage except distinctive operators, revise query, or control QoS. The right of entry manage is suggested to use query rephrasing approaches in Ref. [20]. Query preparations are rearranged and operations are recorded to preparation of filter operations to allow data flow scheme. The design in Ref. [21] uses a query processing to execute right of entry manage on a flow stage. The channel uses security preparations to find the results from SPE after query arranging. Planning SPEs ensuring crucial several safeties has been adopted by authors in Ref. [22]. Xie *et al.* [23] assume safety scheme to defend and keep away from responsive data exposé at DSMS. It emphasizes on query protection concerns with data safety.

13.2.3   Data Privacy and Data Reliability

Mostly, data are in transit with data confidentiality, data integrity, and all kind of security for cryptological protocol issues. SPINS is a much esteemed and finely recognized security set of rules suggested for sensor networks in 2002 [24]. SPINS protocol holds two blocks such as (i) SNEP and (ii) µTESLA. SNEP offers several facilities on data such as validation, privacy, and newness whereas µTESLA ensures validated transmit.

13.2.3.1   Security Protocol

In this part, it considers security protocol as a lightweight security protocol named LiSP is created using well-organized rekeying except any disruptions [25]. The LiSP protocol needs hash functions and storeroom for few keys to reduce important resource utilization. LiSP offers validation and permission of sensing nodes with data privacy methods next to interruptions and inconsistency [7]. A fresh security technique is suggested for sensor data flows in Ref. [4]. This system trusts on Bloom filters using encoding of source data through data packets and carry out security authentication over data flows at the foundation stage. The geospatial with end user security structure for standing sensor networks is suggested among nodes and node-to-sink validations and data secrecy in Ref. [26].

The protocol exercises confidential keys to maintain the origin of data at nodes storage with supporting keys in geospatial areas. The combined data in the midway node is a tough task through sensor network resources. Pietro *et al.* [27] suggested a new aggregation method that offers reliability and privacy on collective data and also identifies fake data through this method. A perceptive relevance lightweight security clarification is suggested in Ref. [28]. A trivial safety system is suggested by Selimis *et al.*, for energy utilization through hardware components in Ref. [29]. This method makes sure integrity and privacy for collected data. Thus wireless networks are used data either stored within sensors or broadcast in the direction of a federal controller for social applications.

13.3   Design of Big Data Stream

13.3.1   Data Stream System Architecture

The architecture is designed for transmit data between sensing devices and the DSM. This transmission is considered by wireless networks with security model (SEEN). The promising computing model has been taken into consideration for several application based on large volume data. Thus Big Data stream (BDS) is considered to process with a less delay. The data processing has been taken for numerous applications such as global monitoring, disaster monitoring, military monitoring and health care in near real time [5, 29, 30]. It follows Refs. [1, 5] to create a DSM based on managing the large volume data using large number of resources. DSM removes duplicate data from adversary to make certain novel sensed data which are accessible at SPE for investigation. Moreover, the DSM is in charge to carry out the security authentication of the arriving data flows to make tally with the executing speed of SPE. Reader can refer to Ref. [30, 31] for more information on stream data processing at data center.

13.3.1.1   *Intrusion Detection Systems (IDS)*

This architecture is also considered both source sensor and cloud data center organized with Intrusion Detection Systems (IDS). When IDS supervise it uses sensor that identifies a sensor's behavior and discovers adversary actions on board and network traffic [32]. IDS create in order setting with spanning port of a sensor and permit to access all packets of the IDS to supervise. LEoNIDS (low-latency and energy efficient network IDS) is a model that decides the energy anticipation control using lower power utilization with expectancy [9]. Lee *et al.* [33] suggested an IDS using the cloud based IDS to provide redesign methods with continually practices finding agents for competent learning and immediate recognition. It helps to work out inter and intra inspect record patterns. Further, it assists to gather data process with feature selection of audit data. Xie *et al.* [34] suggested a new approach to find out hit sources promptly and exactly based on system sensor.

In proposed architecture, data go into the DSM with encrypted format of data flows i.e., it attaches sensitivity level (SL) of data to separate data small package. But in the SEEN method, the encryption of data is considered using dissimilar keys for each data packet at data SL. It focused to preserve dissimilar privacy levels founded on the request with SL of data. Based on calculation, for m-1 keys are needed for m levels of data security with encrypt/decrypt of data.

The data secrecy and keys are explained as follows. Here, it considered three levels of data secrecy as: (a) strong secrecy, (b) partial secrecy, and (c) no secrecy. But two keys (i.e. k_1, k_2) are utilized to encrypt the data for strong or weak secrecy which are as follows: (a) k_1 is used for strong encryption method to supply strong secrecy, and (b) k_2 is used for the weak encryption method to hold up partial secrecy. For no secrecy, no encryption is required for data packets. The diverse security level is formulated as follows.

$$Shared\ K(KSH) = \begin{cases} Security\ level - n & Key\ (1) \\ \quad\vdots & \\ Security\ level - 2 & Key\ (n-2) \\ Security\ level - 1 & Key(n-1) \\ Security\ level - 0 & no\ Key \end{cases}$$

Two ways of encrypting data is required to send out data packets to DSM such as: (i) encryption is needed in the data flow and (ii) encrypt the data packets are needed in the flow. Based on above encryptions, two encryption methods such as (a) strong and (b) weak encryption are used for data sensitivity or secrecy level. The data flow and packets are useful as follows.

(a) The encrypted data flow influences on sensors based on organized with the SL,
(b) The encrypted data packet influences to the sensors based on dissimilar SL with diverse data.

Three steps of data process are needed to maintain DSM such as (a) data collection, (b) security authentication, and (c) data flow query processing. But security authentication is considered for executing at DSM with supporting end user security of large sensing data flows as follows.

(a) Security authentication is needed to sustain the novelty of the data for SPE before the stream query processing.
(b) The Security authentication requires to very closing with a lesser buffer size.
(c) The Security authentication with queries is used with directed acyclic graph where nodes and edges are defined for an operator and data flows between the nodes.

The following significant features deal with above architecture model and security authentication for large data flows [1, 5].

(a) Each data packet requires maintaining secrecy on its SL.
(b) Maximized/minimized buffer size is required at DSM prior to data flow query practicing.

Thus it intends to deal with confront of data reliability and levels of secrecy on concurrent huge data flows.

13.3.2   Malicious Model

The network topology is considered to identify data packet at DSM as per following assumptions.

(a) Wireless networks helps to communicate to massive amount of sensor nodes with large sensing data flows.

(b) DSM is initially organized with nodes to aware of the network topology.
(c) Based on IDS power, source sensors and DSM able to identify loss of attacked data packets and data alterations [4].
(d) The DSM is supported completely safe and secluded as per the proposed model at the cloud data center.

The diversity attacks can be generated by an attacker on large sensing data flows:

(a) The adversary may be taken into custody the nodes to right of entry the data stored in corresponding nodes and tries to use own actions as his needed.
(b) The adversary may block of few or all data packets.
(c) During transit of data packets, the adversary tries to collect the information from them and change data packet.
(d) The adversary can create the beating of secrecy of insightful information.
(e) A repeated hit creates unkindly delayed or unfairly recurring of data flow in network.

It conciliates a node to go down data and set up intrusion in the system to right of entry/interfere with the data. The adversary can interrupt data broadcast through a packet-loss hit. Thus, the packet loss is happened by adversarial model through diverse hits. The attack is also to hold insightful data packets and tries to break the data secrecy. All nodes in IDS identify a packet loss hit and inspect the quantity of loss. It designs the inspecting source device to be truthful to avoid several fake responses. Thus it endures into a certain number of conspiring inspecting source nodes.

13.3.3 Threat Approaches for Attack Models

Generally, attack models are designed based on three threat approaches as follows.

(a) The centric threat approach forever begins by an adversary.
(b) Software centric threat approach begins with model designing.
(c) An asset centric threat approach pursues the gathering of data.

The various concurrent attacks may be performed with matching time at diverse parts of system. Thus the potency of technique is as follows:

(a) The reliability of a large data flow makes sure on data forward from sources to the DSM without modification by adversary transitional.
(b) Validation of large data flows makes sure forwarding the data from genuine sources end user security.
(c) Data secrecy is a set of procedure to restrict right of entry on precise data flows.

Thus, the data cannot be disclosed by anyone except corresponding receivers during transition.

Again, the consequence on data secrecy of a thriving development of liability on the intended structure as follows.

(a) Strong secrecy: Only needed recipients can utilize the data.
(b) Partial secrecy: The emergency information can be disclosed in certain cases.
(c) No secrecy: The conciliation of information in secrecy is not needed.

13.4   Utilization of Security Methods

The selective encryption (SEEN) method is suggested for large data flow to provide the key refreshable and create safety among providers, operation and resource consumption. The prominent features of encrypted methods are as follows:

(a) Proficient key transmitting exclusive of return,
(b) Capable of getting well the missing keys by means of an appropriate recognition,
(c) Faultless key stimulant exclusive of breaking off the data flows, and
(d) Preserve the data secrecy using SL.

The suggested safety method is explained on large sensitive data flows based on several autonomous elements of security such as: (a) system setup, (b) rekeying, (c) new node authentication, and (d) encryption/decryption. These components created several effective and useful suppositions to typify the suggested protection method. The details of independent components are explained in consecutive section.

13.4.1   System Setup

The symmetric key method (SKM) is used to initiate system setup based on the limited accessibility of resources at the source sensors [35]. The following resources are considered for symmetric key encryption:

(a) hashing function need 5.9 µJ and
(b) encryption techniques 1.62 µJ.

Similarly in an asymmetric key,

(a) Two different values such as 304 and 11.9 mJ are required for signature and verification respectively by RSA-1024.
(b) Again, another two values of 22.82 and 45 mJ are required for signature and confirmation respectively by ECDSA-160 [35].

Thus SKM are taken for the early setup for security methods. For procedure for system set up, the practice is initiated by DSM to recognize the validated source. Based on successful validation, DSM distributes the secret keys to the source sensors for encrypted data. The distributed primary key for group phase is as mentioned below:

(a) DSM executes a hash function merged with own secret key to produce an exclusive distributed key using random number.
(b) Next, it encrypts the created distributed key based on initialized pre deployed secret key (k) to produce Centralize Authentication Code (CAC) for the period of the network setup.
(c) The DSM transmits the CAC to all basic sensors.

After getting encrypted data, sensors try to decrypt of the corresponding encryption based on secret key (k) (i.e. $KSH = D_K(CAC)$). The procedure is considered to perform and forward to DSM. The CAC holds identity number ID from source, random number as nonce, and a time stamp to keep away from play again attack.

When the CAC is accepted, it verifies the source ID (S_i) for validation and recovers the matching sensor secret key from its data base (K ← retrieve key (S_i)). The time stamp is verified to keep away from replay attacks [8].

13.4.2   Re-Keying

In this part, the DSM distributes the key for encryption. Based on the rekeying process, LiSP protocol [25] is considered with modification of SEEN for more data centric as a substitute of statement centric. SEEN utilizes a key server (KS) to handles the security keys controlling encryption at the DSM. For encryption, it utilizes 128-bit and 64-bit symmetric distributed key respectively. Distributed keys from KS are executed the rekeying operation for all time. With the shared key, the hash function is executed by individual sensors.

In sequence to build the system extra secure, the distributed key for rekeying ought to be secure and fault tolerant. Here, secure is considered for sustaining the secrecy and validity and fault tolerant which are able to re-establish the missing shared key (K_{SH}). As per SEEN method, two types of control packets are utilized such as (a) Update Key and (b) Request Key. The above keys are explained below.

(a) Update Key needs to update the shared key regularly by DSM,
(b) Request Key is necessary used by sensors if shared key is lost during the rekeying process.

DSM utilize encrypted managing data packets between two keys such as ($K_{SH}(I - 1)$) and ($K_{SH}(i)$). The Update Key maintains key set-up of $E_{KSH}^{(I-1)}(K_{SH}^i(1) \| K_{SH}^i(0))$, for all time. Let the time 't' needs to update the distributed key with start time t'. The Request Key starts, when the sensor did not find difference between two separate time for the shared key i.e., δt (t − t' = δt). The Request Key maintains for all time in the set-up of $E_{KSH}(S_i \| t_i)$, where S_i is the source ID and t_i is time slot are used for encryption along with key (K_{SH}). Then the decryption *Request Key* by DSM to manage data packet based on key (K_{SH}). In that case, the DSM dispatches Update *Key* information to the matching sensors.

13.4.3   New Node Authentication

As per the familiar property of sensor networks, new nodes join to the network and participate as usual node as per rule of networks. Let the foundation node is started by the DSM for the duration of the opening operation [14]. In that case, base sensors initiate the practice by validating the data to obtain the recent key. When the DSM accepts the control packet, it will verify its validity. After success of validation process by DSM, then it pursues the key setup to distribute the recent key. The DSM utilizes the recent distributed key (K_{SH}) in place of creating a fresh key i.e. $K_{SH} = \{H(E(R_1,K_D))\}$. Finally, DSM distributes the shared the keys along with (t_i) to each source sensor $(E_{KSH2}(R_2\|K_{SH2}(0)\|t_i))$. The source sensor obtains the information from its neighbors [12] as per selected time with right information.

13.4.4   Cryptic Techniques

The cryptic practices generate keys as $(K_{SH}(1) \| K_{SH}(0))$ accessible at sensors. Here, $K_{SH}(1)$ and $K_{SH}(0)$ are always used for strong and weak encryption respectively. The integrity and secrecy level is preserved at first part, whereas the source validation (i.e., $AD = E_{KSH}(1)$ $(S_I\|1/0\|T)$ is considered at second part. The validation/authentication part utilize the strong encryption key with source ID for validation, time stamp (T) to keep away from play again attack, and a flag value 1/0 used for strong and weak encryption. With the intention of encryption for the data part of the packet, each sensor executes the XOR procedure. The encrypted precise data is for all time considered on the data SL and for data integrity and secrecy.

The physical layer of sensor networks through IoT system is accountable for getting the perspective data. The concurrent sensed data [15], context information [16], system performance [17] have considered to describe several sensing data based on SL.

When data are accepted at the DSM, it verifies the validation block and utilizes the strong encrypted key to obtain the validation information i.e. $D_{KSH}(1)(S_I\|1/0\|T)$. When it obtains the source sensor ID, it verifies the conformed data packets from valid sources at its own database. After successful validation, the DSM match up to the accepted time frame (T) with its recent time (T') to verify the data cleanness with the intention of keep away from play attack with the help of $(T - T' \leq \Delta T)$. Then, the DSM recovers the matching key i.e. Ki $\leftarrow$ retrieve key (S_i) and verifies the data SL to get key utilized for encryption. The computed fresh key is utilized for data decryption i.e. $D_{KSH}(1)'(\text{DATA}\|\text{MAC})$ for strong sensing data and $D_{KSH}(0)'(\text{DATA}\|\text{MAC})$ for weak sensing data. Then, the DSM matches up to the MAC as uprightness verification. The DSM always maintains the final key $K_{SH}(I - 1)$ for the period of the use of $K_{SH}(i)$.

13.5   Analysis of Security on Attack

The attack definitions and their properties are explained as follows [1, 5]. Here few definitions are mentioned based on attack related security.

Definition 1 (attack on validation): An Adversary M_a attack on validity when an opponent able to supervise, interrupts, and set up itself as an valid node for data flow.

Definition 2 (attack on integrity): An Adversary M_i attack on consistency when it is able to supervise the data flow with attempting to right of entry or change the data packets.

Definition 3 (attack on secrecy): A adversary M_c is an illegal party with capable of accessing the illegal large data flows.

Definition 4 (replay attack): A adversary M_r is an unlawful party with capable of interrupting data packets that makes the reason of loss of data recognition during data flow.

13.6   Artificial Intelligence Techniques for Cyber Crimes

The Internet computing raise significantly matters on information safety and confidentiality. The replicated communications are extremely susceptible to interruptions with many risks. Several sensitive devices are not so adequate for supervising and safety of these communications. The different cyber protection systems require being elastic, malleable and strong, to perceive an extensive diversity of risks and generate clever concurrent decisions [36, 37].

As per the large number of replicated web attacks, individual interference is merely not enough for sensible attack and suitable reply. As per intelligent centric technique, for the most part of web attacks are accepted by cyber or web intelligent agents. The independent agents are fighting with them to perceive, estimate, and take action on cyber attacks anywhere. The several cyber attacks can be controlled by intelligent agents using several security techniques, when several attacks occurred at different sites [38].

Artificial Intelligence (AI) suggested detecting cyber crimes through various possible computing methods. The above techniques are involved to take a significant role in web crime activities. AI always takes the responsibilities to design autonomic computing solutions based on self-governing methods. AI creates the various autonomous computing solutions to the potential of information security in such a way that security is improved using AI techniques for cyber space [37, 39, 40]. The aim of this technique is to be utilized for combating cyber crimes and exercise to use as a successful tool for security, finding and deterrence of cyber attacks.

13.6.1   Cyber Crime Activities

The fast progress of internet computing technology creates several positive impacts for various amenities in lives. On the other hand, it generates several critical issues which are hard to control such as appearance of fresh crimes. Furthermore this technology carries on growing criminal cases change accordingly. Criminal utilizes the technology in illegal way to achieve their own goal. In addition, information technology makes possible global crimes by removing country boundary and generates it in different way of marking which are very difficult to supervise, identify, put off or arrest cyber criminals [41–43].

Computational technology is more and more being both intentioned and utilized a tool for executing crime activities. Several advance electro-computing devices use for criminals to perform inexpensive and simple crimes. Several computing related devices are built up the assistance of humankind, but these are vulnerable to crimes. Criminal always creates the target crimes through information technology systems based on typically several targets. These crimes generate through different computer related crimes such as: "Digital Crimes", "Computer Crimes", etc. Cyber crimes involve with several offences like computer interruptions, mistreat of IPR, economic spying, online obtain by threat, etc. [41, 43, 44].

Many cyber crimes have been issued in several ways of illegal activities by which there is no certain definition concluded on it. But, Gordon and Ford [45] define cyber crime as: "any crime that makes easy or performed using a computer, network, or hardware device" where the facilities are involved in above devices for crime. Dictionary.com defines cyber crime in Ref. [46]. Similarly Fisher and Lab defined cyber crime as Ref. [47].

Brenner explained on crimes that "most of the cyber crime merely signifies the migrated of real-world crime to cyber crime space as a criminals tools exercise to perform previous crimes in fresh ways" [48].

13.6.2   Artificial Intelligence for Intrusion Detection

Artificial Intelligence (AI) emerged as a research discipline to develop intelligent machines. Here, AI is explained as the complex solving problems using machines as:

(a) AI intend to find out the core of intellect and build up intellectual machines;
(b) It generates several techniques for solution of difficult problems without using cleverness.

AI consists of several ways to create computer intelligent machines (self-computed machines) reproduce clever individual behaviour such as judgment, knowledge, analysis, preparation, etc. [40, 49]. The simple problem is solved by using simulating intelligence technique based on definite qualities or capabilities of an intellectual system which ought to reveal. The several features using intelligent machine are explained as follows [50–52]:

(a) Deduction, reasoning, problem solving: These explained by components of AI for solving the problem with logic.
(b) Knowledge representation: The problem is solved through ontology.
(c) Planning: It needs multi-agent preparation and support.
(d) Learning: It used device learning for several applications.
(e) Natural Language Processing: Use information recovery through different text translation.
(f) Motion and Manipulation: Movement of data through direction-finding, action preparation.
(g) Perception: It is important part of AI to determine the several matching or several aspects recognition.
(h) Social Intelligence: It is understanding reproduction
(i) Creativity: Autonomous activities created by artificial perception, and
(j) General Intelligence: It is strong AI used for many fields.

The classic AI techniques have emphasized on individual behavior, information representation and inference methods. Thus, it uses the plan of intelligent through multi-agent technology. Since agent is an independent cognitive entity that realizes its surroundings for working and creates internal choice-building system. This system coordinate to each other and work with together or individual to solve precise problem or group of problems based on intelligent manner.

The role of intelligent agents systems is significant for huge approaches with computation in AI called Computational Intelligence (CI). CI maintains diversity nature motivated practices. These practices offer elastic result for active surroundings such as safety web applications. The natural world motivated practices generate attention in the area of intelligent technologies to imitate biological systems of human being. It creates significant capability to gain several aspects such as discover, remember, identify, etc. The significant example is artificial immune systems (AISs) of such technology [37].

AISs are highly computational systems motivated by organic immune systems which are flexible to change surroundings and competent of nonstop and dynamical learning. Immune systems are most important for every living organism. But AISs are intended to use for cyber security and IDSs in particular [53]. Other example is considered on genetic algorithms for AI technique. Here, machine learning approaches are taken to explain the theoretical concept of evolutionary computation with mimic process of expected selection. They supply most favorable solutions for simple or complex computing problems. The several approaches of AI, CI, AIS and IDS are powerful to develop diversity techniques for classification of security attacks with the help of IDSs [54, 55].

Although several methods are already implemented for securing data over internet networks, still, perennial opponents try to get more new types of attack in cyber systems. Neural networks have the capability to handle many aspects of learning and problem solving practices at different environments. They also offer different techniques for several applications [40].

13.6.3　Features of an IDPS

An IDPS have confident features with the intention to offer competent security against stern attacks which are as follows [58]:

(a) Concurrent intrusion detection: when the attack occurs instantly or subsequently, it can be known suddenly through detection

(b) It be required to minimize false positive alarms,

(c) Human monitoring decrease to minimum, and nonstop process make sure,

(d) Recoverability occurs from system crashes, if it happens accidentally from attacks,

(e) Capable of self-supervising to discover attackers' endeavors to modify the system,

(f) Observance to the safety strategy of the system is being supervised, and

(g) Flexibility to system modifications and user behavior over time.

13.7　Conclusions

The encryption method preserves secrecy levels of large sensing data flows with data reliability. The DSM autonomously sustains two major components such as intrusion discovery and distributed key management. The method has been planned for encryption using appropriate distributed keys. Several cryptographic functions are used with choosy encryption where the DSM powerfully generates rekeys to avoid resending. The rekeying practice certainly not interrupts in progress data flows. The encryption method maintains the original node validation and distributed key revival exclusive of inviting extra overhead.

As per the continuous development of technology, criminal cases increased accordingly. Since technology makes it an easy way to maintain daily lifestyle, it creates several chances for criminals to make numerous cyber crimes to get their goals. Significant communications are especially susceptible. But methods of AI are very much utilized to help individuals in combating against cyber crimes and also they offer several elasticities with learning abilities to IDPS software. Both SEEN and CI make several technological opportunities to detect cyber crimes based on wide knowledge usage in decision making process and cryptographic methods.

References

1. Puthal, D., Nepal, S., Ranjan, R., Chen, J., DLSeF: A Dynamic Key Length based Efficient Real-Time Security Verification Model for Big Data Stream. *ACM Trans. Embedded Comput. Syst.*, 16, 2, 51, 2017.

2. Dayarathna, M. and Suzumura, T., Automatic optimization of stream programs via source program operator graph transformations. *Distrib. Parallel Databases*, 31, 4, 543–599, 2013.

3. Stonebraker, M., Çetintemel, U., Zdonik, S., The 8 requirements of real-time stream processing. *ACM SIGMOD Rec.*, 34, 4, 42–47, 2005.

4. Sultana, S., Ghinita, G., Bertino, E., Shehab, M., A lightweight secure provenance scheme for wireless sensor networks. *18th International Conference on Parallel and Distributed Systems (ICPADS)*, pp. 101–108, 2012.

5. Puthal, D., Nepal, S., Ranjan, R., Chen, J., A dynamic prime number based efficient security mechanism for big sensing data streams. *J. Comput. Syst. Sci.*, 83, 1, 22–24, 2017.

6. Puthal, D., Wu, X., Nepal, S., Ranjan, R., Chen, J., SEEN: A Selective Encryption Method to Ensure Confidentiality for Big Sensing Data Streams. *IEEE Trans. Big Data*, 5, 3, 379–392, 2019, 2016.

7. Shaikh, R.A., Lee, S., Khan, M.A.U., Song, Y.J., LSec: lightweight security protocol for distributed wireless sensor network. *IFIP International Conference on Personal Wireless Communications*, Springer, Berlin Heidelberg, pp. 367–377, 2006.

8. Selimis, G., Konijnenburg, M., Ashouei, M., Huisken, Groot, J., de Leest, H.V., van der Schrijen, G., Hulst, M., Tuyls, P., Evaluation of 90 nm 6 T-SRAM as

Physical Unclonable Function for Secure Key Generation in Wireless Sensor Nodes. *IEEE ISCAS Brazil*, 567–570, 2011.

9. Lee, W. and Stolfo, S.J., Data Mining Approaches for Intrusion Detection, in: *Usenix Security*, 1998.

10. www.cloudflare.com (accessed on: 04.08.2014).

11. Burke, J., McDonald, J., Austin, T., Architectural support for fast symmetric-key cryptography. *ACM SIGARCH Comput. Archit. News*, 28, 5, 178–189, 2000.

12. Arasu, A., Babcock, B., Babu, S., Datar, M., Ito, K., Nishizawa, I., Rosenstein, J., Widom, J., STREAM: The stanford stream data manager (demonstration description). *ACM SIGMOD International Conference on Management of Data*, ACM, pp. 665–665, 2003.

13. Arasu, A., Babcock, B., Babu, S., Cieslewicz, J., Datar, M., Ito, K., Motwani, R., Srivastava, U., Widom, J., Stream: The stanford data stream management system, in: *Technical Report 2004–20, Stanford InfoLab*, 2004.

14. Balakrishnan, H. *et al.*, Retrospective on aurora. *VLDB J.*, 13, 4, 370–383, 2004.

15. Abadi, D.J. *et al.*, The Design of the Borealis Stream Processing Engine. *CIDR*, 5, 277–289, 2005.

16. Gulisano, V. *et al.*, Streamcloud: An elastic and scalable data streaming system. *IEEE Trans. Parallel Distrib. Syst.*, 23, 12, 2351–2365, 2012.

17. Nehme, R.V., Lim, H.S., Bertino, E., Rundensteiner, E.A., StreamShield: Astream-centric approach towards security and privacy in data stream environments. *ACM SIGMOD International Conference on Management of data*, ACM, pp. 1027–1030, 2009.

18. Nehme, R.V., Rundensteiner, E.A., Bertino, E., A security punctuation framework for enforcing access control on streaming data. *IEEE 24th ICDE*, pp. 406–415, 2008.

19. Adaikkalavan, R. and Perez, T., Secure shared continuous query processing. *ACM Symposium on Applied Computing*, ACM, pp. 1000–1005, 2011.

20. Cao, J., Carminati, B., Ferrari, E., Tan, K.L., Acstream: Enforcing access control over data streams. *IEEE 25th International Conference on Data Engineering*, pp. 1495–1498, 2009.

21. Lindner, W. and Meier, J., Securing the borealis data stream engine. *10th International Database Engineering and Applications Symposium (IDEAS'06)*, IEEE, pp. 137–147, 2006.

22. Adaikkalavan, R., Xie, X., Ray, I., Multilevel secure data stream processing: Architecture and implementation. *J. Comput. Secur.*, 20, 5, 547–581, 2012.

23. Xie, X., Ray, I., Adaikkalavan, R., Gamble, R., Information flow control for stream processing in clouds. *18th ACM Symposium on Access Control Models and Technologies*, ACM, pp. 89–100, 2013.

24. Perrig, A. *et al.*, SPINS: Security protocols for sensor networks. *Wireless Networks*, 8, 5, 521–534, 2002.

25. Park, T. and Shin, K.G., LiSP: A lightweight security protocol for wireless sensor networks. *ACM Trans. Embedded Comput. Syst. (TECS)*, 3, 3, 634–660, 2004.

26. Ren, K., Lou, W., Zhang, Y., LEDS: Providing location-aware end-to-end data security in wireless sensor networks. *IEEE Trans. Mob. Comput.*, 7, 5, 585–598, 2008.

27. Pietro, R., Di, Michiardi, P., Molva, R., Confidentiality and integrity for data aggregation in WSN using peer monitoring. *Secur. Commun. Networks*, 2, 2, 181–194, 2009.

28. Zia, T.A. and Zomaya, A.Y., A Lightweight Security Framework for Wireless Sensor Networks. *JoWUA*, 2, 3, 53–73, 2011.

29. Selimis, G. *et al.*, A lightweight security scheme for wireless body area networks: Design, energy evaluation and proposed microprocessor design. *J. Med. Syst.*, 35, 5, 1289–1298, 2011.

30. Puthal, D., Nepal, S., Ranjan, R., Chen, J., A Secure Big Data Stream Analytics Framework for Disaster Management on the Cloud. *18th International Conference on High Performance Computing and Communications*, pp. 1218–1225, 2016.

31. Ranjan, R., Streaming big data processing in datacenter clouds. *IEEE Cloud Comput.*, 1, 1, 78–83, 2014.

32. Roesch, M., Snort: Lightweight Intrusion Detection for Networks. *LISA*, 99, 1, 229–238, 1999.

33. Tsikoudis, N. and Papadogiannakis, A., And Markatos, E.P., LEoNIDS: A Low-latency and Energy-efficient Network-level Intrusion Detection System. *IEEE Trans. Emerging Top. Comput.*, 4, 1, 142–155, 2016.

34. Xie, Y., Feng, D., Tan, Z., Zhou, J., Unifying intrusion detection and forensic analysis via provenance awareness. *Future Gener. Comput. Syst.*, 61, 26–36, 2016.

35. Wander, A.S., Gura, N., Eberle, H., Gupta, V., Shantz, S.C., Energy analysis of public-key cryptography for wireless sensor networks. *Third IEEE International Conference on Pervasive Computing and Communications*, IEEE, pp. 324–328, 2005.

36. Chen, H. and Wang, F.Y., Guest Editors' Introduction: Artificial Intelligence for Homeland Security. *IEEE Intell. Syst.*, 20, 5, 12–16, 2005.

37. Dasgupta, D., Computational Intelligence in Cyber Security. *IEEE International Conference on Computational Intelligence for Homeland Security and Personal Safety (CIHSPS 2006)*, pp. 2–3, 2006.

38. Dilek S., Çakır, H. and Aydın, M., Applications Of Artificial Intelligence Techniques To Combating Cyber Crimes: A Review, *International Journal of Artificial Intelligence & Applications (IJAIA)*, 6, 1, 21–39, 2015

39. Patel, A., Taghavi, M., Bakhtiyari, K., J., Júnior, Celestino, *Taxonomy and Proposed Architecture of Intrusion Detection and Prevention Systems for Cloud*

Computing, Y. Xiang (Eds.), Lecture Notes in Computer Science (LNCS), Springer-Verlag Berlin Heidelberg, Vol -7672, pp. 441–458, 2012.

40. Wang, X.B., Yang, G.Y., Li, Y.C., Liu, D., Review on the application of Artificial Intelligence in Antivirus Detection System. *IEEE Conference on Cybernetics and Intelligent Systems*, pp. 506–509, 2008.

41. Çakir, H. and Sert, E., Bilisim Suçlari Ve Delillendirme Süreci, Örgütlü Suçlar ve Yeni Trendler. O. Ö. Demir, M. Sever, (Eds.), Uluslararası Terörizm ve Sınırasan Suçlar Sempozyumu (UTSAS 2010) Seçilmis Bildirileri, Ankara: Polis Akademisi Yayınları, Ankara, pp. 143, 2011.

42. Dogan, N., Türkiye'de Bilisim Suçlarına Bakıs. *Popüler Bilim*, 8, 3, 14–17, 2008.

43. Poonia, A.S., Bhardwaj, A., Dangayach, G.S., Cyber Crime: Practices and Policies for Its Prevention. *The First International Conference on Interdisciplinary Research and Development, Special No. of the International Journal of the Computer, the Internet and Management*, vol. 19, no. SP1, 2011.

44. Dijle, H. and Dogan, N., Türkiye'de Bilisim Suçlarına Egitimli _nsanların Bakısı. *Bilisim Teknolojiler Dergisi*, 4, 2, 43–53, 2011.

45. Gordon, S. and Ford, R., On the definition and classification of cybercrime. *J. Comput. Virol.*, 2, 1, 13–20, 2006.

46. http://dictionary.reference.com/browse/cybercrime, (24/11/2014).

47. Fisher, B.S. and Lab, S.P., *Encyclopedia of Victimology and Crime Prevention*, vol. 1, p. 251, SAGE Publications, USA, 2010.

48. Brenner, S.W., *Cybercrime: Criminal Threats from Cyberspace*, Greenwood publishing group, Library of Congress Cataloging-in-Publication Data, USA, 2010.

49. Brunette, E.S., Flemmer, R.C., Flemmer, C.L., A review of artificial intelligence. *Proceedings of the 4th International Conference on Autonomous Robots and Agents*, pp. 385–392, 2009.

50. Russell, J.S. and Norvig, P., *Artificial Intelligence: A Modern Approach*, 2nd edition, Upper Saddle River, Prentice Hall, New Jersey, USA, 2003.

51. Luger, G. and Stubblefield, W., *Artificial Intelligence: Structures and Strategies for Complex Problem Solving*, 5th edition, Addison Wesley, Boston, USA, 2004.

52. Artificial Intelligence, Wikipedia, http://en.wikipedia.org/wiki/Artificial_intelligence, (24/11/2014).

53. Hong, L., Artificial Immune System for Anomaly Detection. *IEEE International Symposium on Knowledge Acquisition and Modeling Workshop*, pp. 340–343, 2008.

54. Alrajeh, N.A. and Lloret, J., Intrusion Detection Systems Based on Artificial Intelligence Techniques in Wireless Sensor Networks. *Int. J. Distrib. Sens. Netw.*, 2013, 351047, 2013.

55. Shamshirband, S., Anuar, N.B., Kiah, M.L.M., Patel, A., An appraisal and design of a multiagent system based cooperative wireless intrusion detection

computational intelligence technique. *Eng. Appl. Artif. Intell.*, 26, 2105–2127, 2013.

56. Kaliyamurthie, K.P. and Suresh, R.M., Artificial Intelligence Technique Applied to Intrusion Detection. *Int. J. Comput. Sci. Telecommun.*, 3, 4, 2025, 2012.

57. Patel, A., Taghavi, M., Bakhtiyari, K.J., Junior, Celestino, An intrusion detection and prevention system in cloud computing: A systematic review. *J. Network Comput. Appl., Elsevier*, 36, 25–41, 2013.

58. Patel, A., Qassim, Q., Shukor, Z., Nogueira, J., Júnior, J., Wills, C., Autonomic Agent-Based Self-Managed Intrusion Detection and Prevention System. *Proceedings of the South African Information Security Multi-Conference (SAISMC 2010)*, Port Elizabeth, South Africa, May 17–18, 2010.

14

Cyber-Crime Prevention Methodology

Chandra Sekhar Biswal[1]* and Subhendu Kumar Pani[2]

[1]Utkal University, Bhubaneswar, India
[2]Odisha Engineering College, Bhubaneswar, India

Abstract

In recent years, internet has very quickly changed starting with education, start-ups, and sports to entertainment medium. So internet is the knowledge hub for each and every person having little knowledge about operating the web browser or mobile devices. The use of internet also contains both advantages and disadvantages. The worst disadvantage of internet is Cyber-Crime. Now-a-days Cyber-crime is an emerging threat to all the internet and computer users as well as society in general. Therefore, various countries government, police departments and other intelligence departments are now being strict and reactionary to these emerging cyber threats and spreading of cyber-crimes. Governments have started taking initiatives to eliminate cyber-crimes of all kinds along with cross- border cyber threats, dark web operations etc. Governments of every country including India have started setting up cyber cells across the country and also making them functional by educating police personnel regarding the prevention of cyber-crime. The prime focus of our paper is to give emphasis on various frauds and cybercrime happenings in India as well as different types of cyber-crimes along with possible probable solutions.

Keywords: Cybercrime investigation, cybercrime prevention, cybercrime prevention methodology, cyber threats, cyber security challenges

*Corresponding author: chandrasekhar@utkaluniversity.ac.in

Subhendu Kumar Pani, Sanjay Kumar Singh, Lalit Garg, Ram Bilas Pachori and Xiaobo Zhang (eds.) *Intelligent Data Analytics for Terror Threat Prediction: Architectures, Methodologies, Techniques and Applications*, (291–312) © 2021 Scrivener Publishing LLC

14.1   Introduction

In India we can define cybercrime as an unlawful act or a crime where a computer, mobile devices or any IT enabled devices can be used as a tool or a target. In detail it is an unauthorized access to anybody's computer, mobile device or personal accounts on social media, bank accounts or a personalized cloud space is a cybercrime. An intuition to access business data from Various Data store over the cloud, website and email ids are also coming under cybercrime. The person or organization that performs this kind of activity is known as hacker (Black hat hacker). Cybercrime is a reasonably new alarm for law enforcement department as large numbers of computer owners are connected to Internet; cybercrime also increases accordingly [1]. So to clearly understand about the cybercrime, one has to learn the language and culture of the internet along with the pathways which facilitates various users around the world to connect among them. To prevent cybercrime you need to know all the mechanisms and methodology used for performing cyber-attack. The professionals who prevent cybercrimes are known as White hat hackers [2].

Due to rapid technological changes, our life becomes more. Be it business, education, shopping or banking transactions, almost everything is on the cyber space today. The attention being given to cyber security is often focused on trying to define the problem and assess the true threat level. Cyber security plays an important role in the development of information technology as well as Internet services. Cybercrime is evolving at an astounding pace, following the same dynamics as the inevitable penetration of computer technology and communication into all walks of life.

One of the serious issues in Information Technology is Data Protection or information security which thrusts a major challenge. Of course Internet has become one of the most important and fast growing medium for business development in both private and government sectors. It is being used as the largest communication and information exchange medium now. At the same time Internet is becoming an instrument of numerous types of cybercrimes. It is being used to steal and manipulate the information of users. Important data is being stolen and personal as well as organizational threats are being imposed upon the users which are using Internet.

Not only that now-a-days, Internet is prominently used as one of the prevalent communication and information exchange media. Contrastingly, it becomes an easy way for various ways of cybercrimes such as stealing and manipulating the private information of users. The chances of stealing an Internet user's important information and data become more often be it personal or organizational. Through the Internet the intruders are stealing secret, sensitive information of the users and now-a-days bank account details of the users become one of the prime cybercrimes. Interestingly, when the Internet provides various faster modes of data assessment facilities in the other side it facilitates the intruders for stealing private information of the common users, companies and organizations which is a big concern for all.

Cyber attackers are enjoying a renaissance with the increasing availability of bandwidth, connected devices, and affordable attack tools that allow them to launch evermore complex and potent attacks against a cybersecurity practitioner's (CSP's) residential subscribers and businesses [3]. The threat to cyber security is growing at vast rate. Cyber criminals are becoming more sophisticated and are now targeting consumers as well as public and private organizations. Cybercrimes are rising due to the lack of cyber security. Many researchers have reported many issues related to cyber security in past. This review is an attempt to look at this issue for the whole world in general and for India in particular.

To have a thorough understanding about cybercrime concept, we have emphasized the various terms used in the cybercrime field [4]:

> Internet
   When a network connection is done among a large set of computers around the world, it is known as internetworking or simply Internet. Basically internet is used for sending and receiving email, webpage accessing, transferring files, chat, and a lot of other purposes.
> Web Browser
   It provides the facility to access information through World Wide Web server. Here a url i.e. the address of a particular web server is used to access any information resource. Some of the commonly used web browsers are Google Chrome, Mozilla Firefox, Internet Explorer, Safari [5].
> Internet Service Provider (ISP)
   This medium provides access to users for various requirements [6].
> IP Address
   It stands for Internet Protocol where a numerical label is assigned to a particular device that is participating in a computer network which provides a unique identification for the particular machine. For example, 172.17.64.150 [7].

➤ Email Spoofing

Here a hacker can access your email ID in an authorized way. So email spoofing is a process through which an intruder uses the email id of a user for harmful purposes.

➤ Computer Virus

It's a mischievous computer program which can be executed and replicated by itself same as a biological virus does. It can modify or damage or take control of the other computer programs.

➤ Computer Worm

It is one type of computer virus, which can capable of self-replication and spread to other computers over internet or by using any other transmission medium. It differs from virus in a way which doesn't require itself to be attached to an existing program as well as viruses work on the target computer only [8].

➤ Spyware

Basically this software is maliciously installed on a user's computer without his knowledge to procure unauthorized user's information e.g., Keyloggers.

➤ Adware

Adware is a type of malware, which is basically injected to user's computer by using any non-trusted/malicious websites. The Adware also have self-replication capacity and their objective is to server various non-legitimate and illegal Ads to users, without having the user's consent. Mainly Adware attacks web browsers.

➤ Ransomware

It is also the form of malware, which get injected to user's computer from several sources over the internet. Once the ransomware gets injected to any user's computer, it will encrypt all the user data present in that computer. The hackers, who have injected the ransomware, ask for some ransom amount for giving the decryption key to decrypt the encrypted files.

14.1.1   Evolution of Cyber Crime

The first cyber-crime happened in the year of 1997. It is easy to track the history of cyber-crime and compare this with the enhanced evolution of the internet. Initially the first cyber-crimes were very simple crimes such as stealing information from local computer or local networks by using Flash memory or Floppy drive. The ferocity of cyber-crime goes on increasing from local network or local computer to internet, when the internet gets more popular and basic need of human being.

To summarize Figure 14.1 we can say before 1977, there were also some kinds of cyber-crime happening. As explained in the previous paragraph before 1977 cybercrime means physical theft of information from anybody's computer. These Cyber-crimes slowly started spearheading with Trojans and Advance worms in the year 1977. Later during the year 2004 Phishing attacks came into existence, where hacker made various replicate of trusted website and gained access of user's critical information from that. After that in the late 2007 Botnet attacks and SQL injection kind of attacks came into existence. Then in the year of 2010 as various social media platforms came into existence and slowly people started using it, hackers planned something like Social Engineering and Data harvesting/Identity theft kind of hacking during those time. In starting of the year 2013 hacking started in the financial institutions like banking and insurance sector as that was the time when crypto currency was newly getting used by various users. After that during 2014 UPI (Unified Payment Interface) introduced by various banks for easy money transaction and other banking activities. Hackers are also very much active in these kinds of hacking.

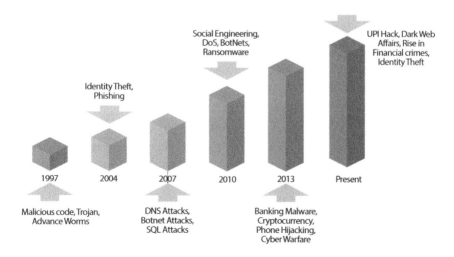

Figure 14.1 Cybercrime evolution.

14.1.2   Cybercrime can be Broadly Defined as Two Types

Any illegal activities, which are not permissible by state of law, are carried out by any person or team using IT enabled Services/devices, e.g. Spreading Hate speech, Accessing and trading over Dark web, performing unlawful business over internet, online betting, Gambling, etc.

Accessing/Modifying any bodies/business house's data without having valid permission to do so. E.g. Website hacking, Email hacking, Data harvesting, etc.

14.1.3   Potential Vulnerable Sectors of Cybercrime

Many times cybercriminals put public life in danger by economically, socially and mentally with the cyber threats. This covers several activities ranging from illegal downloading of music files to stealing credit limits from credit cards and money from bank account. Along with monetary activities, cyber criminals are also motivated for non-financial offences such as frauds related to job, matrimonial frauds, stealing and misusing personal information (Identity Theft), social stalking, etc.

- General Public
- Business houses
- Financial Institutions
- IT companies

Identity Theft
Identity theft is alternatively known as identity fraud; this is a wrongful act of obtaining someone's personal information, which defined their identity. These personal information might be any person's Name, Photograph, Phone Number, Bank account number, Credit/Debit card number, Tax Information (PAN), Driving License, Aadhar card number, etc.

Identity theft has many negative impacts such as:
- ✓   Open Social Media account, Email account on your name.
- ✓   Criminal can obtained access to your bank account.
- ✓   Create fake utility account.
- ✓   Can tell your name during a police arrest.
- ✓   Obtain Duplicate SIM card
- ✓   Fake Identity card, Immigration papers creation.

Due to all these reasons Identity thefts are a severe cybercrime these days, making us elaborate in details about identity theft in details.

14.2   Credit Card Frauds and Skimming

Often hackers make random telephone calls to person by pretending themselves as a bank officer or credit card authorised representative. They will tell you that your bank account or credit card will be blocked and you have to follow certain steps for making them work and mindfully they get your account and card details; sometimes hacker can also be able to take the one time Password (OTP) from you and successfully complete the fraudulent transaction over internet. Having the access to your financial information (Card number, Expiration date, CVV number), hacker can seamlessly perform any online transaction from your bank account.

The skimming is basically a physical process, where the hacker steal all the information of your Debit/Credit card by swiping or scanning your card on a particular device called Card Skimmer. The card number, Creation Date, Expiration Date, CVV number details are stored in the respective card with the help of the magnetic stripe or chip present on the card. Crooks often plant such skimming machines in public places such as shopping mall, ATM machine, sometimes they pretend themselves to be a bank or survey agent and get your card swap/scan through the skimming machine. By swiping the card they will have all the card details with them, which they can use for performing any kind of financial transactions on your behalf. In some cases skimmers can make duplicates of your card without your consent.

Prevention Tips

- Always be alert about your bank account balance and credit card limit.
- Never respond to Fake callers.
- Frequently change your Internet banking Passwords, Credit/Debit card PIN.
- Use Two factor Authentication in all your banking applications.
- Use Official Mobile application of respective bank.
- Never Swipe your card in un-trusted places.

14.2.1   Matrimony Fraud

Popular matrimony websites now-a-days are also becoming a hackers den, with all these theft identity hackers opening accounts in matrimonial websites (both as male and female) and communicating with other matrimony users and trapping them in several cyber frauds. These frauds are alternatively known as honey trap cyber frauds. Initially these hackers communicate with potential vulnerable users over concerned websites chat room, later they communicate over telephone call and WhatsApp. Sometimes these hackers also harass victims mentally and sexually. These are cyber frauds but not financial frauds.

There are several examples of matrimonial frauds known as Black Dollar fraud. In this context, hacker pretends to be from abroad and request the victim to accept some gift (Black Dollar) presented over pre-paid courier, i.e. the victim has to pay certain amount to the courier boy and then he will be given the box containing black dollar. The dollar (Fake dollar) was coated in a black-like material and that has to clean using some chemical. After cleaning the black dollar, we can see the dollar and that dollar is fake dollar.

Prevention Tips

- Never get intimated with anyone in Matrimonial sites, without proper background investigation.
- Don't involve in anything which gifts you freebies.
- Make proper privacy setting in all social media accounts.

14.2.2   Juice Jacking

Juice jacking is a kind of cyber-attack which involves in performing data transfer, malware installation activities in victims mobile phone over USB cable. This happens while changing your mobile phones at public charging stations like hotels, bus stops, airports, railway stations, etc. The USB charging points in these public places can be easily replaced with some modified versions, which can copy the all the data, make a clone of your mobile, also inject malwares into your phone clandestinely.

A clone version of Phone's data can be easily access through any computer/Mac device. Any personal files, photographs, videos, etc. in the phone will be in the hacker's hand. Hacker can use those files in any means. In some cases hackers can crawl your phone and copy only selective information such as Bank account data, passwords, PINs, etc. Later they can use these details and perform any kind of financial frauds.

The malwares which are generally injected to your phone by using juice jacking method are Trojans, adware, ransomwares, cryptominers, spywares, etc. which can do massive damage to your mobile devices. Ransomwares can freeze (Encrypt) all the data inside the device and hacker asks for ransom in order to giving the decryption key.

Table 14.1 Functionality of USB charging cable.

Pin	Name	Cable color	Description
1	V_{BUS}	Red	+5V
2	D−	White	Data −
3	D+	Green	Data +
4	ID	N/A	Permits distinction of host connections from device connection: • Host: Connected to the signal ground • Device: Not connected
5	GND	Black	Signal Ground

14.2.3   Technicality Behind Juice Jacking

Juice jacking works over USB cables because USB design standard is done in such a way that it can convey both data and electricity. Generally an USB connecter contains five pins inside it, only one is needed for charging the receiving end. The other two are used for data transfer by default (Check Table 14.1).

In the mobile devices the data transfer mode is disabled by default, unless you have made any changes to it. Only the power connection end is visible, which in the case of juice jacking is typically not the owner. That implies, when a user gets connected over USB port for charging, they could also be opening up a pathway for performing data transfer between the devices.

Prevention Tips

- Avoid Mobile charging in public places.
- In emergency if you are charging mobile in public places, then at least switch it off while charging.
- Don't connect to internet by using public WiFi.

14.3   Hacking Over Public WiFi or the MITM Attacks

The term MITM stands for *Man-in-the-middle*. MITM is an attack where the communication between two participants is caught off by a third party or hacker. Instead of direct communication between client and server the link gets broken by a third party element (Figure 14.2).

(Victim)

(Server)

(Man in the Middle)

Figure 14.2 MITM attack.

In MITM attack, hackers basically use the public Wi-Fi most of the time, as the information transmitted using public Wi-Fi are generally unencrypted. A compromised Router can take away all the personal data from your computer or mobile devices. For an instance, if you are opening your email using a vulnerable Wi-Fi, then the hacker can easily get the user ID and Password.

In many cases, hackers run fake Wi-Fi signals in public places only to hack people's mobile phone or computers.

Prevention Tips

- Avoid Using Public Wi-Fi.
- Beware of Fake public Wi-Fi.
- Check with the authorities of Public Wi-Fi provider for secure data transmission standards.
- In emergency if you are using public Wi-Fi, then after using it, immediately disconnect and later change the passwords (In Trusted Internet only) of the accounts, that you have accessed using public Wi-Fi.

14.3.1 Phishing

Phishing is a popular cybercrime, which is the act of creating fraudulent websites, sending fraudulent emails, text messages that appear to be from a legitimate source. Using phishing the hackers try to obtain various sensitive information from victim such as Online banking user name and passwords, Email ID and passwords and other such details by disguising oneself as a trusted entity over electronic communication.

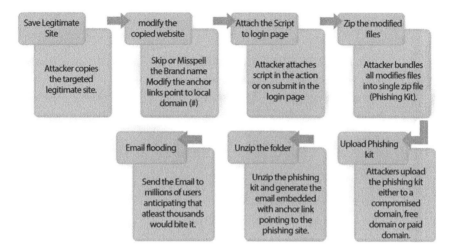

Figure 14.3 Steps of Phishing attack.

As per the above figure (Figure 14.3) the hackers first make a plan for phishing and make a replication of any legitimate website such as Leading Social media website or Popular Online banking website and host he replication website in any webserver and assign a similar domain name to it e.g., Facebook.com is Facelook.com, onlinesbi.com as sbionline.net, gmail.com as Hmail.com. While making similar web design (replication) of any legitimate website hackers generally use very similar logo and exact same to same color combination of the legitimate site so that the victim will not able to identify whether it's the real website or phishing website easily. There must be some login and register page in the phishing page, which is also so similar to the original one.

Then scammers run several email campaigns to populate the phishing websites around the vulnerable users. When any user finds the phishing site either from email campaign or any other medium and enters the Username and Password, the username and passwords will be stored at the database that is being deployed by the hacker to store the victim's details. In this way the hacker will get the direct access of many users' bank account and social media account, etc.

Prevention Tips

- In order to prevent phishing attack, first you need to identify the phishing page or phishing email. You need to check carefully the sender of the email, the subject, the attachment, etc. (Figure 14.4).

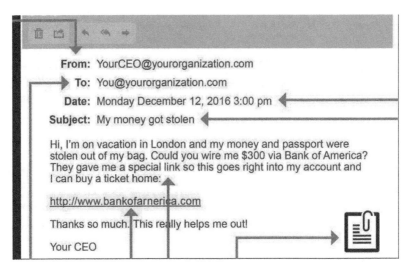

Figure 14.4 A sample email.

- Spam emails can be filtered using spam filter options, which is available with almost all leading email service providers.
- Use latest updated antivirus in your mobile, laptop and other devices, which you use for browsing internet and be sure for enabling the *Internet Security options*.
- It's not advisable to open the email attachments from suspicious sender.
- Don't click any link inside an email, which received from unknown/suspicious sender. First verify the by hovering mouse on it, that where the link is taking to you, then click on the link.
- Immediate report to concerned legitimate brand, if you find any phishing website or email related to their brand/business.
- While visiting any website, lookout for the SSL certificate of the website.
- Never use same password/usernames for multiple accounts.

14.3.2 Vishing/Smishing

Vishing is also a cyber-crime, which is very similar to the phishing concept. In the case of Vishing, the hacker/spammers generally call to potentially vulnerable victims and pretend that they are calling from any legitimate organization. Here fraudster collects sensitive user information over phone.

Smishing refers to the same type of crime like phishing and vishing but the only difference here is spammers use SMS instead of Email or telephone for acquiring sensitive user data.

14.3.3 Session Hijacking

Most of the client server communication over web uses http method of communication and further http communication uses many TCP connections that the server required a method for recognizing every user's connection. When any user opens or login into any website or any web page, then a session is established between the server and user's computer.

The sessions are automatically destroyed when users close a particular webpage or Logout from the website. Each session has unique value and it's stored as a cookie on user's computer (mostly on browsers). The server checks often from the user's end whether any particular the session is connected or destroyed. A session ID generally contains a string variable and it can be passed in different methods such as over the URL, in the http header requisition as a cookie or in some cases in the body of http requisition.

Session hijacking occurs when a hacker takes over a valid session between client (user) and server (Webserver in most cases) anonymously. It is the squeezing of the web session mechanism; which is normally managed by session ID or session token. As shown in Figure 14.5, session hijacking occurred in various levels. A sample Session hijacking can be seen in Figure 14.6.

The session tokens can be compromised in many different ways, some popular ways are:

- Weak session token generation/Predictable session token.
- IP Spoofing

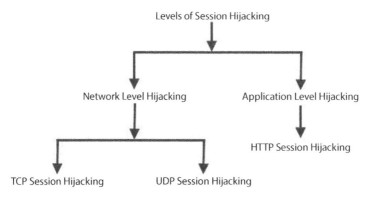

Figure 14.5 Session hijacking levels.

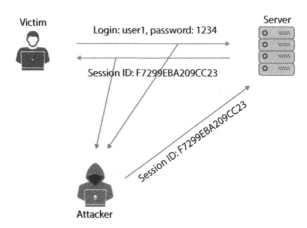

Figure 14.6 A sample session hijacking.

- Cross site scripting (XSS) attack.
- MITM attack.

14.3.4 Weak Session Token Generation/Predictable Session Token Generation

Sometimes while developing any web application, the developer uses a weak session token generation logic, such as an auto increment in the session number as per the number of visitor. In this case, it's very easy for the attacker to identify the session token.

Prevention: Always use strong session token generation algorithm. Sometimes don't try to build your own session generation mechanism, use the mechanism given by the framework. Always try to use secure connection (HTTPS) between client and server.

14.3.5 IP Spoofing

Spoofing means to pretend as someone else. IP spoofing is a technique used for gaining anonymous access to the victim's computer with an IP address of any trusted host. While implementing IP spoofing technique, attacker obtains the IP address of the client and injects their own spoofed packet along with the client IP over the TCP session. So the server will be fooled and it will treat this like communicating with the original host, i.e. the victim.

There are several tools such as: mitmproxy, Wireshark, sslstrip that these hackers use on Kali linux for IP Spoofing.

Prevention

- Promote the use of Transport Layer Security (TLS), HTTP secure (HTTPS), and Secure Shell (SSH).
- Use better packet filtering mechanism or tool. Regular network audit should be also an option for IP spoofing Prevention.

14.3.6   Cross-Site Scripting (XSS) Attack

Cross-site scripting attack is abbreviated as XSS attack. This is basically a client side code injection attack. In XSS attack the motive of the hacker is to execute malicious scripts. The hacker will perform the trick in such a way that the malicious code execution will be done by the victim/users only. The hacker tries to inject the malicious script from the web browser by accessing the web forms of the website. The malicious script may be Java Script (JS), or shell script or any xml file. Once the hacker successfully uploads the script into the web server, then the real attack will take place when the user tries to access the malicious file/script or code.

By performing XSS attack hacker can gain access to the victims file on the web server, victim's computer through the browser. Hackers are able to change all the files and database on the particular server, the malicious script can further mutate and getting auto injected to all the files and directories of the webserver. In some cases the hacker can gain the overall access to the victim's computer through the malicious script injection.

Generally hackers target all the forums, comment and contact form section of the websites and from there they try to inject the codes. The webservers which are using un-sanitized user inputs are most vulnerable to XSS attack.

As displayed in the Figure 14.7, here are the steps for the XSS attack.

1. From the very beginning, the hacker injects the malicious code into the database or the file system of the webserver.
2. The Webpage is being requested by the victim.
3. The server serves the required page as requested by of the victim to the browser (victims), the victim also receives the malicious code along with the webpage.
4. The malicious code gets executed on the victim's browser, in this instance by executing the script, the victim's cookie will be sent to the attacker's server.

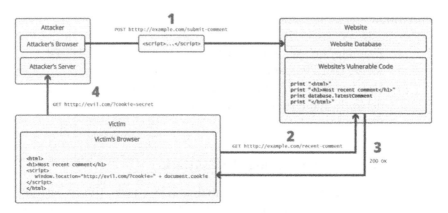

Figure 14.7 Steps of XSS attack.

5. Now the attacker can extract the victim's cookie as and when the http request reached the server.
6. Attacker can use the stolen cookie for many anonymous activities.

Prevention

- Sanitize all the user inputs while taking input using any web form.
- Perform regular security audit of the web application and look for malicious code inside it.
- Never execute any user's input without verifying its type.
- Encode data on output.
- Use content security policy.

14.4 SQLi Injection

SQL injection is an injection type attack to any database. It's one of the very old hacking techniques. Nowadays we are calling it as SQLi Injection. This attack helps in executing malicious SQL script in the database, which can control the DB server behind any web application. A perfect SQLi Injection attack can fetch all the sensitive records such as Username, Passwords, credit card information and any other personal information, which are stored in a particular Database. Using SQLi injection attackers can constantly get a backdoor entry to any Database and keep on extracting the user information regularly [9].

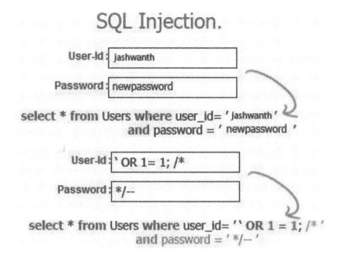

Figure 14.8 SQL injection interpretation.

As shown in Figure 14.8, the SQL injection statement executer will get the same output from the Database as an authenticated user will get, while entering the correct username and password.

There are many types of SQL injection such as in-band SQLi, Out-of-band, and Blind SQLi. The SQL injection attack is not.

14.5 Denial of Service Attack

It's popularly known as DoS attack. DoS Attack is a cyber-attack, in which hacker aims to access a computer, server or other device by getting it accessed through a malicious actor in such a way that the malicious actor will put a heavy load on the server until it consumes all the resources of it and as a result the server or service will not be accessible or unavailable to the real users. In DoS attack the malicious actor tries to interrupt server's normal function by putting heavy load artificially [10].

DoS attack generally functions by putting enormous load on the target machine until the normal traffic request is unable to proceed as a result the normal request will be denied to server, hence it is called Denial of Service attack.

For example: A website is hosted in a server whose capacity is RAM: 4 GB, 2 Core CPU and 50 GB of space. As per the application architecture, the particular website can handle a maximum of 2,000 concurrent users at a time. In this scenario hackers will send multiple number of

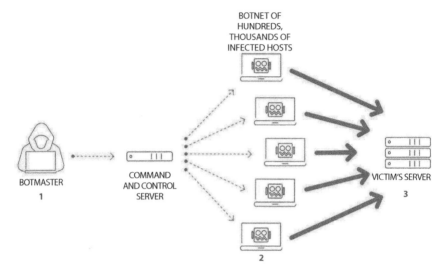

Figure 14.9 A sample DOS attack.

requests to the Webserver (Figure 14.9—Victim's server) using botnet. As the server's concurrent user limit is 2,000, if the hacker will send more than 2,000 requests at a time then the server's core will not be able to process that much number of requests and it will be unavailable for legitimate users.

In Figure 14.9:

1. Attackers sends LUNCH commands to botnet from a command & control server.
2. BOTS sends Attack traffic to victim's server.
3. Attack Traffic overwhelms the server, making it unable to respond to the real requests.

Prevention

- Deployment of strong Server firewall as well as firewall in the application level can prevent the Dos or DDoS attacks.
- Botnet IP should be blocked from application level and Server Level.
- Setting server alarm, which will notify the Server Admin on receiving abnormal request from suspicious IPs.

14.6   Dark Web and Deep Web Technologies

Everyone is using the Internet, which is a very sophisticated medium for people for surfing any information they need, and helps people to communicate and in accomplishing millions of tasks. While searching any information over the Internet through any search engine, we only see those information, which are crawled by several search engine. Here is the strange fact, the internet we are seeing is only 10% of the entire internet, and rest of the 90% is not available for use for general users. The Dark Web and Deep lies in those 90% [11].

14.6.1   The Deep Web

The deep web is also known as Undernet or invisible web or hidden web. The 10% Internet we are able to browse or surf is like the surface of the entire internet, the Dark web lies underneath the surface of the internet. Deep web are those parts of the internet which can be accessed by conventional web browsers, but those are not indexed by any search engine. Many organizations are running various activities out of the sight. Those activities can use deep web for better hiding purpose. The Deep web can contain various databases, web resources, which can only accessed by the owner of the data or the person who is given the access. Figure 14.10 represents the pictorial view of Dark Web, Deep Web and surface web.

Generally search engine create indexes of several data found over internet and arrange them in proper order for effective searching, so that people

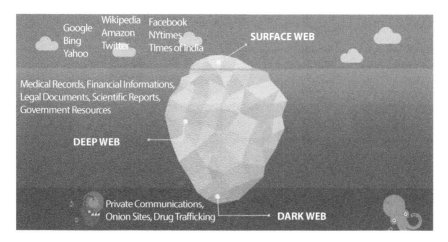

Figure 14.10 Differentiation between dark, deep & surface web.

can get the most appropriate search result for their desired search query. Search engine employs some automated crawlers and spiders for indexing various resources all over the internet. But in case of Deep web the technical architectures are much complicated that a search engine can never find the data and web resources stored on deep web for indexing [12].

Lots of data on online isn't available for public access. Companies or banks have private databases, or some websites, which are not meant to be indexed on search engines and they are remain unsearchable. The deep web is a rich repository of confidential information such as medical Records, Financial Information, Legal Documents, Scientific research details, Government records, etc. [13].

14.6.2 The Dark Web

Dark web is that place of the internet which is difficult for a normal internet user to reach. The dark web is also the part of World Wide Web, but it is an encrypted online content, which can never be indexed by search engine. Dark web runs on Dark net. Dark net can also be denoted as Darknet, which is an overlay network, within the internet, for accessing which we need specific software and special configuration or some sorts of authorizations. It uses a unique customized communication protocol [14].

Dark web is the place, where everyone wants absolute anonymity. The darknet helps in encryption and special privacy browser such as tor. Darknet helps in encryption and special privacy browsers such as Tor. Tor uses Onion Routing Network or what we often call as Onion Router. The Onion Router is a free software that directs traffic through a massive

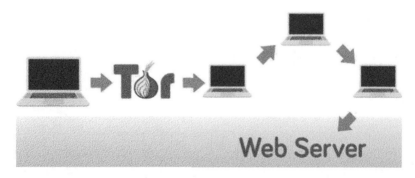

Figure 14.11 Tor browser functionality.

network consisting of thousands of relays. Due to this reason, the origin of the request and the destination of the request can never be tracked. Tor uses a series of virtual networks (Figure 14.11) by connecting through a series of virtual terminals. The tor network is managed by The Tor Project Inc., which is a Massachusetts-based research-education based non-profit organization.

For which dark web is used for all the illegal activities such as Drugs Trading, Gun buy sell, contract for killing, stolen credit card details, etc. In the dark web you can find almost everything, which you can never find on the surface web or those that are illegal on the surface web. You can find several market places on the Dark web i.e., Dream Market, Hansa AlphaBay, Silck Road, Sheep Marketplace, Atlantis, etc. All these market places are used for different illegal purposes [15].

14.7   Conclusion

It is evident from the past studies and records that when the technology advances at the same time cybercrimes also increases. It is a surprising fact that cybercrimes are performed more by the qualified people so it propels all to know about the basic principles and ethics of internet use. Definitely cybercrimes and hacking are posing a big threat for safe internet use. We can utilize the various techniques and occurrences from past incidents so that cybercrime can be reduced comparatively. Also stringent Cyber laws are required to change and evolve as swiftly as hackers do for effective way of controlling cybercrime. So, there should be balance between protecting citizens from crime, and providing their rights intact. The prime advantage of internet is its vastness and free use. But again the question arises whether it can provide stiff action against cyber criminals. It is seen that as security becomes steep, intruders also advance in their path accordingly. There will be a lot of unexpected difficult challenges which will stay ahead of cyber criminals and cyber terrorists that can be prevented with a close and positive partnership and collaboration of both the individuals and government. Our aim is to focus upon a safe, secure and trustworthy computing environment for all. Definitely it is very vital for maintaining our national security and economy. Although various steps are taken by the Indian Govt. for decreasing cybercrimes and safe internet use, yet cyber law cannot afford to be static. It should be strictly changed keeping in pace with the advancement of technology and time.

References

1. Neufeld, D., Understanding Cybercrime. *Conference: 43rd Hawaii International Conference on Systems Science (HICSS-43 2010), Proceedings,* Koloa, Kauai, HI, USA, 5–8 January 2010.
2. Ndubueze, P.N., *Cyber Criminology: Contexts, Concerns and Directions,* Ahmadu Bello University Press, Kaduna State, Nigeria, July 2018.
3. Ghate, S. and Agrawal, P.K., A Literature Review on Cyber Security in Indian Context. *J. Comput. Inf. Technol.,* 8, 5, 30–36, 20th October, 2017.
4. Cagnin, C., Havas, A., Saritas, O., Future-oriented technology analysis: Its potential to address disruptive transformations. *Technol. Forecasting Social Change,* 80, 3, 379–385, March 2013.
5. J. Dubovský, Google Patent, Jul. 14, 2016, Pub. No.: US 2016/0203337 A1.
6. https://en.wikipedia.org/wiki/Internet_service_provider.
7. Gunjan, V.K., Kumar, A., Avdhanam, S., A Survey of Cyber Crime in India. *Conference: ICACT 2013At: Rajampet, Andhra Pradesh, India,* September 2013.
8. https://blog.malwarebytes.com/threats/worm/.
9. Maraza, B., *Revista Internacional de Ingeniería y Tecnología (EAU),* Published on Dubai, Bremen, Science Publishing Corporation, Jul 29, 2018.
10. Syed, N.F., *IoT-MQTT based denial of service attack modelling and detection,* Edith Cowan University, Australia, 2020, https://ro.ecu.edu.au/theses/2303.
11. https://www.youtube.com/watch?v=z5W-tIIK8Ts.
12. Merelli, I., Pérez-Sánchez, H., Gesing, S., D'Agostino, D., Managing, Analysing, and Integrating Big Data in Medical Bioinformatics: Open Problems and Future Perspectives, in: *High-Performance Computing and Big Data in Omics-based Medicine,* vol. 2014, Article ID 134023,01 Sep 2014.
13. Dark Web. Bloomenthal, Andrew, Reviewed By Anderson, Somer, Updated Jul 7, https://www.investopedia.com/terms/d/dark-web.asp.
14. https://en.wikipedia.org/wiki/Darknet#:~:text=A%20dark%20net%20or%20darknet,a%20unique%20customised%20communication%20protocol.
15. https://www.techrepublic.com/article/dark-web-the-smart-persons-guide/.

Index

Printed and bound by CPI Group (UK) Ltd, Croydon, CR0 4YY

27/10/2024

14580469-0003